GEORGE NELSON DESIGN

GEORGE NELSON DESIGN

Whitney Library of Design
an imprint of Watson-Guptill Publications/New York

The Architectural Press Ltd./London

Copyright © 1979 by George Nelson
First published 1979 in the United States and Canada
by Whitney Library of Design,
an imprint of Watson-Guptill Publications;
a division of Billboard Publications, Inc.,
1515 Broadway, New York, N.Y. 10036

Library of Congress Cataloging in Publication Data
Nelson, George, 1908-
　George Nelson on design.
　　1.　Architectural design.　I.　Title.　II.　Title:
On design.
NA2750.N34　　　745.4　　　78-32097
ISBN 0-8230-7204-5

Published in Great Britain by The Architectural Press Ltd.,
9 Queen Anne's Gate, London SW1H 9BY
ISBN 0-85139-232-6

All rights reserved. No part of this publication may be
reproduced or used in any form or by any means—graphic,
electronic, or mechanical, including photocopying, recording,
taping, or information storage and retrieval systems—
without written permission of the publishers.

Manufactured in U.S.A.

First Printing, 1979

Photographs by George Nelson unless otherwise noted.

The following essays have been reprinted with permission:

"Peak Experiences and the Creative Act."
Mobilia Press, ApS No. 265/266, 1977.

"The Hidden City."
Architecture Plus, Nov/Dec 1974.

"The End of Architecture"
Architecture Plus, April 1973.

"Interiors: The Emerging Dominant Reality"
Interiors, November 1975.

"The End of the Topless Trinities"
The Livable City, No. 5/3 (September 1978),
The Municipal Arts Society.

"The City and the Mayor," published as
"New Haven and Its Mayor"
Holiday magazine, May 1966.

"Tents"
Interiors, December 1978.

"Great Writers"
Copyright © 1973 by *Harper's* Magazine.
All rights reserved.
Reprinted from the April 1973 issue by
special permission.

Foreword to "How to Wrap 5 Eggs" by Hideyuki
Oka. Bijutsu Shuppan Sha (Japanese edition, 1965) and
Harper & Row (English edition, 1967).

"The Future of Packaging," published as "The Most
Recent of All Packaging Problems," pp. 16–17 in
Packaging 2, 1970, The Graphis Press.

"The Universal Necessity."
Reprinted by special permission of
Design Canada, Government of Canada.

To Jacqueline, constant collaborator, with love

Contents

Introduction, 8
Peak Experiences and the Creative Act, 11

ENVIRONMENTS
The Hidden City, 25
The End of Architecture, 35
Interiors: The Emerging Dominant Reality, 45
The End of the Topless Trinities, 59
Scenarios for the Post-Modern City, 65
The City and the Mayor, 83

OBJECTS
Tents, 101
Mobile Seating, 111
Great Writers, 119
"How to Wrap Five Eggs," 125
The Future of Packaging, 131
The Future of the Object, 135

STATEMENTS
The Office Revolution, 153
The Universal Necessity, 161
Plagiarism, or How to Be Creative When No One Is Looking, 169
Miniaturization, Ephemeralization, Dematerialization, 175
Design and Technologies, 179
Design and Human Needs, 185

Introduction

In a society saturated with visual illiterates it is inevitable, I suppose, that some of the misconceptions of the methods and aims of the contemporary artist should spill over onto design. This transfer takes place, despite the fact that design is an intensely practical matter, because every artifact has a physical appearance and thus invites esthetic judgments.

Because of this it is essential to keep in mind that design is an ancient activity and that for a very long time it was the prime survival tool. Humanity in its infancy was confronted by a world of predators which were larger, faster, stronger, better clothed, and armed, and it was only with the design of tools, traps, and weapons that a degree of parity was achieved. In those distant times design and making were all of a piece, a condition which persisted right up to the Industrial Revolution, when the fragmentation of work took over and it became possible to identify a separate process called "design."

The word itself is a source of confusion for many, and the dictionaries, until recently, were not very helpful either. All one really has to know is that design is a process in which needs or wants represent the problem, while ideas represent possible solutions. A solution that seems workable is checked out with a list of criteria, such as suitability of possible materials, inventory of available tools, taboos which might be associated with the article in question, and cost in whatever currency is in use.

To design and prototype a new commercial plane may take 20 million workhours, a number beyond any person's life span, and under such conditions the designer as solo performer tends to fission into a team of specialists. But the basic process is simple in essence and it rarely varies except in degree of complexity.

One of the constraints on the designer is that he cannot function without a client. As usual, we have to acknowledge exceptions, which mostly turn out to be craft articles. But for anything more involved the designer needs his client, with whom he forms a symbiotic relationship in which one pays and the other spends.

A poet, in theory at least, could scribble a masterpiece on a blank wall or a shopping bag and the same might occasionally be said of the painter, if his aspirations were not too extravagant. But the designer burning with visions of a new Xanadu or a utopian housing project must find someone to come up with the front money. There have been some marvelous designer/client twosomes in history, but, like marriages made in Heaven, they are more enviable than plentiful.

The old patrons—feudal barons, Princes of the Church, Greek tyrants, Renaissance aristocrats—have all vanished, and big corporations and governments now pick up the tab for monumental office buildings, public plazas, oversize abstract sculpture, and other artworks. All too often the patron has been transmuted into a committee, not necessarily a bad thing in itself, but the ensuing dilution of vision is less likely to encourage the creation of great art or architecture.

To add to the general confusion, designers, like the scientists of an earlier generation, have been discovering that their work keeps spilling over its traditional boundaries. Architects, identified with the design of buildings, are moving into interiors, graphics, and large-scale planning, as well as entrepreneurial ventures. Industrial designers, primarily concerned with products, have expanded to take on exhibits, market surveys, commercial interiors, building systems.

The walls of Jericho, so to speak, are crumbling, and in their place there is a shift from specialist to generalist as the connections between things take on an importance formerly reserved for the isolated things themselves. This goes on in all fields of endeavor. Einstein announces that while God is mysterious in His ways, we can be sure that He is not being whimsical or malicious. The statement is comprehensible to nonmathematicians, although its full implications may not reveal themselves immediately. The point, however, is that Einstein has spoken, not as a mathematician-physicist, but as a philosopher. Rachel Carson, with a single book, blew the first whistle on the environmental polluters, and Rene Dubos, a specialist in the life sciences, has turned out an influential series of writings on the human condition. Economist E.F. Schumacher attracts a global following with his message that small is beautiful. The list of distinguished specialists now wearing generalist hats has gotten very long.

Traditionally we are not an intellectual people and we do not go in much for speculation or introspection. Action has been our thing since the day the Pilgrims landed, and if one sticks to the numbers—the ounces of gold and silver, tons of coal or steel, the thousands of miles of express roads, tens of millions of family dwellings—it has worked in impressive fashion. But now the warnings are coming with greater frequency: we may not exceed the limits of what the planet can bear; the depletion of basic materials is upon us; we must not go on wasting resources. It will take more lumps on our heads and maybe an educational catastrophe or two before we fully believe what we are hearing. Even so, we are not doing too badly: the fish, I hear, are running again in the Hudson River.

Given all these stirrings on so many fronts, it would be surprising indeed if generalist attitudes had failed to affect designers to some degree. This book is such a testimonial to the impact of change, an expression of personal philosophy which is not that different in essence from statements coming out of the life sciences, sociology, psychology, and other disciplines.

The similarity of these messages does not come from people reading over the shoulders of other people: it simply reflects the fact that the scene, from almost any point of view, presents roughly the same information.

What seems to come out of such information is the proposition that the central problems of our time are no longer technical, but moral or, if you prefer, religious. Until these problems have been confronted—which is the same as saying until humanity takes the next step towards maturity—technology will continue to remain without direction and push us still further in the direction of a transistorized Dark Age, following some nightmarish script like George Orwell's *1984*.

It is an odd prospect that lies before us: at the very pinnacle of our technical achievements to find ourselves thrust back into a reply of the most ancient of dramas—the great myths of antiquity in which the epic struggles between the forces of light and darkness were personified in the violent figures of battling gods and demons.

The forces of darkness are those pressing for the further dehumanization of mankind and their power is that of the great industrial societies. Those in opposition have no official status and they are located in a shapeless mass scattered through the population—a grassroots movement with no single focus or thrust. Its strength and size are unknown and untested, but its leading figures are very articulate and there does seem to be a trickle of defectors from the antilife legions of the establishments.

The designer seems to me to be in a peculiarly favored position to observe all this if only because everything he does can be evaluated as an enhancement of life or its opposite, and he has to become sensitized to these issues whether he is conscious of what is going on or not.

This, I think, is what these essays are mainly about. Written over a period of about a dozen years, they show a gradual intensification of the values expressed early on, rather than a significant change in the outlook.

One last thing should be made clear: the meanings of words like "specialist" and "generalist." These are not the titles of the captains of opposing teams but descriptions of mental states shared to some extent by everyone. Any graduate, going from school into a first job, is going to be given small jobs where he is expected to concentrate on very small areas. With time, and also with a bit of luck, his field of view widens and formerly absorbing problems now look smaller. Specialists with curiosity and energy are unable to resist looking up from their work from time to time, becoming more aware of complex wholes, the connections that hold them together, and some of the dynamics of systems. For most of the people we think of as brilliant and sensitive observers of the large scene, work in their chosen specialty goes on.

There is no contradiction: the generalizing view is no better or worse than any other except in relation to a context. In times of rapid change, when new social configurations are being only dimly perceived, the person who sees them as a whole is the urgently needed clarifier and intellectual leader. At other times, when society is in general agreement on fundamental values, the concerns of the designer can blossom into a delight in small things.

None of these simple pleasures are for us. Not now. We are the apprehensive passengers on a Titanic II, better informed than our predecessors, equipped with the latest in radar and sonar, but also lacking their touching confidence in their own survival technology. Is it possible—we wonder uneasily—is it possible that an iceberg might strike twice? It is not conducive to relaxed enjoyment of the decorations in the main salon.

Peak Experiences
and the Creative Act

The International Design Conference in Aspen (IDCA) takes place every year in the Colorado mountains, usually in the latter part of June. Traditionally it brings together speakers from all over the world and from a wide variety of disciplines, but in 1977 it was put on by the members of the IDCA board themselves.

The theme was "Shop Talk" and the speakers' role was to talk about any aspects of their work they found relevant. My contribution had to do with a problem which has fascinated me for years: the nature of the creative act and its connection with peak experiences.

As things turned out, presenting the talk in an atmosphere of extraordinary warmth and receptivity became in itself a peak experience.

Santa Sophia, Istanbul.

I believe peak experiences or moments are the most durable and rewarding things that can happen to one in the course of a professional career. But once this is said it gets complicated because the peak experience tends to be associated with what we call the "creative act." Not necessarily or inevitably, but it tends to be.

I remember one which didn't involve *doing* anything, but getting *exposed* to something. I was eighteen, a sophomore in college, and I was walking across the campus when it began to rain. In front of me was the old art school, which was also the architecture school, and I thought if I walked through I would get out of the rain for a while until I came to Chapel Street on the other side. So I went into the art school. The corridor walls were hung with a series of ten-day design projects by some student architects. The title of the project was "A Cemetery Gateway," and the presentations were watercolor and tempera renderings. They were the most exquisitely beautiful and exciting things I had ever seen in my life. I fell in love instantly with the whole business of creating designs for cemetery gateways. This was when, without any further question on my part, I decided I had to be an architect. I was at Yale and up to this point had no notion of what sort of career might present itself, but after that walk through a corridor in a beat-up building to get out of the rain, there was no further doubt.

So I went to see the Dean, and I said, "I think I want to be an architect, but I really don't have any talent. Through my entire childhood any art course I ever took was a disaster. In fact, I could not even draw an apple and make it recognizable. How am I going to be an architect and make drawings like those designs in the corridor if I don't have any talent?"

The Dean was a pretty wise old bird—a three-hundred-pound wise old bird, which is a lot of wisdom. And he knew a number of things that I didn't know. One was that the student projects were really awful, and the exquisite beauty and imagination I saw in them were somewhere in my own fevered mind. He wasn't worried about talent because he was accustomed to students who seemed to have no talents at all. Furthermore, this was in the mid-twenties, and he was very hard up for students because everybody wanted to be a customer's man on Wall Street and get rich overnight. So I had no trouble getting accepted.

He said, "You are only a sophomore; why don't you make architecture your major, take the following courses, and get a head start?"

At this point I had no idea what architecture was except a lot of pretty renderings of cemetery gateways. Presumably there could also be gateways to post offices, municipal garbage dumps, or courts of law. I was carried away by the fact that I was going to be allowed to take a crack at this, but also scared of failing. So I signed up for a correspondence course in pencil sketching, completely confusing the creation of architecture with the making of pencil sketches.

A man named Ernest Watson made pencil sketches, and he had started a correspondence course; I think he must have had all of six or eight customers at his peak. He sent a kind of Bristol board that he loved to draw on, instructions on using pencils, and a few little sketches of his

Student sketches, George Nelson, 1930.

Primavera, *Sandro Botticelli. Courtesy Alinari/Editorial Photocolor Archives.*

own, which to me were a sort of peak achievement. I got to work and found that I couldn't make sketches the way Mr. Watson did. So I cut up his beautiful drawing paper into small cards I could carry in my pocket, and in the twenty minutes between classes I would sit and make marks with a pencil.

The reason I did this was because at a very early age I was forced to learn to play the piano by my mother, who had dreamed of becoming a pianist, and as her first born I got the full impact of her frustration. I don't know how they teach piano now, but in those days you had to do finger exercises. There was someone named Czerny who had produced dozens of books of finger exercises, so the notion of doing them with a pencil came very naturally.

I took these cards and I got, let's say, an HB pencil, and I did my little exercises. First I'd stroke very gently to see how it would work on a slightly toothy surface, and then I'd do it harder and harder. The next time I would do it with a B pencil and a 2B pencil. By the end of the term I could pick up any drawing pencil from 6B to 6H and know exactly what kind of tone, value, and texture I was going to get on that particular kind of paper. I did this because I didn't know of anything else to do.

Then I got into a sketching class, and we were sent out to do a gateway in Harkness quadrangle which wasn't like a cemetery gateway; it was a gateway to culture, fortune, social status—who knows—but a very nice Gothic gateway with fine shadows. I made my drawing on Mr. Ernest Watson's paper, went to the first class, where it was hung up on the wall, and when the teacher came to mine, he stopped and said, "Ha! we have a master in this class." I thought, "Is it really that easy?" What I suddenly learned was that at most levels, competition is not very difficult, not because you are necessarily bright or talented, but if you do your finger exercises you come out ahead. So all this came out of walking through a building and seeing some student drawings which really were not very good.

Other peak moments of a passive sort occurred off and on during the years, and curiously enough, no matter what produced the impact the effect was always the same. In the early 30s when I was living in Rome at the American Academy, I went to Istanbul, a city about which I knew absolutely nothing except that there was a place called Santa Sophia. So I went to see Santa Sophia, walked in, and was knocked absolutely flat—just crushed by the terrific power of the place.

Last year I went back to Istanbul and spent five days admiring everything, but I couldn't get that "zap" again from Santa Sophia. I could remember what had happened the first time, but I couldn't get it again. It is a marvelous building, and I knew more about it than I had thirty or forty years before. It looked about half the size I remembered, it was lovely to be back there, but this time nothing knocked me down.

There were other moments: a freezing day in Florence, when for the first time I got into the Uffizi Gallery and found myself in front of the Botticelli *Primavera*—those zany girls with flowers in their hair—and again "whammo." The tremendous power of this thing was somehow inside yourself because it worked on you *then* and didn't necessarily work earlier or later. Everybody must have memories of such encounters.

One afternoon in Chartres, it was a blustery day with clouds going across the sun so that the stained glass would swell and shrink like an accordion, and someone up in the organ loft was learning how to play Ambrosian chants. There was an odor of incense, a few old women praying, and . . . "Zap!"

One of the odd ones was at the Museum of Modern Art in front of *Guernica*, a painting I had seen at least eight or ten times. This time it killed me. I went back later to try to resuscitate that magic instant but couldn't do it. So there are peak experiences that have to do with not creating anything at all but encountering something that absolutely shoots you off—in the sense of a critical mass coming together and exploding.

Anyway, I got through architecture school and was made a teaching assistant. The great crash of 1929 had happened, but we weren't yet aware of its full impact. I was feeling pretty smug and looking forward to a tranquil life as an academic because it seemed all so safe and pleasant. But if you are lucky, you are not allowed to stay safe. You're thrown into jeopardy. After one year I was dropped, because the school was now beginning to feel the pinch. I was at the bottom of the totem pole, so off I went. And now a real panic, because jobs were vanishing and my nice safe teaching spot was gone, and I thought, "My God, what do I do now?" Then I thought, "Well, I guess I had better go and win the Paris Prize." A bit presumptuous, but what else could I do? I had been at Yale, which had consistently won Rome Prizes. Catholic University, a bedraggled school on the outskirts of Washington, D.C., always won the Paris Prize. I'd saved up a bit of money and went to Catholic University to win the Paris Prize.

I was also mad at the Dean who had fired me, and I

thought, "I'll show him," which was very childish, but it did keep me working around the clock. It was like training for an athletic contest: I got up at seven in the morning, worked until two in the morning, no dates, no movies, no nothing . . . just work, work, work. I did this through all the school year, no other courses, no distractions. I lived in a little rooming house near the school. I dove into the Paris Prize competition, almost made it, didn't quite, but had developed such terrific momentum that when the Rome Prize came along I moved in without really thinking much about it and won. I remember the telegram: don't tell anybody now but you won. What the Rome Prize meant to me was two years in Rome with all expenses covered. The Depression was now really hurting: my father like millions of others had lost everything he had, and the prospect of two years in Rome was like a free trip through Dante's *Paradiso*. Sooner or later, the two years will be up, but you're going to be safe, you're going to be safe. It took years to get over the illusion that safety was worth a damn.

I went to Rome—a 23-year-old kid from Hartford, Connecticut, middle class, very quiet family—suddenly propelled into an international society in an imperial capital 2,000 years old. It was a change. The American Academy had a semidiplomatic status so we were invited to embassy and society parties, a world beyond my wildest imaginings. It was Fellini's "Dolce Vita" thirty years before he made it. But other things were going on at the same time. I found a bicycle lying around the Academy, appropriated it, and started in a methodical way to see the city. At the end of a year and a half of trying, I gave up. There is no way to see this city. There is no end to it. But I learned a couple of things.

In the early thirties there was a great controversy whether modern architecture was here to stay or not. Back home, there was considerable doubt about it. Architects were still covering their buildings with pilasters and columns and arches and all that, which, I must say, look better today than they did when we were in rebellion against them. But in Rome the extraordinary thing I learned was that *everything was modern*. You would be walking down a street past a 15th-century palazzo and sticking out of the wall of the palazzo would be a ruin of an arch; the palazzo was built around the ruin centuries older than the palazzo. Then, because business wasn't good in Rome either, a corner of this palace had been remodeled and somebody had put in an ultramodern candy shop. So there were these three epochs coexisting in one

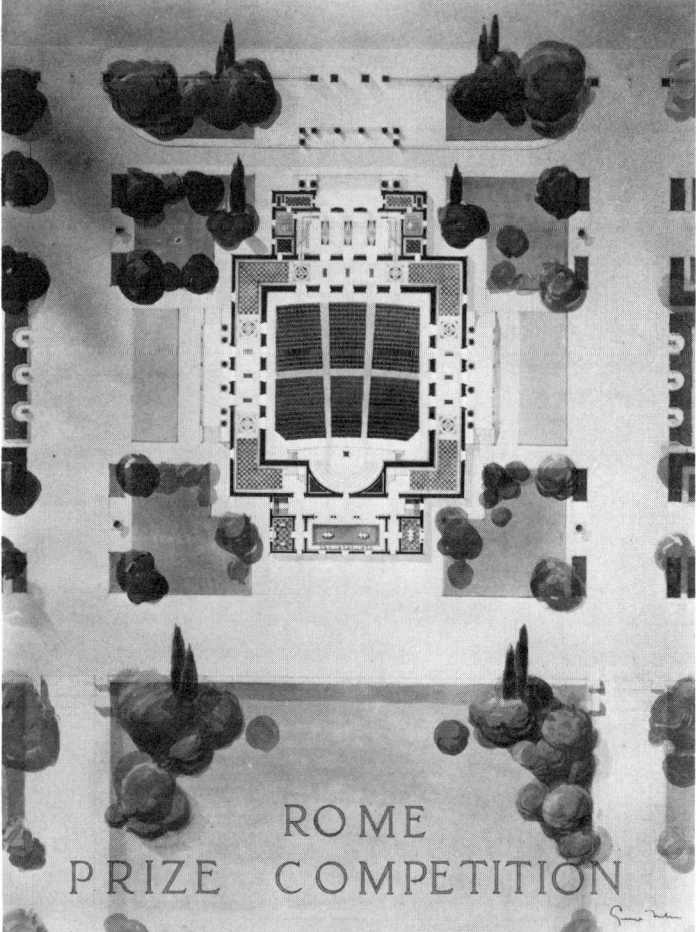

Rome Prize Competition, George Nelson, 1932.

American Academy in Rome. Courtesy the American Academy in Rome.

building. And suddenly you realized the obvious, that everything that is worth anything is always modern because it can't be anything else, and therefore there are no flags to wave, no manifestoes, you just do the only thing you can honestly do *now*.

The two years in Rome passed very, very pleasantly. There were twenty-six students; the Fellows in the Academy lived in a big villa on top of one of the seven hills where the views were incomparable, attended by thirty-four servants. (I wouldn't mind doing it all over again.) But in the second year I realized that I was going to have to leave and go back. What I was going back to, according to the American papers, was architects selling apples on street corners. So panic ensued. From safety into jeopardy, again. The panic lasted two or three months. Then it became apparent that panic was not productive. The question changed to, "What assets do I have as a student in a foreign country that I could put to some use?" It occurred to me that architects at home had no idea what was going on in the world of European modern architects. I thought, "I will go around Europe on my travel stipend and interview leading modern architects. I will photograph their work, write articles, get them published, and with the money I can somehow get along." So panic changed into a more cheerful state of mind simply because there was something to do. The force of the drive to survive was terrific.

I remember one day in the spring when Le Corbusier was scheduled to come to Rome to give a lecture. Normally, the idea of grabbing this great man by the arm and saying, "Please, I need you for a few hours; come and tell me all about it," was unthinkable. But I was so afraid of failing that I did it.

He gave the lecture, there were about six or eight hundred hysterical students in the hall, and somehow (this part is a total blank in my memory) I got him! And took him across the street away from all those cheering students to a cafe where we sat for two hours and he told me everything. It was very good. I got my interview and gave him money for the pictures he promised to send. He never did send them, so I solved the problem by making forgeries of his own sketches.

I later went to Berlin to see Mies van der Rohe, who was living in a mansard on top of a big old building. Mies did not speak English; I had some German. It wasn't as fluent as I would have liked, but he was very kind to me, maybe because he was lonely. He wasn't being persecuted by the Nazis, but they weren't giving him any jobs. The kind of things that Mies and the Bauhaus represented were strictly verboten.

All Mies wanted from me was news of Frank Lloyd Wright. Then came the shameful realization that, as a graduate of a U.S. architectural school, I had barely heard this man's name and knew nothing about him except some scandalous newspaper tidbits, and this was our greatest national resource in architecture. I was not unique in my ignorance.

There was only one picture in his handsome attic space, a precise German engraving of an Ionic column capital with a piece of the shaft and the base. I was surprised to see a great modern architect like Mies with an Ionic column in his study and said so. Thanks to my bad German, he misread what I was saying, and he came up to me, put his arm around my shoulder, and said, "Isn't it beautiful? You know," he continued, "the others [the others meant all other architects in the world, no doubt] copy this kind of thing, but we love it and appreciate it." I was very lucky. I had good teachers when I was growing up.

Back home, I got a job with an architect, to my surprise, and hated it. For the first time I realized that I was not cut out to be an architect; what had appealed to me in architecture was something else.

The articles written on my travels, the interviews,

started getting published, and the editor of *Architectural Forum* called one day, asked me to come to his office, and said, "I've been seeing these articles of yours in *Pencil Points*. Why didn't you send them to us?" A very competitive man, Howard Myers. I said, "Sir, if you would look in your files, I think you will find a rejection letter." And sure enough, they did. One thing led to another and pretty soon I was working for Howard Myers. It was another stroke of luck. He was not an architect, but adored architects and architecture. For six or seven years, he was like a second father and the toughest disciplinarian I have ever had in my life. And I grew up a little bit thanks to him. On *Forum,* I met all the top architects in the country and many from abroad who came here to get their work published.

The information pile-up started again. First, in Rome—I didn't know what I had stored, but there was a lot of it. And now here I was, a junior editor on a *Time-Life* magazine all because one day when it started to rain I walked through a dilapidated corridor in an art school.

One of the projects I was handed as a beginner at *Forum* was to look at a pile of airviews of cities with about 150,000 to 200,000 people. They all showed the city center—the business district—and what was called in those days "the ring of blight." This was made up of the houses of well-to-do people, abandoned by their owners, as business pushed out, now rooming houses, Chinese laundries, marginal business places.

I don't remember what the assignment was, but as I looked at one city center after another, I got curious; the blight was always in the same place. The city center was always roughly about the same size. And it was the first time that I got a dim perception of the city, not as a product but as an organism. In nature, when an organism dies or decays, it marks the beginning of a new cycle of growth. What about this ring of blight? What is it going to become? It has to grow into something else. And for no reason I could understand, I started measuring downtown areas. What I discovered was that the whole area was walkable, and "walkable" was the trigger that shot off the "zap" again. These instant images of the ring of blight, excavated the way a dentist would clean out a cavity, turned into a ring road and parking with a pedestrian precinct on the inside. Suddenly the old downtown began to look humane and interesting and lively. This was in 1942. I made a project based on the city of Bridgeport, Connecticut, which was sponsored by the Revere Copper and Brass Company and published as a two-page advertisement in *The Saturday Evening Post* in 1943.

At that time, *The Saturday Evening Post* was about the biggest weekly magazine anywhere. I think they claimed 7 million readers. True or false, it was very big. And the project was published under the title of "Grass on Main Street." The reason it was called "Grass on Main Street" related to the 1932 campaign for the presidency between Herbert Hoover and Franklin D. Roosevelt, when Hoover, in the heat of combat, said, "If you elect that Bolshevik, grass will grow in Times Square." Well, I was not very political, but I was so enchanted by the picture that I voted for Roosevelt. Grass never did grow on Times Square, but you couldn't blame FDR for that; it was Hoover who made the promise.

Anyway, another peak moment occurred when "walkable" and its implications exploded into awareness. The fact that this was not really new—medieval cities were all pedestrian—didn't matter. What mattered was that I had done it all myself under my own steam. It was my creative act.

And if it happened to be historically not original, it didn't make the slightest difference. The feeling was good. I had come alive, I'd become identified with a sort of marvelous reality, and there I was. This happened a number of times.

I got involved in a book project with my co-managing editor, Henry Wright. The book was to be called *Tomorrow's House,* and Simon & Schuster were publishing it. They had given us advances, and like any young writers we had spent them and hadn't done the work. After we began to get phone calls which became increasingly irate and insistent, we got to work. I think that probably Henry and I, at that moment, knew as much about the modern house, its practitioners, the different brands of modern houses, as any two people in the country. We were crammed with information; we were dealing with the subject all day long. We were well-qualified to write the book, except when we got to the chapter on storage: we simply could not write the required 5,000 words. This produced frustration of an acute sort. We had done all sorts of research; we knew, for instance, that housewives' pet peeve was inadequate closets. (This was the beginning of the American possessions explosion.) We also knew that closets were very good for clothes, but not so good for golf clubs or coffee percolators or watering cans, but we couldn't break through anywhere to write 5,000 words.

I was sitting in my office, staring at the wall, miserable; we had just had another angry call from the publisher. I was looking at the wall and something in my head said, "What's inside, how thick is that wall?"

I thought, "Who cares how thick the wall is, it's probably 4 or 5 inches, go away."

And again, the real feeling of a dialogue with an unwanted visitor: "What is inside the wall?"

"Hollow tile with plaster on top of it."

"What else?"

"Nothing."

"Do you mean there is a vacuum?"

"Not a vacuum, air."

"Air" was the trigger. Suddenly all these unrelated things crashed together, and I realized that the essential element in any storage unit of any sort or any size was *air*. A closet has so much air; a kitchen cabinet has so much air. And I thought, "My goodness, if you took these walls and pumped more air into them and they got thicker and thicker until maybe they were 12 inches thick, you would have hundreds and hundreds of running feet of storage. It didn't take enough inches off the room on either side to be noticed." This was the birth of the storagewall.

Now as it happened, there were storagewalls in Europe in the 18th century. They didn't look like ours and they were developed for other reasons. Henry and I didn't know this. But again there was a genuine creative act because of going through this massing of information, through the frustrations, through the explosion, into the insight with all the good feelings that come with it.

The storagewall today is like a hairpin; nobody even thinks about it; people use it in all sorts of places all the time. However, when the storagewall was published in papers we never heard of that were read in the furniture industry, we were crucified because we had made an invention or design which was going to destroy the case goods industry. These storagewalls could now be built into houses and people wouldn't buy case goods.

There was one company in Zeeland, Michigan, headed by a man named D.J. DePree, who seriously looked at the threat of built-in storage. His designer had just died, they needed another one; they were a case goods manufacturer basically at that time, but DePree was an extraordinary man. He decided that if someone is doing something better and therefore poses a threat, we must join with the threat because this represents superior performance.

So one day, he came into my office and said, "How would you like to be our designer?" And I said, "I don't know, who are you?" and he told me a little bit. But I said, "I've never designed any furniture; I've never even seen the inside of a furniture factory. Why don't you find someone who understands these things," and he went away. He didn't come back for six months, suddenly reemerging, a good, solid Dutch midwestern figure with his big hat. I didn't know at the time that knowing this man was going to be one of the biggest things that ever happened to me. I said, "Glad to see you, but why are you here?" He said, "You know, before poor old Gilbert Rohde was cold in his grave, we got telegrams from designers all over the country, all of whom had seen the inside of a factory, and we took your advice and we went to see them and their stuff was horrible. So we figured we really weren't risking very much if we got a designer who didn't know about furniture or furniture production. Anyway we've got a factory; do you want to see it?"

This started a relationship I have no way of describing adequately, nor is there any way I can express what I owe this man—but it was another beautiful learning experience. D.J. DePree was a deeply religious person, a Calvinist, a Fundamentalist. I'd never met a real live Fundamentalist before. He knew, for instance, how old the earth was; it was 4,612 years old, I think. He knew the temperature of the fires in hell. My generation, which saw itself as more or less atheist or agnostic, found this funny. In a near-insane society it takes more than that for a good laugh, so I didn't find it funny. We spent most of our business meetings arguing religion, and one of the things we presently discovered was that having started from the extreme left and right, so to speak, we always went around the circle . . . and then we met.

And when we met, in a sense, we embraced. It was very curious. I got to realize that what was really important about this man, whose ideas, which to me were as crazy as mine were to him, was what they did to him. And what they did to him was beautiful. I've been lucky in my teachers, very, very lucky.

So now I was an industrial designer. How nice! You walk through an art school, you get to be an architect, you really don't like most of it. You become a magazine writer, and then because you write one thing too many, you are an industrial designer.

I had another zap moment or peak when I opened my office in 1947. It was important to me to have certain status symbols around, and one of the symbols was a spherical hanging lamp made in Sweden. It had a silk covering that was very difficult to make; they had to cut gores and sew them onto a wire frame. But I wanted one badly.

We had a modest office and I felt that if I had one of

Storagewall, 1944. Life *magazine, photo by Walter Sanders.*

Bubble Lamps, George Nelson design for Howard Miller Clock Company, 1952.

these big hanging spheres from Sweden, it would show that I was really with it, a pillar of contemporary design. One day Bonniers, a Swedish import store in New York, announced a sale of these lamps. I rushed down with one of the guys in the office and found one shopworn sample with thumbmarks on it and a price of $125.

It is hard to remember what $125 meant in the late forties. You could buy a brand new Ford convertible for $640, complete with rumble seat and white wall tires. This automobile, with motor, lights, gas tank, and wheels, was only five times the cost of this one lamp. I was furious and was stalking angrily down the stairs when suddenly an image popped into my mind which seemed to have nothing to do with anything. It was a picture in *The New York Times* some weeks before which showed Liberty ships being mothballed by having the decks covered with netting and then being sprayed with a self-webbing plastic, and again, whammo! We rushed back to the office and made a roughly spherical wire frame; we called various places until we located the manufacturer of the spiderwebby spray. By the next night we had a plastic-covered lamp, and when you put a light in it, it glowed, and it did not cost $125. But note again the irrational jump from dissatisfaction with a product that was overpriced to remembering an item in the newspaper that seemingly had nothing to do with it.

In all the experiences I have been describing, what we get is an invariable pattern. It is not mine; it's everybody's. First you collect and analyze information, then apparently the nonrational part of the brain goes through a mysterious search for bits of information that have no meaning to the logical part of the brain, and then—if you're lucky—these irrelevant items come together and something happens.

For the process to work, for the creative act, the logical, analytical part of the brain has got to be put out of action. This goes against normal behavior. Because in our kind of technical industrial world, we've been brainwashed from birth to believe that everything can be discovered by observing, measuring, analyzing, and thinking, but it simply isn't so. The entire history of scientific discovery, mathematical discovery, bears this out. We cannot *think* our way into creative behavior.

There is a story about a 19th-century French mathematician named Henri Poincaré, who became famous for a series of equations. He worked for months trying to find a solution, got nowhere, became increasingly frustrated, and was many times on the verge of giving up. One day, as he was walking down one of the boulevards, he remembered he had to do something, got on a bus, and as he entered the carriage, he *saw* all the equations. Just like on a blackboard. A very common story. It's common with people like that anyway.

There's also the great-grandfather of all these people, Archimedes. He was a Greek, late in the third century B.C., who was given an impossible problem by the king of Syracuse. The king had a crown and wanted to know if the gold in it had been alloyed with silver. He said, "Archimedes, you're a genius, go find out." Well, Archimedes was a mathematician as well as an engineer, and he knew that there was no way he could possibly measure the crown. It was too irregular. To tell whether a thing was all gold or not you had to know its volume; you also had to have the weight of an identical volume of gold and then you weighed it. But he had no way of figuring out the volume of the crown and became frustrated by his efforts to find one. Again that familiar preliminary mental condition. He went home, got into his bathtub for the ten-thousandth time, sank down, and watched the water rise. He had seen this happen every time he had taken a bath, but what he saw this time was the displacement principle: an irregular body will displace its exact volume in a liquid, which can then be measured. Then he started shouting, "Eureka!"—which means, "I have found it!"—as indeed he had. They must have heard him for blocks.

There is something significant to note in all these tales: anyone who has such experiences never says, "I *did* it"; he always says, "I *found* it." Interesting. It was there all the time. I *found* it. The creative act is always *finding* something.

I remember a conversation with Erich Fromm some years ago. I was a customer of his at the time. I forget the context, but Fromm asked, "Did you ever hear of a man who got an erection by an act of will?" And I said, "Well, come to think of it, no." You cannot emulate Archimedes by an act of will either. In some strange way one must be passive and receiving in order to do this.

We're beginning to learn some of the reasons why these things happen and how. Research into the structure and behavior of the brain indicates that its hemispheres or lobes are specialized. The left lobe seems to work very well with linear problems like language and analysis; the right hemisphere deals primarily with visual matters, synthesizing activities, and nonlinear situations generally. What we call "inspiration" seems to stem from the right lobe's phenomenal ability to go switching through memory banks to pick up seemingly irrelevant items that come together and make sense, which the left lobe can't do. Maybe the excited, enormously satisfied feeling of a great event occurring is the happy surprise of finding that for once in your life both lobes are actually cooperating. In a direct, practical sense, this means that inspiration doesn't just happen to anyone. It is not like getting struck by lightning. The left lobe must do its homework, collecting the data and taking the problem as far as it can, and then the right lobe has to get into its own act, which is this mysterious searching for things that can be fitted together.

There is a story about Louis Pasteur that bears this out. Pasteur became one of the famous men in Europe because of his discoveries in bacteriology, and there was a big reception for him in Paris. He was approached at this reception by a colleague who was so envious that he had no way of concealing it, and after congratulating Pasteur, he said, "Dear colleague, are you aware of the extraordinary fact that so many of the great discoveries of our century have been made by accident?" Pasteur looked at him as one might look at a new variety of insect and said, "Yes, I have noticed this; and have you, dear colleague, ever noticed to whom the accidents happen?"

One of the most common misconceptions about creativity is the notion that it has to be associated with certain professions or activities. Even an observer as sympathetic and perceptive as Dr. Abraham Maslow confesses that he was a victim of this view, and he wrote about it: "I soon discovered that I had, like most other people, been thinking of creativeness in terms of products . . . assuming that any painter, any poet, any composer was leading a creative life. Theorists, artists, scientists, inventors, writers could be creative . Nobody else could be."

The reality is different. There is no such thing as a creative profession. There are as many hacks in architecture, graphics, and industrial design as there are in banking, garbage collection, or any faculty in any university. *Only individuals can be creative.* Also, all individuals are born with the potential. Why all people don't get to be like Louis Pasteur is the mystery, for the door is open to every healthy baby.

There are other curious aspects of this creative act and the extraordinary feelings that come when it happens. As I said, there is no way of willing it. The ground must be prepared in some way, and then, maybe, it happens. But you can't say, "Today at eleven forty-five I'd better stop what I am doing and be creative." There is no possible way of doing this. Another aspect of this question of creativity is that the importance to the creator of whatever may be discovered or invented has no connection whatever with the value society may put on it. What the creator creates is to him a total thing and a magnificent experience; what this is worth to the society is a different matter. For instance, if some genius concocted a $2 detonator that would make our sun go nova and vaporize the entire solar system, we can be sure that he would be plastered with medals from Colorado to Irkustk. But the satisfaction of the achievement of blowing up the entire planetary system is no greater or less than discovering, for instance, that pedestrian malls are nice things to have in cities.

A couple makes love: does the girl say, "What a pity he isn't Rock Hudson or Elvis Presley?" No. If they are feeling good, they are very happy, and this is as good as it has ever been for anybody else. This is important to know. It's a totally inside, personal thing.

What the creative act really means is the unfolding of the human psyche in the sudden realization that one has taken a lot of disconnected pieces and *found,* not *done,* a way of putting them together. This is when the solitary individual finds he is connected with a reality he never dreamed of, with a feeling of internal power without limit, and the knowledge that he is truly and fully alive for one miraculous instant.

All these feelings or insights are of extremely short duration. The analogy I think of is a strobe light, twenty-five-thousandths of a second—but you get enough light out of it to make a photograph. Peaks are of very short duration, possibly because none of us could live through a longer exposure.

But this leads to curious speculation. You might think of your working life—forty or fifty years—as a sum total of maybe six minutes and fourteen seconds of peak experiences. That is really all there is. What this brings up is the possibility that we may have to learn to think about the meaning of time in other ways.

To understand these moments whose effects can last a lifetime, one goes back to the creative act and asks, "What is it, really?" Well, it's frustration and search, it's research, it's inspiration, it's explosion, and all the rest of it. *But at its base it has to be an act of love.* This is why it can't be willed. Dick can't say it's time now for me to love Jane or vice-versa. It happens. And the sudden flowering which comes from this act of love is not really a pop lyric, it's a very practical matter. For instance, how do we light a candle? We get a match and light it. Okay, but will it light if there is no oxygen? No, it will not light. So, in a certain sense, love and the oxygen in the atmosphere are basic prerequisites for making certain things happen.

The other really extraordinary thing about love *is that it sets the lover free.* If you think of the self—the isolated, alienated self—going around in its little prison and suddenly it encounters another self. There is nothing more than a startled glance, and the bars of the prison dissolve. Then solitary, isolated individuals become part of a much larger thing, and they are free in a way they were never free before.

Fromm described loving as an intense awareness of the reality, the miraculous living reality, of another person. It can also apply to things. I watched Wright design a building once . . . five hours of the most incredible concentration I've ever seen, and at the end of it, he sort of woke up and looked around—I was sitting in a corner hoping I wouldn't be thrown out—and said, "Come here, George. I want to show you something." He pointed to his drawing: "I was supposed to get this church done two years ago, but I really didn't have the right feeling about it. Today I got it and look—here's the church and here's the little loggia that goes to the minister's house." And he said, "You know, George, it's a very modest house, the church doesn't have much money, but it is a noble dwelling!" This was the difference between Wright and any other architect I ever met. He was loving that dwelling because it was *noble.*

Love is also of necessity an affirmation of life, and it is not so easy to do—particularly in the society in which we happen to find ourselves, which is almost totally obsessed with death. But the lesson of the people we look up to is that it is not impossible.

I'll end with a story about Wright. I followed him around like a puppy for about ten years. He was my hero, I wanted his secret. "How do you get to be a great architect? How do you do buildings that people can't stop walking around in because they are so alive? How, Mr. Wright? Show me, tell me." And I always kept hoping that somehow he would let slip a phrase that would clarify the whole problem, and I wouldn't have to thrash around anymore.

One early spring evening, I was out on the terrace at his desert camp, looking at one of those spectacular Arizona sunsets. The place was deserted. I think the apprentices were off somewhere making dinner or cleaning up. Anyway, the terrace was empty. I heard a door slam, looked back, and there was the old man coming out of his apartment. He'd apparently had a pretty good day. He was wearing his porkpie hat, his stiff collar, his cape, his cane, and he was feeling sociable. He saw me standing there, sauntered over twirling his cane, made some small talk about sunsets or Arizona or whatever, when suddenly he said, "George, do you know what architecture is, what architecture *really* is?" I replied, "Mr. Wright, why don't you tell me?"

Behind us on the terrace there was a big palo verde tree—a desert tree that has a green trunk and branches, spines in place of leaves, and at that time of year, February or March, it bursts out with the most beautiful, delicate yellow blossoms you can imagine. He waggled his stick, pointed back at this tree, and said, "Architecture is like that palo verde tree bursting into bloom." I sagged with disappointment. I had thought he was going to tell me something. Then he made a little more talk, but I was burning with disappointment. Then he went off about five or six feet, suddenly stopped, turned back. He said, "Well, maybe it isn't quite like that palo verde tree bursting into bloom; maybe it's more like a boy falling in love with a girl." And I thought, "You old blackguard, you had the chance of telling me. Why didn't you?"

It took me ten years to realize that he had told me the most important thing he could possibly tell me. I've been lucky in my teachers, but sometimes too slow as a student.

ENVIRONMENTS

The Hidden City

The notion of making buildings invisible, or less visible, after millennia of efforts by emperors, prelates, and architects to make their projects supremely conspicuous, could only arise when the volume of building in cities began to pass the overkill mark. The projects shown here were done by my class at Harvard's Graduate School of Design in 1973 and they are a fair sample of reasonable expressions of the concept. The Graham Foundation of Chicago provided a generous grant which allowed the presentations to develop more fully than is ordinarily possible with student projects.

There is no claim of originality in this concept: underground structures are not new, and there are excellent examples in many places to illustrate how buildings may become "quieter" visually through the use of berms. The real effort here was to organize, or perhaps to distill the meaning of many projects, into a body of theory

Dunehouse, Atlantic Beach, Florida. Architect: William Morgan, FAIA.

with possible value as another tool for the urban designer. The only worrisome aspect of the proposals is that if they are too widely accepted we are going to have to cope with a national shortage of topsoil. Maybe this could be the push that would launch us into municipal composting as a sensible and valuable aspect of city life!

One day I had lunch with a friend, who went to a lot of trouble to explain to me what visual pollution was all about. As an inhabitant of New York, it didn't seem to me that there was much anyone could tell me, but my friend was from Ohio, where he works as a designer in a barn in the country, and he had concluded that visual pollution was caused by billboards, by telephone poles and wires, and by gas stations.

It was a nice day and after lunch I walked back to my office, meditating on this information. It was a pretty neat formula he had worked out, and presumably if we got rid of these three blights, visual pollution would end. It was all so pat that I got uneasy. It was too much like politicians' talk: "Reelect me and I will give you a century of peace, but please don't get upset if I drop another half-million tons of bombs while we are waiting." That kind of thing.

It also struck me that walking in New York, where there are precious few sights that gladden the eye, reveals large quantities of visual pollution, but as it happens we do not have billboards to speak of (except in Times Square where they look rather nice and lively) and we have no telephone poles at all, since the wires have long since been put underground. As for gas stations, all you have to do on Manhattan is run out of gas and then try to find one. Apparently you don't need billboards, telephone wires, or gas stations to pollute an urban environment, although, of course, they do help.

For a long time after that walk I found myself speculating on the sources of visual pollution from time to time, but without much in the way of results. One night when I had trouble getting to sleep I ran through a collection of private images of cities remembered—San Francisco, Zurich, Hong Kong, Rio, Paris, Helsinki—and before I fell asleep it seemed clear that the main source of pollution in New York had to be the architecture, but it seemed also clear that you couldn't say architecture equals urban ugliness, since there were so many examples to the contrary. Yet there are certain configurations of buildings and spaces which add up to hopelessly unattractive cityscapes and others which do not. Precisely what are the qualities which turn an environment one way or another?

As we scan our private lists of great and not-so-great cities, Venice, for many people, stands out as the queen of cities. Even if some of us would not put it at the top of our list, it is always up there near the top. Why? The first thing that comes to mind is that Venice has canals instead of streets, and it is remarkable how much more pleasant in every way water is, compared with asphalt, or boats compared with cars. If anyone wanted to make a rule out of this: "cities with canals are easier on the eyes than cities with streets," I would not debate the issue. But Venice is more than canals.

You can walk your feet off in that compact city, going through alleys and squares and across bridges without ever coming across anything identifiable as visual pollution. In addition, movement through the city, whether by boat or foot, is exciting, for the variety of scale and the transitions from tight enclosures to great spaces are endless delights. The city "fits" the human occupant in a series of rich and dramatic ways. It is never dull.

Modern cities lack these qualities. They offer instead a kind of urban eczema composed of scattered high-rise offices and apartments, miles of four-story neighborhoods, and more miles of bombed-out slums, the whole scene laced with traffic and parked cars everywhere. It is hard to get *inside* in a modern city. One is always jammed between hard building fronts and car-filled streets. Modern cities reject their inhabitants, which is logical enough, since they were never planned with people in mind, and the newest of them, like Brasilia and Chandigarh, don't seem a bit better. The proudest boast of the planners of Brasilia was that there would not be a single traffic light in the city. All this means to me is that the only way to live in such a place is to be permanently sealed in a bus or motor home which never stops moving. Venice doesn't have traffic lights either, of course, but the concept is different.

There are obviously exceptions to what I am saying: Chicago, for example, has many elements which can only be classed as amenities. But the point, nonetheless, has to be made: the contemporary city, lacking those monumental structures and open spaces which came into existence as expressions of faith and power, tends to be formless and lacking in enlivening changes of pace. One has only to think of a relatively minor city such as Guadalajara, with its four magnificent squares checkerboarded in the center of town, and to compare it with its more up-to-date counterparts anywhere in the U.S.

All cities have expressive form. That is, their configurations reflect contemporary realities, whether religious be-

Grand Canal, Venice.

liefs or economic arrangements or opinions on the divine right of kings. One problem which plagues the modern city is that there is very little to express: the Church has lost its meaning and power, the men with great wealth have become uneasy about displaying it, and we can't even imitate those good-looking medieval walls, except perhaps in Disneyland. The most monumental structures we put up in cities, the highrise buildings, have been boiled down to simplistic extrusions whose forms are determined by land prices and by the battle between entrepreneurs and building trade unions, neither of which is an exciting subject for glorification. In the Communist countries, where the entrepreneurs are replaced by public bureaucracies, things are no different: we see the same extruded slabs, with detailing still less sophisticated technically. The modern city, sprawling over miles of countryside, has thus become painfully familiar to us as a formless network of roads woven into great masses of building lots, spiced with roadside strips and automobile junk yards. We apparently have almost nothing to express, and we express it. No wonder there is so much vandalism.

Questions: Can we do anything, even theoretically, about the endless visual boredom so typical of the contemporary city? If architectural sprawl is a prime source of visual pollution, can anything be done about it? Are we capable of even conceiving a solution that might humanize the dying cities? Or are we moving into a kind of "Brave New World" where there will be no need to worry about such problems?

Given what has already been said, we might accept the proposition, if only for the sake of furthering the argument, that a city with a half or a third of its buildings discreetly eliminated, much as a dentist cleans out a cavity, would be a visual improvement over what we now have. But could we even imagine doing such a thing? Buildings are generally there because people need to use them. And yet, I am impressed by the possibility that less, in the case of cities, is better than more. Michigan Boulevard is Chicago's great street primarily because for much of its length some of the buildings are missing, replaced by parks and river crossings. Could any of us imagine this street improved by any architect alive, with buildings continuous on both sides? I doubt it.

It doesn't even matter whether the buildings which do fill one side are "great" or not: it is enough for us that half of them aren't there. If you run through your own memories of streets you like, whether from actual experience of cities or photographs, I strongly suspect that a good percentage of them will, like Michigan, be incompletely built. The quais in Paris and Moscow are one-sided streets. There is the Stockholm waterfront, Dutch towns like Delft, the Nevsky Prospekt in Leningrad, the Copacabana in Rio, the rue de Rivoli in Paris, and any number of great squares in London and Dublin. It always seems to work out, although the old-line architects may not like it: less architecture in all these examples seems to come out as less visual pollution, because there is more form, more variety, more urban richness, more contrast, more rhythm.

But we can't tear down half the buildings. Not even the Communist countries, with none of our land acquisition problems, can tear down half the buildings. So we have to look for a compromise, and the one that suggests itself to me is that if we can't eliminate them, perhaps we can make them invisible. Is there any way to do this?

Actually, there are two possibilities. One is familiar to us: build underground. This is being done in many places. The other, not familiar, is to build above ground, using structures like low-profile Aztec or Mayan pyramids, covering them with topsoil and planting nasturtiums, poison ivy, or whatever comes to mind. Such structures would of course be visible, *but not as architecture,* which I see as their great virtue. A facade-happy architect might see it differently. These earth-covered structures would look like artificial or natural hills, depending on how tricky we got with the interior planning and the landscaping.

Now we come to a very reasonable question: why should anyone build a building covered with earth? Esthetic considerations are out: we cannot say that the city would be more beautiful, or more suited to the sensory needs of urban people. A technological society cannot operate with values, like esthetics, which are not quantifiable. The same goes for humane considerations. Still, there are reasons which might register, even with a technological barbarian. This proposition has to do with windows.

Being creatures of habit, all of us, we have a stereotype view of the big city, which shows us a skyline made up of buildings perforated with windows. But the startling fact is that as we survey the services accommodated within cities, there is a very large number of building types which not only do not need windows, but *do not want them.* Here are a few: warehouses (both cold and warm storage), telephone exchanges, power sub-stations, data centers, opera houses, department stores, movie houses, concert halls, museums, convention centers, sports arenas, shopping malls . . . you can take the list from there.

Given this one hint based on windows, we can hope for a breakthrough in the monotonous urban scene. This is not Utopia, not a great big shiny dream city of some indefinite future. It is just one simple anti-architectural device which might give an urban environment the relief it desperately needs.

We can begin to imagine some forms this concept might take. The structures are not really true pyramids, for space requirements would tend to make them longer than they are wide. They are probably not very high, for you can't go much over a 30-degree slope and still hold the earth covering without retaining walls (not that these are out of the question). But if we go back to the incomplete list of building types, we find that these as a rule do not go very high. Buildings that do go high generally need windows, anyway.

One of the interesting characteristics of pyramidal structures is that they are larger at the base, which suggests that roads could go through them and ample parking could be provided. If daylight is wanted inside, there is nothing to stop us from putting in a half-mile of skylights, very much like the galleria-type shopping malls. We can also attach small structures to the sides of our hills, like Mediterranean villas. These could be small office clusters related to activities inside, or perhaps restaurants, or even a few houses for the lucky owners. All this would be visually interesting and there would still be plenty of room for hillside parks, toboggan runs, waterfalls, or whatever else the ingenuity of owners and architects might come up with.

I do not see any very stringent limitations on the size or shape of these structures. They could be five or ten miles long if there were space needs on this scale, curved as well as straight, complex in their plans as well as simple.

If we imagine a city in which all of the major windowless services are clustered in hills, some unfamiliar images come to mind. For one thing, a city of one million population might give the impression of a city of 600,000 or 700,000. This would be an instant gain, for there would be a reduction of apparent bulk and congestion, an increase in elbow room. Equally important, I think, would be the creation of strong contrasts: a play between hard and soft, man-made and natural, large and small. Another contrast suggests itself: a new distinction between automobile and pedestrian. If the service mounds accommodated the main roads and facilities for parking, one could conceive of plans which would permit the development of adjacent pedestrian areas, possibly serviced by monorails, subways, electric minibuses, and moving sidewalks. A vivid illustration of existing possibilities of this sort is to be found in the air terminal in Tampa, where little electric shuttles free of noise and pollution move hundreds of thousands of people in a pleasant, comfortable fashion.

The most interesting design problem is not the artificial hills themselves, but the relationship between these soft swellings in the urban landscape and the more traditional building types around them. One could imagine pedestrian valleys formed by these planted structures, combinations of very large and very small open spaces, visual experiences at a variety of levels. One might object that such structures would waste a great deal of valuable land. This might be true, but we would first have to define what we mean by "waste." A typical shopping center is never thought of as waste by developers, but most of the land involved is covered with asphalt for parking. A civilized society might consider this something of a waste, too, since the land under the asphalt is permanently destroyed as far as life support is concerned.

If such a shopping facility were built in the fashion I have been describing, however, it might take less space, since the parking is under the shopping (where it belongs anyway). An eyesore could become an amenity, and this might have an effect on the uses and the money value of the surrounding area. Given the shopping center of today, there are few people who would want to live next to one, and as a result the adjoining properties are generally given over to parasitic marginal uses. But if one were to sweep the prevailing mess under one or more earth-covered mounds, the entire aspect and meaning of the area would change, presumably for the better. The same could be said, probably, for light industrial and warehousing uses.

There is something else in the wind these days which may have an interesting effect on the acceptability of these hollow hills: this is the developing energy shortage. If you look at any chart of power consumption for the past thirty or forty years, you see a line which rises faster and faster each year until it now approaches the vertical. In other words, there seems to be no visible limit to our demand for energy. But if you compare this with a chart of energy *production,* the line doesn't go up as fast. The difference between the two lines is the energy gap, and the gap is due to become a crisis.

The Oakland Museum. Architects: Kevin Roche, John Dinkeloo and Associates; top photo courtesy the Oakland Museum; bottom photo by Alexandre Georges.

Under such conditions, our invisible city components should come off very well indeed. Wind drag is minimized by the low mounds, and the structures themselves could approach the insulation values of a cold-storage warehouse. Solar energy could be tapped through skylight design for the cold season, and bounced off in hot weather. The more we look at these earth-covered shells, the more interesting the design problems and possibilities. The mere fact that services associated with urban blight can be so enclosed that they become civic amenities could change many of our notions about urban planning and redevelopment.

Some years back something was done in New Haven which suggests the kind of thing which might happen. At the east end of the center city there is an old square, full of elms and surrounded by interesting buildings, mostly residential. Nearby, a light industry area had had a blighting effect on the square and it had begun to decay. Then an express highway was built in between the two, with the road set high up on a landscaped earth base which effectively isolated the two areas from each other, and the square's prestige returned rapidly. We may anticipate similar results from our synthetic hills.

The real value I can see here, aside from the advantages already mentioned, is that we can introduce new elements of scale, contrast, and spatial rhythm which are sorely needed. And I can't imagine anything nicer happening to those pool-table towns all over the Midwest, where a few hills could work wonders in the flat landscape.

At the Graduate School of Design at Harvard, this past year, we have been tackling the problem of the invisible city, exploring some of the possible uses of artificial hills and trying to see how these might relate to the more familiar kinds of buildings. The results may not make sense, you know. We may find that they present short term financial problems at the outset. Or that they would work effectively only in new towns. Or that there is a national shortage of topsoil to cover them. We have to realize that the right to experiment includes the right to fail. But in one sense, ventures of this kind cannot fail, because the exercise alone is bound to deepen the discussion about cities. Merely trying something of this kind modifies our established attitudes about what a modern city really is and could be. Exercises of this type do not revolutionize cities: they broaden and enrich our view of the problem.

Let me recapitulate, briefly. First, we have the observation that a substantial degree of visual pollution in cities is

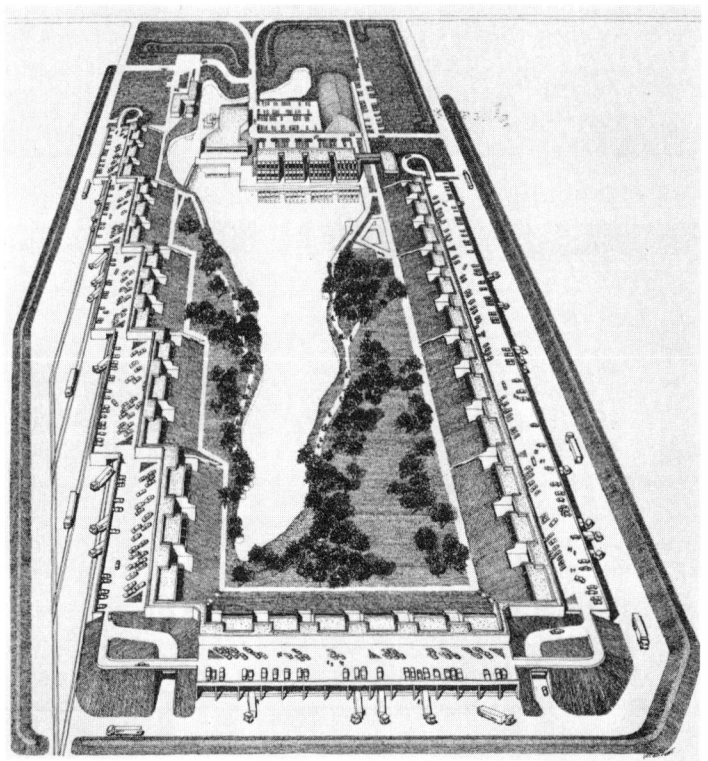

The airview shows a main highway at the top and a motel on the small lake. Facilities for light industry and offices are located in a U, serviced by a peripheral road. Earth berms contain storage and some manufacturing space. The scheme is a model solution for combining such activities in, say, a residential neighborhood. Harvard Student Project, "Industrial Park" by John Becker. Illustrations by Albert Lorenz.

Bicentennial Park, a project for a parklike exhibition and sports development: the uniform characteristic of the student schemes shown is the coexistence of tranquil surrounds and high-density use of the terrain. Such a tool for improving urban environments is still awaiting the exploitation it deserves. Harvard Student Project "Bicentennial Park" by John Becker; illustration by Albert Lorenz. The project was assisted by a grant from the Graham Foundation for Advanced Studies.

created by the buildings themselves. Second, we have the proposition that if offending buildings cannot be removed, many services can be so housed that the buildings become invisible as buildings. Third, this possibility of the visual elimination of architecture exists because so many facilities have no need for windows. Fourth, the community could acquire many amenities and benefits through the procedure described.

If we were scientists rather than architects and designers, what I have been doing would be described as the presentation of a series of related hypotheses. Progress in science is closely connected with such presentations, for it is taken for granted that it is the right and the obligation of the scientific community to attack such presentations in every possible way so that the hypothesis is established as valid, modified to meet objections, or demolished. Whatever the outcome, the community benefits. We could use a lot more of this in architecture. The only such example that comes to my mind at the moment is the published work of Paolo Soleri.

One of the real difficulties in dealing with urban problems is that they have a very low social priority, which in turn means that the money they need is spent elsewhere. As a broad generalization, one can say that any problem intimately related to people gets a relatively low priority in any of the advanced industrial societies, which are much better at dealing with physical things than with living organisms. One result of all this is that we tend to see city problems as operational rather than human. And yet any city, whatever its physical plant, consists essentially of living, interacting organisms. The central cities all over the country are dying, not because the power has been shut off or the buildings are falling apart, but because those people who can afford to do so are running away from them.

Paris, in the time of Francois Villon, was a stinking medieval pesthole, crawling with pimps, whores, thieves, con men, and murderers. And yet this drunken rascal produced some unforgettable poems about the city he loved, and especially about the women of the city. Have you read any poems lately about the women of Chicago?

Cities can kill their inhabitants with rat bites, malnutrition, drugs, disease, violence, and slum fires. (A lot of this can happen in the country, too.) Cities can also kill by starvation of the spirit. If there are things the modern city can do better than the old ones, they are to cripple the spirit, beat the essential humanity in man to its knees, blind those who can still see, and lobotomize the survivors who can still think and feel.

I am not about to suggest that these maladies can be cured by putting up some earth-covered structures. That would be arrogance carried to the point of insanity. These hypotheses indicate some possible physical improvements, but they are also symbols. As symbols they stand for the belief that vision, at this point in time, is more important than new technology, for technology has reached the stage at which efforts to remedy its own mistakes seem to take us closer to disaster. The vision needed is nothing more or less than a series of images of physical realities so conceived that one could hope for an improvement of the human condition.

This is what I am asking you to think about. It is the most intelligent and constructive thing a designer can do in a time of global crisis, and of social and moral transformation.

Dunehouse, Atlantic Beach, Florida. Architect: William Morgan, FAIA.

The End of Architecture

In the early 70s I spent two years commuting to Harvard's Graduate School of Design, working in the studio with groups of architectural students. I loved the whole thing and probably would have gone on with it indefinitely but for the fact that flying the shuttle from New York, with all the attendant commotion in getting to and from airports, combined with the loss of two days a week from my office, became too high a price for the fun. Before this came about, however, I learned that the other price a visiting professor was expected to pay was a lecture to the entire school once a year and this obligation led to "The End of Architecture," a title I found eminently suitable for a student audience which was still at the beginning.

I have always felt that in dealing with student audiences one does not fool around: there is a responsibility to tell them, as precisely as possible, what one believes to be true and why, and to emphasize the high level of their responsibilities as

Park Avenue, New York. Photo by Gil Amiaga.

future designers, and to leave some awareness of the nobility of their calling, both in terms of past history and present possibilitites.

There were many such talks during this period and "The End of Architecture"—for me—comes closer to saying what I had on my mind than most of the others.

A road meanders toward the coast. It passes through villages, goes up hill and down, passes farms, finally comes to the cliffs over the sea, and stops. It is the end of the road. But the journey does not necessarily stop. With a boat, it could go on.

For uncounted years, starting long before they learned to put thoughts into writing, people have been building: mud walls, rock walls, marble walls; roofs of straw, clay, wood, stone; posts, lintels, beams, arches, corbels, vaults, domes, trusses. . . . Eventually they looked around, and named it architecture. It is the largest category of designed objects. The objects are hollow: they have outsides and they have insides. They dominate the natural landscape: wherever the road goes on its way to the sea, there were fields and forests, and there is architecture. Now architecture has competition, for in place of the fields and forests there are the strips, the neon jungles snaking out from the towns, eating up the surrendered landscape.

Our life span is three score and ten, give or take a few decades. Buildings last longer. So, as the race slowly grows and develops, two kinds of permanence become familiar: the permanence of nature and the permanence of architecture. The Argentine poet Borges writes that it is "Hard to believe that Buenos Aires had any beginning. I feel it to be as eternal as air and water." The human animal has always needed a sense of security, and until very recently these two kinds of permanence were his twin environmental pillars. Now, both are threatened. In Los Angeles, they have tried plastic landscaping on a freeway. In all cities, the highway bulldozers chew great holes in the shattered urban structure.

I suggest that the end of architecture, as we are accustomed to think of it, is being hastened, paradoxically, by the triumph of modern design. The new scale of building, now moving towards megastructures and megacities, will have the same effect. The collision between architecture and technology is leaving the former battered. We are presently going to become aware that the greatest source of visual pollution in cities is the buildings. The architect is gradually being changed from a professional to personnel, to use Paul Goodman's phrase. "Expression," that quality in architecture which allows us to distinguish a church from a town hall, is disappearing. So are windows, in more and more categories of building. The emergence of the first completely enclosed towns within a decade or two is more than likely. The space needs of automobiles are eviscerating older cities, making it clear that all current types of buildings, as grouped in urban settings, are obstructive hangovers from a period when civic form was determined by pedestrians, horse-drawn vehicles, and trolley cars. While these forces have no common origin, they are all exerting pressures in a common direction.

If architecture is thought of as building created by architects, we collide immediately with the fact that very little building, anywhere or anytime, has come from architects' drawing tables. Even if we think of architecture as building-*plus*, that is, as structures designed to gladden the eye and nourish the spirit as well as keep off the rain, there is very little of it. Nonetheless, there is a broad consensus that this "little" is precious. Even the visually illiterate sense that Chartres is more than a hall, the Parthenon is more than a bleached ruin, and Monticello is more than an old-fashioned house built by a wealthy man. Great buildings, like great paintings, books, plays, or poems, are highly concentrated testimonials to the ability of the human animal, under suitable conditions, to get up on his two feet and make like a complete man. In addition, they have scarcity value: there have never been enough of them.

When conditions are not suitable, architecture, in the sense just given, is at a serious disadvantage, more serious than the plight of painting or theater, for there is no such thing as an architecture of protest. An "angry" building is an impossibility: it cannot be designed, let alone built. "Suitable conditions" are hard to define. No society has ever tried to create such conditions. Their emergence has always been fortuitous. About all we can do is pinpoint the small places and brief periods when great buildings did appear in substantial numbers, and try to figure out by hindsight what the ingredients might have been. Without stopping here to delve deeply into such questions, I think we can say that some common qualities would be: a general feeling that life has meaning; a sense of individual liberty in the effective elements of the population; and a shared faith in the main values of the society.

These conditions do not exist at the present time in either capitalist or communist societies.

In addition to those rare events we label "great" architecture, there is also the larger output of decent, well-conceived, attractive and sensibly functioning building. This too appears to be under attack on several fronts.

One of the most serious of these threats has come, quite unconsciously, from the architects themselves. During the first half of the 20th century a struggle developed between the establishment architects, who wanted to continue their eclectic way of designing buildings, and a younger group which insisted that honesty of design, in the sense of functional planning and the expressive use of modern materials and techniques, was long overdue. This movement, like the eclectic approach it was fighting, was international. By the 50s it was clear that the modernists had won.

Now when an architect decides to use modern materials and techniques in an honest, logical way, it does not take long before he is up to his ears in systems, standard elements, and modules, and as soon as the modules show advantages of cost or speed, industry begins to turn them out. When there is an adequate range of such elements in the catalogs, it inevitably occurs to someone that it shouldn't be that hard to put whole buildings together and sell them directly to users. Presently the landscape begins to fill up with standard office buildings, trailers, prefabs, mobile homes, and modulars. More and more are being sold, complete with furnishings and accessories. In theory there is no reason such buildings should not be decent and attractive, but, in reality, the effect is usually that of a flattening out of experience, a diminishing of life.

In general, this is true of technology wherever it takes over. Changing modes of travel offer an illustration. When a person walks or rides behind a horse, there is time for many experiences: details of the landscape can be enjoyed; if someone is encountered along the way there is conversation. Shift the movement to a train and there is still a lot to see. Even on Japan's Tokkaido Express, at 125 mph, it holds true. But take a jet and nothing is left but a cramped seat, a magazine, and perhaps a drink. As technology advances, experience recedes. Not always, and not inevitably, but generally. The symbolic expression of all this is the lunar landing: there, if a man were permitted to experience the environment directly, he would instantly die.

Another element with which architecture has to cope today is the new scale, the enormous increase in the size of the staging areas required for more and more activities. Airports have increased their size tenfold in a relatively short time. In the military area, given the capability of weapons now, a major war could begin and end within 48 hours because the fronts no longer have adequate depth. A suitable staging area for a war of greater duration, with a minimum sporting element left in the goings-on, would now require at least two planets. The interstate highway system has consumed two million acres. Suburban developments take even more. Shopping centers consume hundreds of thousands. Urban renewal programs gut whole sections of cities. Cities sprawl out into megalopolitan regions of 50, 80, or 90 million inhabitants. Visionaries like Paolo Soleri design concrete beehives for a million people.

All this creates new problems for the architect. They may not be insoluble, but they are unprecedented kinds of problems, not merely bigger ones.

A common basis for architecture in the past has been the existence of intelligible individual and social relationships. They may not have been humane or amiable, but they were there. When temples like Karnak were built, the cost in physical labor was enormous, but no one questioned the importance, even the necessity, of what he was doing. No matter how onerous the conditions, the relationships were human and universally understood. Even when things became intolerable and the people revolted, the changed relationships were still real.

We are now a long way from these simple times. Today the orders issue from anonymous corporate bureaus and are executed by in-house staffs or offices which have also become public corporations. The architect who designs a 1,000-house tract or a 30-story apartment building has no idea whom he is designing for. At best, he can only read reports which statistically define a market: average income, $16,327; 2.368 children per family, etc., etc.

As we move up the scale to the so-called "significant" buildings—large commercial complexes, religious edifices, government and other institutional structures—we run into another curious fact: nobody seems to believe, with much conviction, in any of the institutions.

There is no need to credit the young with this: their conspicuous display of scorn for established values, their sit-ins, card burnings, and draft evasions merely put headlines on attitudes already held, silently, by millions of their elders. The case with which "loyalties" are switched from one corporate employer to another, the obsession with retirement which begins decades before the day, preoccupation with boats, choppers, campers, travel, with anything but work, the universal cynicism about political leaders, all these familiar manifestations are evidence enough. It has become difficult to find people with any interest in what they are doing for a living, and millions, the sociologists tell us, actively hate their work.

All this is reflected in architecture, which becomes progressively more bland, blank, mediocre, characterless. Thus the social critics cry out, not without reason, about the dehumanization of existence. Boredom, the chronic illness of our time, finds its portrait in buildings.

This takes us to a point architects rarely talk about: that the visual pollution of which we have suddenly become so conscious is not created primarily by billboards and litter, but by the superabundant clutter of buildings. Most cities would look and feel better if half the structures in them could be made invisible.

The swallowing up of isolated buildings (another form of elimination of superfluous architecture) is actually beginning to happen with the megastructures. Le Corbusier suggested this in his plan for Rio. He had noted that efforts to remake obsolete quarters in old cities invariably bogged down in legal problems related to condemnation, whereas the highway builders seemed to have no such difficulties. His inspired response to this observation was to suggest that buildings be constructed on the rights-of-way, with the highways on top. The result was linear buildings which might be five to a dozen miles in length. The scheme was not built, but it is not hard to see that the idea at its very worst would have reduced clutter. There are already a few such structures in Rio—not yet five miles long—which look well on their hilly sites. But the question arises, do we have architecture here, or technological anthills? People like Yona Friedman in France and N.J. Habraken in the Netherlands seem to visualize cities as endless structural cages, filled in to suit whatever type occupancy is desired. Others have suggested that we build in the spaces under existing elevated roads in cities.

Whatever one's opinions of such proposals, there is in all this a very clear, almost unanimous expression of a trend, the move away from differentiated buildings to relatively anonymous large-scale space enclosures. I suspect the reason for much of the excitement about Pier Luigi Nervi is not so much his brilliant engineering, but his creation of gigantic and exciting interior spaces. It is almost impossible to remember a Nervi exterior but equally impossible to forget the interior.

Wherever we look, the message seems to be that we are moving from the monument to the bell jar. Hans Scharoun's Philharmonic Hall in West Berlin is fantastically beautiful inside, a disorganized nothing outside. One could describe a cave in the same terms used for the concert hall. Or perhaps for Santa Sophia in Istanbul. As a nonhistorian, I suddenly find myself regretting that I know nothing about the feverish last years of the Byzantine Empire. It is possible that we have something in common.

This much seems clear: what we think of as the "reality" of architecture, which has so long been a conspicuous expression on the exterior (just think of Venice or Paris or Florence for a moment) is now shifting with considerable rapidity to the interior. Such a transformation is not necessarily bad, but it does give rise to questions about what is happening to architecture as we are accustomed to think of it. My own hunch is that a lot of it is going to simply vanish, first by becoming increasingly uninteresting and then by being swallowed up into megastructures or by being buried in the earth or covered with topsoil and planted.

Now let me pull the noose a bit tighter: I have seen at least two proposals for covering entire towns with domes, and there is a persistent rumor that such communities are now being planned for the Arctic. Buckminster Fuller's suggestion that midtown Manhattan be covered with a dome two miles in diameter has been widely publicized. Another, which looks similar, has been designed by a team headed by Frei Otto. In such concepts we find the bell jar blown up to megascale. What are the chances that we are going to get domed cities? I don't know, of course, but my guess is that the chances are roughly 100 percent Let me give you two examples of the way such things work.

When air conditioning first appeared on the scene, its best customers were restaurants and movie houses. In a very real way, it was forced on them: those who put it in did more business, and those who did not, lost business. Then stores began to follow. However, since air conditioning was considered expensive, it was generally believed that its blessings would be limited to those who could pay and that those who could not would somehow get along. But this isn't the way things turned out: even cars are now air-conditioned.

When the first shopping centers were built, people parked their cars and went in and out of shops by way of a sidewalk, just as they did on Main Street. Then some unsung genius reinvented the shopping mall (the GUM store on Red Square in Moscow, late 19th-century design, and the Galleria in Milan are early examples), added air conditioning, and did very well. The shopping mall, despite its added costs and higher rents, seems to be taking over.

The enclosed city is going to have a similar history, simply because it is possible. The synthetic environment,

Dome of the Sports Palace, Rome, Pier Luigi Nervi. From Aesthetics and Technology in Building *(Cambridge, Mass.: Harvard University Press, 1965). Photo by Oscar Savio.*

*R. Buckminster Fuller's proposed dome over Manhattan.
Courtesy Buckminster Fuller Archives.*

under development for thousands of years, is not going to stop short of total realization. The first covered cities will probably be built in difficult locations: in the Arctic, on the Equator, on the Moon or Mars. Then it will be discovered that the idea can be sold. When its commercial viability has been discovered by the entrepreneurial wolves, the sheep will follow.

What happens to architecture then? You don't need buildings under a dome: tents or thatched huts will do perfectly well. Given a very large bell jar, climatized to meet the exact specifications of the Garden of Eden, the only functions left which have been traditionally met by buildings are security and privacy. So what happens to architecture in the enclosed cities?

Here too, obviously, the dominant reality will be the interior space. It may be objected that architecture is more than a matter of facades and visible mass. True enough, but it is hard to think of an architecture deprived of these elements. As we move around in cities, we have access to various interiors, but the overwhelming sensory experience in streets is created by the visible bulk of buildings.

One more point should be made. Architecture has long been the business of architects, whether they called themselves priests, craftsmen, or master builders. It has been a professional calling, carried on with love, dedication, and long study.

This is changing too. Big, successful offices are being bought by conglomerates, or are going public. Furthermore, some of the more enterprising architects are discovering that they can get more work, and make much more money, by becoming entrepreneurs. Can a public corporation act, think, feel like a profession? Furthermore, as the client-architect-contractor-subcontractor configuration gets replaced by large turnkey enterprises, these invariably create their own staffs. In theory, there is nothing to prevent a corporate design and planning group from turning out work of superb quality, and there are indeed occasional examples of just that. But, generally speaking, the professional who becomes personnel shortly turns into a bureaucrat, concerned for his job, his status, and his pension. More often than not he ends up doing what he is told to do. As he becomes a skilled bureaucrat, he knows what he has to do before anyone tells him, thus preserving the illusion of independence and personal freedom. This process of transformation in which a man becomes a mouse, or, as Kafka put it, a cockroach, is not due so much to the organization of the corporation as to its aims, which are almost invariably not human aims.

Thus we finally confront not only the dehumanization of architecture, but of the architect as well. There is nothing special in this process: it is going on all through the society.

It is difficult to present a series of observed trends, as I have done here, without at the same time creating the impression that these trends are irreversible. This is not necessarily so. If domed cities are to be part of our future, it will only be so because millions of people, habituated to more and more sealed environments, do not resist the development. If the unrestricted breeding habits of humans were replaced by a disciplined concern for future generations, all the megaproblems of mass housing, metropolitan regions, and the rest would presently evaporate. If the top priority of society were the growing of healthy people, the brutalizing, oppressive aspects of technology would disappear.

We have a lot of "ifs" here. Nevertheless, in theory, a free society can decide to reverse any trend it judges undesirable. The trouble here and now is that we have lost confidence in our ability to control our destiny and have retreated into helplessness, alienation, and a search for privacy. We do not feel like citizens in a free society. Even so, we are not entirely without resources. One is the new and rather shapeless force described as the counterculture.

The counterculture is a force, not because of any organized power, but because it is a body of ideas, attitudes, feelings, and behavior shared by substantial numbers of individuals. These people, as already suggested, are not confined to any social or age group. The endlessly demonstrated failure to make a viable, healthy society, the meaningless nature of "affluence," and the disastrous waste of social energy on insane ventures have been disturbing to far more people than just to alienated youth.

The ideas of the counterculture include outspoken disapproval of war, organized bigness, power, and authority. Science and technology are suspect. On the affirmative side, the counterculture favors respect for the individual and the natural environment. There is a clearly shown desire for community, life-enhancing relationships and activities, commitment.

Such ideas are infiltrating the society at all levels; and as they gather force, we can begin to hope that the "suitable conditions" mentioned at the beginning may somehow again emerge and allow the ancient creative impulses to flourish. A nice thought. I have no idea what the odds are but it is *absolutely imperative that we act as if they were overwhelmingly favorable.*

We have to stop and examine the last statement. The artist, architect, designer—any individual who wishes to use and deepen his creative capabilities—is as fully entitled as the next man to feel pessimism or even despair as he looks around him. At the present moment he would be an insensitive clod if he did not. Nonetheless, when he confronts his chosen work, his own problems connected with that work, he must take a positive position with regard to them. This necessity has nothing to do with his being considered a fine, cheery fellow by his neighbors and associates, but is because the problems cannot be attacked, let alone solved, if the approach is negative. Any valid creative effort is by its nature an affirmative expression, and anything else is a psychological impossibility.

But even a new "suitable condition" will not revive the decaying modern-architectural realities of the past few decades. The megastructures are moving in to stay and none of us will live to see the monument displace the bell jar. It is also possible that the trend towards an impalpable, impersonal, undifferentiated kind of shelter is not something we ought to resist. It could be that in an unexpected way it expresses another move out of our race's tormented and violent adolescence and towards maturity.

As the race makes such a move, it will have a diminishing need for architecture used as ego props and amulets. We know this from our records. Buddha left a family palace, a first-class status symbol if there ever was one, and took up residence under a bo tree. St. Francis of Assisi did much the same thing. Gandhi spent more time at a spinning wheel than in Cadillacs. Einstein lived, quite contentedly it appears, in a nondescript frame house in Princeton.

If this is where some of the discernible trends are taking us, then we have something real to work with. If our future is to be filled with factory-made, spidery geodesics, weightless systems in tension, fragile modular shells of glass, light metals and plastic films, then surely one way to look at all this increasingly sophisticated anonymity is to see it as a fresh chance to create a real habitation for man, collective in its outward expression, infinitely varied and personal in its inner reality. It is not too hard to see these feathery urban networks in one's mind's eye, as graceful and unselfconscious as a forest.

It doesn't matter so much whether architecture is coming to an end or not, for the central problems of our time are not architectural, but have to do with the humanizing of technology, with getting this runaway monster under control. Technology cannot possibly be humanized unless people become human first, which is no mean task when we consider the extent to which the present passive acceptance of mass violence and truly insane brutality has gone.

The only possible mission today for architecture lies in the creation of humane environments. There is nothing else. The realization may come as a shock, but there is nothing for us to celebrate, glorify, or memorialize. I doubt if there will be monuments to the dubious heroes of Vietnam. Our leaders do not inspire reverence or gratitude. It is hard for an architect to feel passionate dedication to high-rise office buildings or shopping malls, which are rapidly moving into the category of building overkill, anyway.

The mission is to create people gardens, environments fostering human growth and development. The problem is to learn what such environments might be and how to design them. Learning is going to be painful, for we are out of practice. Perhaps we could get started by just trying to get our souls out of hock from the supermarkets.

Whether we have come to the end of architecture or to some dimly perceived new beginning (my guess is that we have come to both) there can be no doubt that we are in the middle of a transformation of unprecedented magnitude, not only for architecture but for all our activities.

In such a situation, one would think that the first thing the individual architect might do would be to form his own judgment about what is really going on. The pictures I have presented include a tendency for individual buildings to coalesce, taking on the form of large mixed-occupancy complexes with no special exterior character.

Within such frameworks the interior becomes the major reality, the most expressive element in the total scheme. Given the rapidly developing catalogs of industrial elements, many building types are moving in the direction of manufactured packages. The architect as a professional is gradually becoming the architect as a corporate type, inevitably taking on corporate values. The enclosed city seems to be a future reality, with shopping malls as the first completed step. Architecture as ego-reinforcement is on the way out; disposability is on the way in. The many proposals to bury buildings or cover them with earth indicate that many of the old meanings of architecture are already disappearing.

With all this fissioning, coalescing, packaging, and hiding of building, one may suspect that we are presently going to be confronting the problems of a synthetic environment in their purest form, with interiors and urban design as the major activities along with engineering. The old slogan, "the house is a machine for living," will no doubt give way to "the city is a machine for living." It could be pretty grisly. To some small extent the outcome will depend on how the architects align themselves with the forces which enhance or degrade the quality of life.

These speculations represent a highly personal scenario; other concerned individuals will write their own. But despite the innumerable variations one could imagine, I cannot believe that the creative role for the designer *now* can be anything other than the production of humane environments. Anything else, given the social context, is anachronistic, inconsequential, egotistical, and empty posturing.

The real problem for the designer is not only to find clients: *he must first determine what a humane environment really is*. What seems to be needed is observation, study, interdisciplinary friction, and thought, directed towards the creation of a new cultural base, which is an indispensable prerequisite for a revised set of social priorities.

The humane environment is not a slogan: it is a mystery which can only be penetrated by humane people. There is precious little to be learned about it from our surroundings or from the schools, and the society has shown little interest in it, although the signs of change are visible.

The end of architecture, as I have been describing it, marks one of those very rare moments in history when another step in the direction of human maturity appears to be almost within our grasp.

Interiors: The Emerging Dominant Reality

The best time for spinning theories—I think I am quoting someone—is when things are coming apart at the seams, and the theory presented here—that interiors may well take over as the major elements in the urban environment—is in this sense timely.

Aldous Huxley, in the preface to his book of essays *Aldous Huxley on Art and Artists,* remarks, "Thinking intently of the work in hand, one is apt to forget the work with which one is no longer concerned. (Hence a certain tendency on the part of writers to repeat themselves. What feels, at a given moment, like a brand-new inspiration may in fact be something written years ago, forgotten and now pushed up again into consciousness by the subliminal self.)"

Now that Huxley brings it up, I do remember that this theory began to take shape quite unexpectedly at a Smithsonian lecture in Washington and what propelled it into consciousness was the 35th anniversary issue of *Interiors* in 1975.

GUM Department Store, on Red Square across from the Kremlin, was built in 1876 by a Scottish entrepreneur. It is a multistory assemblage of shops and cubbyholes rented out to traders and retailers. It is not the first of the great 19th-century covered shopping streets (Paris has some from the 18th and the early 19th centuries), but it may well be the largest.

No matter how far we go back in time, wherever we find buildings, whatever their purpose or nature, they always have outsides and insides. I am not offering this as a celebration of the obvious, but simply as a comfortable small fact. We can do things with it.

One of the first things we can do with it is note that while all interiors and exteriors are equal, in a certain sense, some are definitely more equal than others. A pyramid (Egyptian or Mayan, it makes no difference) has a great deal of exterior, very little interior. The same goes for the Washington Monument, Chichen Itza, and those wild astronomical structures in Jaipur. At the other extreme of the scale we might cite the Houston Astrodome, a circus tent, or a geodesic dome, all interiors with no exteriors of any consequence.

Assuming that architects are people who give us the plans of buildings, which then become supporting structures and outer skins (not really true, but good enough for illustration) and that interior designers move into these empty shells and fix them up (also not quite true, but never mind), we then get a picture of a kind of Yin-Yang fitting together of external and internal, container and contained. The interesting thing about this relationship is that the two are almost never equally balanced, as we have just seen. The beautiful old Chinese symbol, half white and half dark, is constantly being distorted by a kind of triangular tug-of-war between the function of the building, the technology available, and the values of the society.

In the heart of Paris there is a grand opera house, designed by Charles Garnier, one of the fanciest, fussiest piles of stone ever put together in one place. In Sydney, quite recently, another great opera house, by Jorn Utzon, has also gone up. Both buildings are large and expensive, both seem to work perfectly well for the staging of operas. Beyond these similarities, the two buildings seem to have nothing in common, whether form or spirit, and the relationships between insides and outsides are entirely different.

Social Values Outweigh Function and Technology

Going back to the three criteria mentioned, function, technology, and social values, I think one could make a pretty good argument in favor of the last as the most significant, and I am going to try to get back to this later on.

I could never qualify as an architectural historian, but one does see a lot of things in moving around. I still remember my first trip into southern Germany's Baroque country a long time ago, with Richard Lippold. Thousands of people—many of them designers—know that Lippold is a very special kind of sculptor, but what they may not know is that he almost became a concert organist. I was interested in looking at the churches and he was interested in listening to them. I didn't know it at the time, but musicians feel about Baroque organs the way they do about Amati cellos and Guarnerius violins.

A German Baroque church, first seen on a leisurely approach, is a kind of medium-to-large stuccoed barn, set in a meadow or planted field as a rule, with a variety of fittings on top, such as clock towers and onion domes, that tell you it is a church. For some reason or other, the architects for these edifices weren't very interested in the outsides, although a few are pretty ornate and all of them look fine in their rural settings.

The interiors are something else. Once inside these seemingly modest and inconspicuous structures you have to hold on to your socks, because the visual blast comes through the door at something like force 10 on the Beaufort scale. There is nothing like it anywhere. A swarming of cherubs, saints, flowers, angels, marble (real and fake), twisting pulpits, paintings, chapels, candleholders, altar clothes, votive offerings dripping off walls, vaulted ceilings, hit the unprepared viewer without warning and turn his spinal column to jelly.

The churches we visited were usually empty, and if the doors were unlocked, Richard would sneak up into the organ loft and turn loose while I set my camera on a tripod and took flash pictures. The combination of a Baroque organ in a Baroque church is the great-grandfather of the multimedia experience, particularly if you add in the smell of candles and incense.

This was 18th-century interior design, with some powerful sensory extensions, in a specialized type of building. One might say that the inside-outside relationship, in terms of significance and impact, was on the order of twelve or twenty to one. I also learned that Johann Sebastian Bach, no less, was at work at exactly the same time (right on the edge between the 17th and 18th centuries) and when his music and the inner architecture are put together, it's just like the XJ-12 engine at around 4,500 rpm. Everything goes together in a very right kind of way.

Another church that has a similar interior-dominating quality is Santa Sophia in Istanbul, but there is a small difference that is important. The Byzantine church took its form from a structural invention that made it possible to set a dome very smoothly on a rectangular understructure, generating large spans and impressive heights. In

Baroque church, Birnau, Germany.

buildings like Santa Sophia you can sense the inevitability and intellectual power of a great piece of geometry, and it shows on the outside. The Baroque architects couldn't have cared less about structure: they were interested in religious architecture as *theater,* and consequently there is nothing on the outside to warn the visitor about what is going to hit him when he goes in.

One of the very good things about architectural history is that it is constantly demonstrating that the number of ways to skin a cat is close to infinite.

Design, viewed even casually over a few centuries, gets to look like a very dynamic occupation, and the endless shifting of the inside-outside relationships from one time and place to another is one of the things that makes it so.

Every once in a while a momentary balance is achieved. The marble temples of classical Greece provide as good an example as any. The outsides consisted of a rectangular block of columns set around an inner block, with the whole surmounted by entablatures, pediments, and a gable roof. Inside the temple there was a full-height chamber containing a large statue of the deity. The Greek temple had no congregation: priests or priestesses took care of it and people came in as the spirit moved them, said a prayer, usually asked for something, left a little offering, and went out again. No services and sermons. It must have been nice. There was none of the mass lockstep so popular with the over-organized religions, just a one-to-one relationship. This solitary, intensely personal act was undoubtedly part of what gives the fragile ruins of temples like Sunion their almost magical evocative quality.

Generations of architects and artists have been brainwashed about the beauty and importance of Greek building, but a great part of its appeal, never acknowledged in the textbooks, is that practically all of it lies in ruins. The Parthenon, by all accounts the greatest of them all, is no longer a building, but a shattered fragment in a remarkably dramatic location. In its intact state the temple was solid and heavy, polychromed and carved, and I find it very hard indeed to believe that it was nearly as lovely as the ruin, with that incredible, liquid violet Greek sky pouring through between the glowing columns. In any case, I would guess that in the Greek temples the insides and outsides came out around fifty-fifty. But as soon as it is said we realize that some illusory numerical balance is not what we are after. Architecture is not created by bookkeepers.

The incredible thing about these modest Greek structures is the flawless craftsmanship, the infinite attention to the smallest details, and the overall elegance that results from seeing to it that all the parts come out right. But "balance" in terms of inner and outer is meaningless: what we have to look for is something else. The place to find it is in the Gothic cathedral.

Medieval builders were obsessed people: they believed in the Virgin Birth, the physical existence of Heaven, Purgatory, and Hell, and they were unanimous about getting to the Holy Land and lambasting the infidels. As builders, what they wanted was to put up stone structures higher than any had ever gone before, and this meant that weight, which had been an aid to stability in the buildings of Greece and Egypt, was suddenly a crucial problem. To deal with it they thinned down all structural members such as vault ribs and columns, using a great variety of moldings to maintain cross sections and at the same time take out weight. They also broke through side walls with flying buttresses to spread the loads, and they replaced masonry walls with glass whenever they could. The result, in the most developed examples, was a stone cage of startling delicacy, a sort of spiderweb set in compression rather than in tension.

To comprehend what the Gothic builders were really about, the best way is to visualize something one cares greatly about because it represents one's private image of the absolute top in quality and elegance. A light plane, a racing sailboat, or car all fill the bill, but what comes to my mind is a bicycle. One has to think of a bike with a Columbus double-butted frame and Nervex lugs, Nisi tubular rims, a Regina chain, Weinmann brakes, a Campagnolo derailleur and crank set all weighing in at around 18 pounds, and the meaning of a Gothic cathedral becomes much clearer. It is perfectly reasonable to think of the Gothic church as a $1,200 bike with stained glass windows.

In thinking of these great structures as the outcome of a long process of stripping, refining, eliminating, redesigning, we again come to the analogy of the bicycle, where everything is part of a harmonious flow of forces, where the integrity of the design is apparent wherever you look at it. In the cathedrals, the inside-outside "balance" I have been talking about simply doesn't exist: surfaces, structures, details move throughout the entire fabric and again, wherever you look the dynamic interweaving is always the same.

The builders were crazy, of course, at least by modern accounting standards, and what they did without sophisticated engineering data and methods was simply unbelievable. But they finally got theirs at Beauvais, where they went up higher than ever before, and the roof fell in. Anyone who builds a bike of the kind I described is also crazy: who needs it? It is only when one decides that the great church and the little vehicle are art works that it begins to make a kind of sense.

Harmony, Space, and the Bauhaus
In a way, it is easier for us to comprehend what the Gothic builders were about than the Greeks. We are accustomed to light frameworks, and a main thrust of building technology is always to try to do more with less. What we are not quite so familiar with is what happened when these approaches were taken in the cathedrals. Given a masonry building, given the need to eliminate excess weight, what happened was an interior and an exterior that were indistinguishable from each other. There was no "balance" any more, just a totally harmonious experience in which the traditional distinctions simply were not needed any more. It was an incredible breakthrough, and in the centuries that followed there has been little to match what these people did. I would imagine that the closest we have come, here in the U.S., was in the work of Frank Lloyd Wright, who was not a cage-builder, but a man who believed, with Lao-Tse, that the meaning of the spaces contained was more important than that of the container. Wright's buildings have never been given their due, at least on this basis, for most of what he was trying for was blotted out by the success of the Bauhaus approach, which was primarily based on a reconciliation with industry and only incidentally concerned with spaces and people.

To connect some of the threads moving through this mini-exploration of insides and outsides, it doesn't hurt to remember that Early American, that now-nostalgic style so greatly admired by department store decorators, supermarket decorating magazines, and roadside furniture emporiums, was an import from Europe, chiefly England, Holland, and Germany, and that with exposure to the ferocious climate of New England many of the items, like half-timber houses, were quickly discarded because they didn't stand up. Georgian stone details were thinned down for execution in wood, which was available everywhere, while in many places the only stones around were the hardest kind of granite. Buildings other than houses, such as churches and meeting houses, were simply enlarged modifications of the standard dwelling and topped by appropriate markers like steeples.

The main thing about interiors in those days was keeping them warm, and so small rooms, small windows, low ceilings, wood paneling, and large fireplaces added up to a system designed to keep the occupants alive through the winter. If there was ever an interior that wanted to keep as far away from the outside as possible, the Early American house had it. The fact that many of these rooms were very handsome is due in large part to a very strong and lively tradition we put under the general heading of "Renaissance" and the highest authority for architects like Thomas Jefferson was Palladio, whose cool, perfectly symmetrical villas in northern Italy represented the dominant standard of taste.

Palladio's main business was the creation of stately homes for stately people. The exteriors were everything, and the most one can say about his floor plans is that the rooms had to find their place inside the facades. That many of them were very fine indeed is due to the fact that the rooms were spacious and, like the outside, symmetrically laid out. The thing the decorators had going for them at the time, something we have almost completely lost, was a back-up of superb professionals: cabinetmakers, carvers, plaster workers, metal people, weavers, painters, and sculptors, all of whom had learned their trades through long apprenticeships in a commonly understood tradition.

It is worth recalling that the major role of painters and sculptors was that of decorators. The greatest names of the Renaissance were represented on ceilings and walls, and the subjects of the paintings were generally bucolic, with a strong insertion of the themes of classical mythology, all of them part of the education of a gentleman. Thus, when we look at typical rooms, we find toothsome wood nymphs, Cupids being awakened by Psyches, Diana hunting with her maidens, and a generous assortment of ladies being seduced by lustful gods in the form of bulls, swans, showers of gold, and the like. Pink-tipped bosoms, generally C-cup or better, were very much appreciated by the upper classes, and the genteel erotic atmosphere of these boudoirs and salons went very much with the spirit of the times.

From the Age of Faith to the Age of Science
Outsides and insides had very different functions, and this showed. The imposing exteriors, no matter how tasteful, served as a reminder to the masses that there was an iron fist inside the embroidered glove, and the job of the interiors, open only to the peer group of the host, was to reinforce the image of all established status. Naturally, oneupmanship was part of the game, just as it is now.

The whole period from the breakup of the Middle Ages to the beginning of the Industrial Revolution was pretty much a piece, and while interiors naturally reflected the patterns established outside, the two had relatively little to do with each other, aside from proximity. In buildings open to the public, mainly churches, the sharp decline in the old religious fervor was clearly spelled out by the theatrical nature of the interiors. The God of Abraham had somehow become a Master of Ceremonies, with people like Borromini, Veronese, and Tintoretto taking care of the stage decorations. It all worked very well for close to five centuries, until the lid blew off.

The lid, in essence, was the preindustrial way of making things, and the prevailing values were materialistic, in sharp contrast to the beliefs that shaped the social structures of the Middle Ages. It took a considerable head of pressure to blow it, for it had all the accumulated weight of the centuries from early Egypt to the mid-19th century.

What happened, to continue this series of outrageous oversimplifications, was that science had finally gotten to the point where it was able to trigger a series of technological breakthroughs. Things like the development of a reliable metallurgy, the use of steam for motive power, and a new feeling that Nature was now an open book, completely subject to the control of man, were all part of the new scene. Sir Isaac Newton, who had lived until the second quarter of the 18th century, had a lot to do with this feeling, for he had convincingly postulated a kind of clockwork universe, reassuringly reliable in its behavior, with all its mechanisms open for examination and adjustment. Naturally in those countries where industry had gotten under way, feelings of optimism were rampant.

One of the meanings of all this, for the purposes of our story, was that metal construction suddenly came into its own. Steam had made locomotives possible, now that the metalworking knowhow was there; and the same information was applied to rails and bridges, and finally to the great open train sheds that still embellish the city of London. These sheds had spans previously considered impossible, and they represented a new kind of public interior that had no precedent in earlier building. The peak of this development, as far as public awareness went, was Eiffel's tower for the Paris Exposition of 1889, a structure that fell only a few feet short of 1,000.

Steam power meant that people could travel on a scale that was also without precedent; and in a few years architects and artists were coming back from the most exotic places. Their drawings were published and widely disseminated, and suddenly architects were able to design the most fantastic buildings without ever having to draw

The Grand Palais in Paris, a French contemporary of the GUM store, is a magnificent blend of ironwork, glass, and unimpeded floor space. As a busy exhibition center today, the interior is still as exciting as the best of the shows mounted inside.

on their imaginations. Just as asparagus beetles never appear until the first stalks are above ground, so did the first new house clients appear. They were in every sense ideal: they had plenty of new money, neither knowledge nor taste, and an insatiable appetite for recognition and social status. The architects had a ball: never had there been such fantastic examples to copy, along with clients who wanted only to be conspicuous.

There are two ways to look at the riotous manifestations we lump together as "Victorian": one is to see them as the quintessence of vulgarity, the other is to see them as a series of inventions which gave interior design an entirely new scale and meaning. The Bauhaus, always sternly Calvinistic, took the former view. Today we are far enough removed to see what was going on behind the overstuffed rooms and the jigsaw decoration. One invention for which we should be grateful is the open plan. Up until this time, problems of heating made it essential to develop spaces that could be closed off. Central heating removed this problem, and it became possible to create interiors with the skimpiest of barriers between living spaces.

With the open plan, it was no longer necessary or desirable to group windows in the symmetrical Palladian patterns. Glass was now coming out of factories in large, flat sheets and people could put in as much as they wanted. Furthermore, the size and number of windows was dictated as often by interior needs as by formal design requirements for the facades, thus giving rise to the inside-to-outside kind of design we now consider proper for all kinds of buildings. "Form follows function," said Louis Sullivan, and "function" tends to be expressed by interior arrangement. On this basis we might consider the Victorian period as the first time in centuries that the interior was back in the limelight. Unfortunately, the light stayed on only until 1914, when something else began to happen.

What happened was Modern, a movement born in rebellion against the eclectic excesses of the Beaux Arts styles, and like many such uprisings it was strongly moralistic in tone, addicted to witch-hunting and other Puritanical pursuits, and unbending in its condemnation of those who refused to put their feet in the path of righteousness. I forget exactly when Adolf Loos made his famous pronouncement, "Ornament is a crime," but it scared hell out of a lot of backsliders and deprived two whole generations of the good clean fun that comes from embellishment. It took the grafitti artists of the New York subways to remind the faithful that a plain surface can really be very plain indeed and that Nature abhors a vacuum.

By the time Modern established some standing for itself—say late 20s to early 30s in Europe—something else began to happen that made hash of the manifestoes that had been coming out with the regularity of Old Faithful. This was the accelerating pile-up of technological miracles and the concomitant rise of great bureaucracies. The promise of a burgeoning industrial base was the abolition of poverty; the promise inherent in the bureaucracies was that anyone who could stand the boredom could get a full week's pay for a day's work with job security and pensions. Not bad, if one wanted to throw in one's entire working life in exchange for a slow death in Florida. Apparently many people thought it was a good deal.

Promises, promises! Poverty didn't get abolished, and if anything it spread to more people than before. The corporations grew like Topsy, at first on the basis of productive ability and later with the use of acquisitions and high-pressure marketing. Management types came out of the business schools like Kentucky Fried Chicken off those homelike conveyors and presently there were a lot of business jets flying around, taking care not to collide with those highrise towers the parent companies were putting up. Franz Kafka described the whole scene in books like *The Castle,* long before White's *The Organization Man* appeared, but he was dismissed by those most in need of his treatment as another of those neurotic kooks out of Mitteleuropa.

The Topless Corporate Highrise
And what does all this have to do with insides and outsides? Actually, quite a bit.

Consider the most conspicuous item in the current cityscape. This, of course, is the corporate highrise. If you look carefully at any big city skyline today, you will see that some of the towers have terminals on them: pyramidal roofs, the shiny Art Deco cap of the Chrysler Building, little classical temples, and other motives suitable for topping off high buildings. All the rest, the most recent ones, have no terminals at all. They are simply sliced off at the top floor, rather like a rectangular salami, and that's that. The change came around 1930, when Raymond Hood produced the Daily News building on Manhattan's 42nd Street, and the critics hailed the bravery and honesty of an architect who decided that when a high building reached full height, it should simply stop. None of that wedding cake stuff for Raymond Hood. He then went on to become one of the architects for Rockefeller Center, and presently this cluster also

Railroad station, Milan.

came out topless. We now have a picture of a kind of an international phenomenon: towers that look as if they had been extruded like toothpaste up to 50, 70, 100 stories. The skins of these buildings fit into a number of formulas which create vertical, horizontal, or waffle wall patterns, and the materials are metal, concrete, and glass. These towers run from $50 to $100 million each, these days, and it is incredible that they look so poverty-stricken. The poverty is spiritual, but this is not a word to be found in the vocabulary of business.

Granting that the outsides, for all their neat simplicity, do not delight the eye, what about the insides? These are packed solid with tight little boxes, not unlike filing compartments, in which people do things on telephones or with pieces of paper, and sometimes interior designers are retained to lay out and design the spaces.

Downstairs there are lobbies with elevators and newsstands, sometimes with shops and restaurants. If the building is big enough, there are several levels of such services. In Montreal's Place Ville Marie there is a monster network below street level, a kind of city-under-a-city where one could imagine people living for months without ever having to surface. Tokyo has similar networks. We are now in the period of too many people and too much of everything else, and things get a bit crowded. But these mechanized, electrified grottos are *interiors;* the exterior is an asphalt pavement.

The Worship of Mobility
The intense preoccupation with mobility, typical of all industrial societies, has spawned a huge number of new things and situations, all of which are developing a character of their own. A plane interior, for example, is not a room but a highly specialized tunnel in which people sit crowded together. The design of the tunnel and its contents is severely limited by considerations of weight, fire, ventilation, lighting, and so on. So there emerges a general type of interior we associate with planes. But it doesn't stop there. The meaning of the plane is so powerful in the eyes of the people who have only reverence for the idea of moving around that presently its interior takes on authority and significance. At this point it is perceived as something worthy of emulation in buses and railroad cars, and presently we may see a far-out boutique whose interior is more than slightly reminiscent of a plane.

Cars, where many people spend more time than in their beds, have a similar effect. I was startled recently, while working on a problem of office furniture, to find that wherever we touched the design it seemed to have a quality suggestive of automobile interiors. We hadn't thought of any reason why a work station should resemble the inside of a car, but there we were. Primitive people enrich their work with designs taken from nature, often passing these recollections through a geometric sieve. Why shouldn't people today, whose heads are stuffed with sensory recalls of the feel of vehicles, not respond in the same way?

Airports and terminals develop distinctive vocabularies which then serve to establish another kind of mobile character. The older terminals consisted of blocks which sprouted fingers as more and more traffic demanded an increase in gates. Finally, when walking to the end of a finger was getting close to the amount of time needed for the flight, a drastic change was initiated by Eero Saarinen for Dulles airport outside of Washington. He shrank the fingers back into the terminal and replaced them with "mobile lounges." At Tampa the main terminal block is linked to small satellites by automatic trains. There is something absolutely right, to a contemporary person, in this replacement of a cumbersome tunnel and the long, dragging walk that goes with it by a relatively weightless little shuttle that "makes" the tunnel by its own traces through space. One thinks of those photographs made by someone drawing in the air with a flashlight. The "picture" is transitory, weightless, an experience in time and space. It would be surprising if architecture did not make its new moves in some such direction. Perhaps the first step is what is now going on, buildings so sterile and monotonous that no one will miss them if they do vanish.

We have now looked, in very sketchy fashion, at two conspicuous types of buildings: corporate office towers and structures associated with mobility, and, strange as it may seem, these cover almost everything modern society believes in. We have to add, of course, the establishments dedicated to retail business, the shops, stores, supermarkets, shopping centers. Their common characteristics include no windows except for display, and an inside-outside relationship in which the interiors are everything. These places need parking for a mobile clientele and all the exteriors do is keep the rain out, or perhaps provide a support for advertising. "Architecture," in such structures, is reduced to a very primitive minimum of support elements, mechanical systems, and a skin of some kind. All decisions are made by the money men. The entire multimillion-dollar complex comes down to shopping spaces separated from vast asphalt deserts by a container which is in effect an oversize bell jar.

The population has been brainwashed for decades to believe that buying is virtuous, bringing good fortune to the buyer and full employment to the nation. Do you remember the Chrysler president who, when car sales slumped so badly, suggested that the President of the United States inaugurate a "Buy a Car" week? There was no question in his mind whether buying was virtuous or not.

Large numbers of people spend a great deal of time in these retail spaces, looking around at merchandise on display and buying or stealing whatever takes their fancy. The interior carries the full burden of providing functional layouts for the goods on sale, and of creating whatever atmosphere is believed to have seduction value.

We now have touched on three major building categories, and I think that perhaps it is enough. Bureaucracy and corporate power produce those towers with windows you can't open; the craving for mobility spawns interstates, vehicles, and terminals, and seems to generate a special style of its own; buying takes place in large, open, air-conditioned containers. In all three the interiors are clearly more important than the outsides. I think we can stop here, because these are the three great building symbols of prevailing values. Now that God is dead, we can be sure without looking that the churches are going to be cozy clubhouses with attached classrooms, and since Man doesn't matter either, we can be equally sure that his dwellings will have neither grace nor nobility.

Now, I think, it is time to get on with the matter of social values and their connection with my persistent hunch that interior design is coming up as a dominant activity in the restructuring of the urban environment.

Last summer there was a flurry in the papers about a sudden shortage of tops for Mason jars. *The New York Times* explained that behind this was the fact of *8 to 10 million new gardeners* scattered around the country. I had been going around for the past year predicting that the most sacred of all middle class American cows, the immaculate, weed-free front lawn, was presently going to be dug up and planted to flowers and vegetables. The basis for this pronouncement was a visit to a supermarket where I could not believe the prices on things like tomatoes.

I don't know how many of those 10 million new gardeners did dig up their prize lawns; after all, anyone with a front yard is likely to have one in back, too, but clearly a lot of people had been as startled as I to find what it cost to purchase a cucumber or a cauliflower. Apparently one can raise as much as $500 worth of fruit and vegetables in a smallish garden; anyway, the result was a silent mass movement of interesting dimensions. This created the shortage in Mason jar tops, because any garden will spin off a surplus that can be canned and used later. All this is fairly obvious.

What is not quite as obvious is the chain of events that can be triggered by such a decision. One is the discovery that growing things can be interesting, and the battle with the bugs has real drama in it. Another is that people who have gardens move around less, thus saving gas and rubber. It is sometimes hard for the committed gardener to tell whether he is working or playing, and the whole idea that entertainment can actually be active comes as a big new idea to many urban people. In the process of planting, weeding, and cultivating, waistlines tend to go down, which cuts into the sale of books on how to reduce while drinking beer and gazing at the tube, and this saves not only beer money, but countless acres of forest which would otherwise be cut over for paper for books on easy dieting.

What can happen from a tiny shift in personal values is a new awareness that life can be this way rather than that way. When millions of people make this shift at once, we get a change in social values, for the multiplier effect starts working. Economics also gets involved, for ten million gardens producing only $100 average value add up to $1 billion not accounting side effects.

The whole subject of gardening, like bicycling, is unexpectedly rich. An interest in organic gardening can take a person from noxious pesticides to other methods of control, from chemical fertilizers to composting, from an indifference to a mistreatment of the natural environment to a passionate concern for the future of the planet. All of this can come out of getting fed up with the price of tomatoes.

A convenient truism, not unlike the observation that buildings have insides and outsides, is that *the price any society will pay for anything is a direct reflection of what it believes in,* that is, its value system. To prove our devotion to mobility we have paid some $90 billion for interstates, the price of 100 million cars, several hundred thousand gas stations, repair and service shops, airports, jet fuel, planes, etc., etc., etc. The tab attached to this expression of faith must be in the neighborhood of a trillion dollars. Such expenditures are always rationalized on some grounds or other: travel is broadening, business cannot be done in one spot, goods have to be moved, and so on. All of this may be perfectly true, but the underlying base is faith, and it isn't necessarily rational.

The U.S. is now alone among the "have" countries in still having a chronic slum condition in every one of its major cities. Why? Countries less rich than we have gotten rid of them because of a belief that slums are undesirable, even intolerable. We have not.

Our notions about almost anything we do rest on assumptions we believe to be rational and practical, but it is hard to prove or disprove these assumptions. The reason for going into this seemingly remote matter of social values is that they are changing radically and rapidly these days, and whatever we now do in cities and buildings will reflect these changes. Most of them appear to favor an increase in the development of interiors.

Consider just a few of the changes that have taken place within recent years. Before John Portman's Hyatt Regency in Atlanta, it was taken for granted that the only "practical" hotel was a solid block with public rooms at ground floor and perhaps the mezzanine. But the Atlanta hotel has a courtyard some twenty-odd stories high. It broke all the rules set up by the accountants, but it worked. The reason it worked was that this spectacular interior indicated that the hotel, in addition to having to make money, was concerned with the pleasures of its patrons. This was enough to change occupancy ratios.

Some of the new highrise towers are doing roughly the same thing. The good old galleria, the covered street or plaza, is appearing at the base of towers like the Galleria in New York and the IDS building in Minneapolis. Again, we find large public spaces, so designed that their use is a pleasure, are coming in after almost a century of neglect. What is happening, it seems, is that urban amenities are back.

Great Living Rooms vs. Hitler Bunkers
The pedestrian mall has spread throughout the world. The only difference between such a space and a galleria is whether it is open to the sky or covered by a large skylight. From this point of view it is perfectly proper to view such spaces as urban interiors, whether they are covered or not.

There is a lifestyle in the older cities of Europe that helps make clear the value of such urban "interiors." Some years back I did some work in Paris with one of those rare craftsmen who still know how to make the "automates," those mechanical dolls that so delighted people in the 18th century. He and his wife lived like any blue-collar couple on the sixth floor of a walkup, right under the roof. They had two rooms, including a primitive kitchen, plus a creaky bathroom. And yet they seemed well contented with their lodgings. One day when I went out with his wife to help with the shopping, I discovered why. Down in the street there was a small square,

IDS Crystal Court in Minneapolis is one of the best of the new examples of large enclosed public spaces. The soft lines and curlicues of the late 19th-century structures are gone, which is why the modern enclosures rely so heavily on masses of plants. Architects: Philip Johnson and John Burgee.

Piazza San Marco in Venice is still one of the greatest public "rooms" anywhere. The disciplined fussiness of the facades is one reason and the easy modest scale is another. Even German and American tourists almost relax here.

The shift from passive to active use of public fountains is worldwide, and the new pedestrian mall in Munich is one of the good examples of a traditional amenity being given new meaning by the adherents to a new lifestyle.

surrounded by a railing and fitted out with benches. Along the streets around the square was the usual assortment of neighborhood shops. On one corner there was a bar which doubled as a tiny restaurant. Most of our shopping time was spent in passing the time of day with old neighbors and the shopkeepers, and at some point we went into the bar for a cup of coffee and more conversation. They had no serious housing problem, for *all this was their living room;* it had everything they needed in the way of supplies and sociability right there. A marvelous humane solution from any point of view, but for us it will take a bit of doing, for our goal, particularly in the suburbs, has been a dwelling as self-sufficient as Hitler's bunker, coupled with a social existence the poorest Bolivian peasant would consider utterly uncivilized.

Values are changing. "Quality of life" is a phrase one hears all the time now, and all the examples cited above have to do with that and nothing else. As the impotence of both government and big business to enhance the quality of life becomes more apparent, individuals start looking for solutions on their own. As the various crises in which we are enmeshed get worse, these grass-roots movements will be accelerated. It looks as if the interior, whether public or private, will become the leading expression of these new attitudes simply because buildings (and building codes) cannot be changed around overnight, because they are well along the road to becoming stock industrial products, and because the increasing monotony of the urban scene will by itself be enough to drive people indoors. The role of technology in all this, one may hope, will be less antihuman, not from philanthropic motives, but because a public with a changed awareness of what it believes to be desirable can exert enormous pressures without saying a word.

There are other factors: suddenly, these days, one hears entrepreneurs saying that their future work will consist of a lot of rehabilitation. New building costs have gone through the roof and most cities have a large supply of well-built old structures that need only modernization. In Sweden, I understand, rehabilitation is now official public policy, and new building permits are granted reluctantly, only if there is no suitable old building available. The motor driving such developments is primarily economic, much as the decision to start a garden is related to the price of tomatoes. The result could be reconditioned cities. It hardly needs pointing out that the main work on a rehabilitation project has to do with its insides.

What is the connection between the shifting role of interiors and the interior designers? I doubt if it is preordained that all new interior projects will go to interior designers. The architects have been casting envious eyes at the field and a certain amount of preparatory propaganda has come out of the AIA. It also seems unlikely, whether we designate pedestrian precincts as "urban interiors" or something else, that the work would go to members of ASID; there are too many special skills, and the landscape architects seem to have most of them. Then too, a great deal depends on the designers themselves, who so far have not identified themselves very conspicuously with a concern for the human condition. It sounds as if a shifting of professional lines as well as social values will probably go on. The immediate opportunity would appear to lie in a change in the values of the designers themselves and a realization that if technological society is finally sawing itself off at the knees, some awareness of the desirability of working towards an amelioration of the meaningless, alienated existence that millions call living might open up new views of possible constructive, creative activity.

To achieve this, it is essential to develop some reasonably clear-headed personal assessment of the current scene and immediate trends. One hypothesis I like is that there is a double trend: a tendency to move into an increasingly dehumanized social climate, mediocre in all its manifestations, with a nervous Establishment edging towards a police state and the free distribution of tranquilizers. The other is to put one's bets on (and efforts into) moves towards a people-oriented technology, a restoration of human dignity, a less frenetic, competitive, materialistic set of attitudes. Interesting work for the designers seems to lie along the second line, for the attitudes encourage the reconstruction of cities, the segregation of cars from people's lungs and limbs, the revival of creative activity, the entire gamut of amenities which lead people to become fond of and protective towards their cities. Again, the urban interior, whether roofed or not, seems to be the place to do most of it, and to the extent that a sense of community reemerges, interiors are high on the list of places where it is best expressed. Interiors are lightweight, open to individual production, impermanent, and hence less burdened by ego-ridden pseudo-concerns for posterity.

There is no assurance whatever that of the two paths indicated a moment ago, the one the Good Guys take (our side, of course) is the one everyone else will take too. *But it is absolutely necessary to act as if they will.*

The End of
the Topless Trinities

Three things come to mind as accompaniments to the rise of technology: a speed-up of events, so that a "period" may begin and end in decades rather than in centuries; the global village is here, more or less, so that a local manifestation may affect the entire planet almost instantly; industry today works with systems and standard components, so that many formerly similar things now tend to be identical.

A consequence of all this is that interesting variations on a common theme now tend to vanish in favor of an iron monotony. This quality has been noticeable in the highrise towers built all through the global village, and the combination of a tower, a plaza (more like a slice of a parking lot than a real plaza), and an oversize abstract sculpture have moved from an interesting combination of elements to a deadly cliche.

World Trade Center, New York City: once looked at, the awesome height and mass of the Trade Center has nothing further to tell us, other than to hint that when the IC chips have fully replaced human bodies, the buildings will be easier to maintain. The sculpture holds up very well, trading its own extraordinary impression of contained power for size. Architects: Minoru Yamasaki and Associates. Photo by D. Brewster; courtesy The Port Authority of New York.

Viewed through New York eyes, the Topless Period seems to have been launched by Raymond Hood in the late 1920s when his Daily News Building was unveiled to show a shaft that went up full height and then stopped. No spire, mini-temple, pyramid . . . nothing. This inspired omission was hailed as the "ultimate solution," and Hood's appointment as one of Rockefeller Center's architects released a flood of flattops for office towers that is only now subsiding.

Rockefeller Center also introduced the other two elements of the Topless Trinity: the plaza and its monumental sculpture. The project became a community amenity overnight, as well as a strong expression of the burgeoning wealth and power of the multinational corporations. The three-part formula dominated corporate building design until the beginning of the 70s.

Even government, in a suitably more modest fashion, followed suit. Calder Plaza in Grand Rapids, Michigan, has a main building only about a dozen stories in height, and the sculptor's great red steel beast dominates the scene like a prefabricated tail wagging an architectural puppy.

In New York's World Trade Center a spherical sculpture of more modest dimensions is the third leg of the tripod, a sensible solution, for nothing could compete with the 110-story twin shafts.

At Rockefeller Center, Paul Manship's Prometheus *is the pivot point of the first of the great Topless Trinities. Photo courtesy Rockefeller Center Information Bureau.*

Renaissance of the City, *sculpture in Peachtree Center, Atlanta: the forms are executed in rough fiberglass. Photo by Clyde May.*

The glassed-in Egyptian monoliths, rather like H.G. Wells' Martians, have been striding across the country for some thirty years now, ornamenting one decaying city center after another. Each has a Top of the Something Bar and Restaurant, and in the really fat projects the restaurants revolve. The view directly below generally reveals a clutter of small parking lots and boarded-up little buildings, but the middle view, with an elevated highway and perhaps a river, is better.

What we really got with the topless towers was not architecture, but a diagram: New York's skyline, now crammed with flattops, is the world's largest bar chart of corporate growth.

Inevitably, the Topless Trinities are beginning to show signs of age and wear. One straw in the wind was Philip Johnson's ISD complex in Minneapolis, an attractive heresy which ignored the obligatory abstract sculpture and put the plaza under a greenhouse. Hugh Stubbins' Citicorp tower ends in a chisel edge, becoming the first building in years that can actually be recognized in New York from a distance. Johnson and Burgee are putting the new AT&T headquarters in New York on the Pazzi chapel and plan to top it off with a Baroque pediment.

Architecture seems to be moving once again into what Sean O'Casey liked to describe as "a state of

Australian Mutual Provident Society, Melbourne: the contemporary sculptor clearly feels uncomfortable with themes having a human connection. Architects-Engineers: Skidmore, Owings & Merrill; photo by Wolfgang Sievers.

In Fort Worth, John Portman's black glass shaft rises out of a generally sleazy environment and is an elegant but rather chilling image of a possible urban future, in which glass fortresses rise out of deserts of asphalt, litter, and rubble. Photo by Alexandre Georges.

chassis." It couldn't happen to a nicer profession.

Being action-oriented folk, it is not our habit to speculate on the meanings of the events in which we marinate; but a last lingering look at a vanishing phenomenon, before it is classified as another instant antique, may provide some information.

In the brief years between 1912, say, and the Great Depression, there was a uniquely American glorification of the joys of business success, expressed in the first skylines by towers with an exuberant rash of terminals in every imaginable style. This ended abruptly when Hood's flattops took over, and these too provided a social mirror which reflected a childlike faith in the dream of endless growth. A topless tower can be put together like a stack of poker chips; in a symbolic sense there is no limit to its growth. The message that also comes through these structures is that of completely depersonalized corporate entities, an expression accurately matched by Andy Warhol's early portraits of Campbell's Soup cans.

The chisel edge top and the broken pediment are simply new ways of saying, "This is where it stops." The new values and sensibilities include an awareness that limits do exist, that diversity is more humane than a monoculture, that there are better ways to live than Orwell's *1984*.

Under the bombardment of this new software, the cold monoliths with their parking-strip plazas and sanitized abstractions begin to lose their hard edges, like reflections in a puddle of oil, fissioning into Renaissance Center's glass stovepipes in Detroit and Pennzoil's faceted geometries in Houston. Harbingers of a new Golden Age or just more thalidomide babies? Posterity, no doubt, will set us straight in due time.

If some of the new probes recall Brunelleschi going back to the ruins of Rome and thus innocently inventing the Italian Renaissance, the only question to be answered is, can anyone really dust off a 550-year-old act and come up with a hit the second time around? If the answer is negative, there are always other acts.

In the meantime, the Topless Trinities seem to have had it, like MacDonald's shrinking arches, and we can be grateful for small blessings.

The notion that the new office towers are less in the way of architecture and more in the nature of 50-story bar charts can be checked by almost any view of Manhattan.

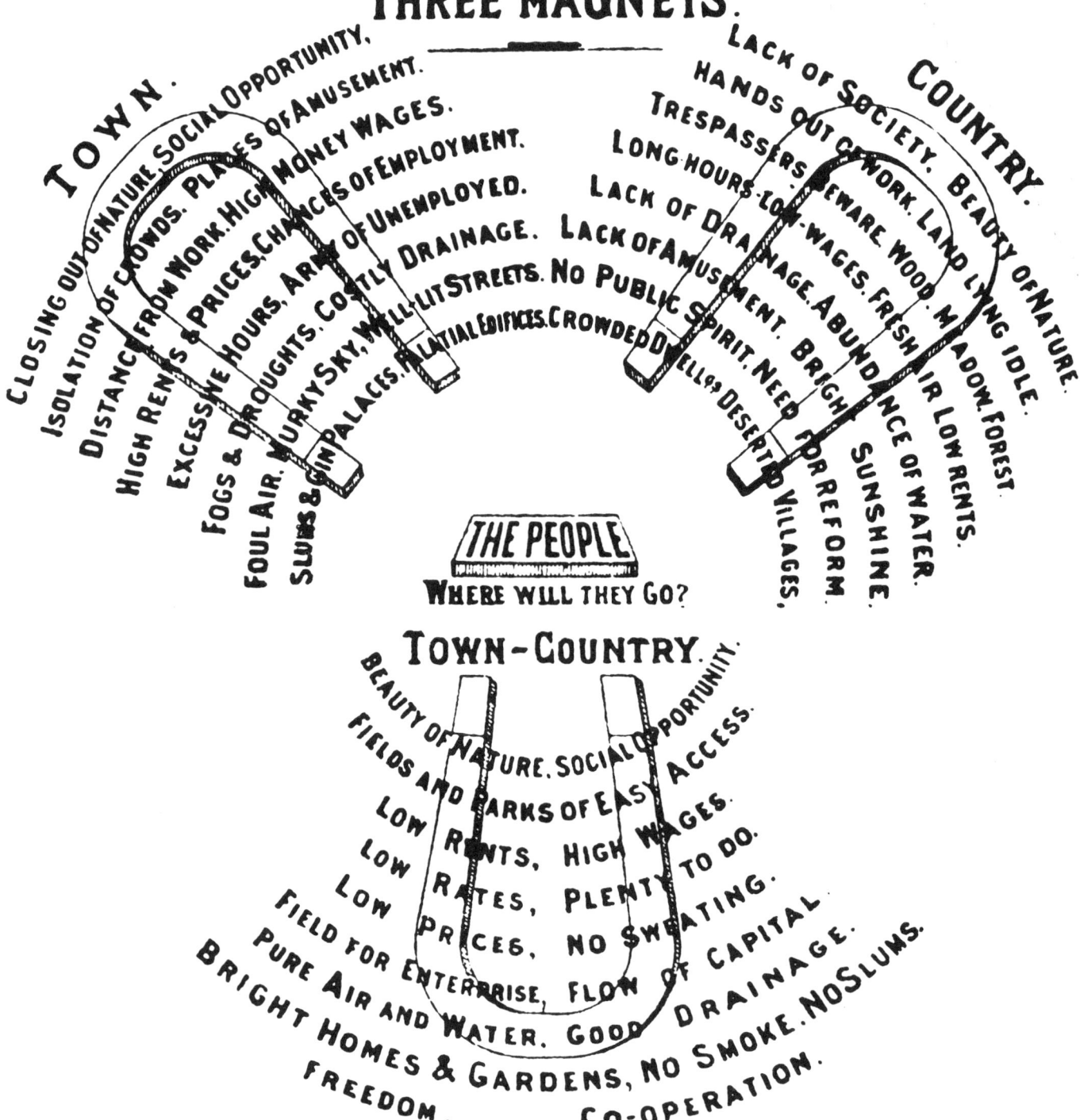

Scheme by Ebenezer Howard for a Garden City, 1898.

Scenarios for the Post-Modern City

The way to look at the proposals for new kinds of cities discussed in this essay is to see them as evidence of truly astonishing social change.

Ebenezer Howard, a court stenographer by trade, invents the Garden City as a way of beating London's exorbitant real estate prices. Chambless caps a commuter train right of way and calls it a town. Le Corbusier creates an urban pattern copied the world over: it is totalitarian. Soleri's fantastic geometries could illustrate any canto of Dante's *Inferno*; Tange's Toyko is also authoritarian, realistically he asserts. A brilliant group of people, working away at their dreams for close to a century, and what the late arrivals say, without exception, is that unless the post-modern world is run by police, it won't run. We might compare these proposals with some more or less contemporary novels: Huxley's *Brave New World* and Orwell's *1984*. The architects and writers have come up with the same scenarios.

All societies, even the most primitive, are complex, evolving structures and hence contain elements which strike some of their members as imperfect or deplorable. Such reactions are generally shared by those who live in misery and others (St. Francis of Assisi is a good example) whose lot in life is tolerable or better, but whose sensibilities or vision lead them to view the imperfections as intolerable. Up through the Middle Ages such rebellious attitudes were taken care of by assiduous propaganda describing the goodies to be provided in the Afterlife. With the growth of science and the decline of credulity, the business of soothing the unhappy masses was taken out of the hands of priests and picked up by reformers, heretics, revolutionaries, and writers.

Two elements coincided with the decline of credulity: one was a steadily accelerating change and the other was the piling up of enough written history to permit people to scan social evolution. People who have a known past with more content than "Abraham begat Isaac and Isaac begat . . ." begin to be able to project alternative futures. This new ability became visible in the early 1500s when Thomas Moore wrote his *Utopia*, a word picture of a redesigned society. In Greek, "utopia" means a "non-place," an imaginary locality. By extension it has come to mean a better, or even an ideal, place, and the literature is extensive.

One difference between a writer's utopia and an architect's or artist's is that the latter can be seen. Another is that the writer tends to emphasize the social arrangements which make his utopia possible, while the designer tends to show how it looks and works, but not how it might happen. The implications of the designed utopias, however, are clear enough: vastly strengthened powers of condemnation or outright socialization of land, regional and local planning with teeth in it, and presumably, a population which no longer goes around with spray cans defacing buildings and public vehicles.

Because of the radical changes needed to make their visions emerge as reality, few authors or architects have seen their dreams come true. Nevertheless, at least one of the concepts described below actually made it: Ebenezer Howard's Garden City, which was built in England, not once, but twice. Perhaps it is stretching the word to call his proposal a Utopia, but it was certainly a vision not previously advanced and it did offer a new way of life which seemed to be dramatically better than the old one. What may have saved Howard from oblivion was the fact that he was not an architect and he could not draw pretty pictures. As a result, he had to create something which would appeal even to bankers.

Garden City

Ebenezer Howard prepared himself for an unanticipated immortality by spending most of his life as a stenographer in the law courts of England, an unlikely beginning, to say the least. As a youth, he spent some years as an unsuccessful farmer in Nebraska, an equally unlikely prelude. In his spare time he was an inventor, creating devices which history has neglected to celebrate. Possibly there is a clue in this hobby of his, for the Garden City concept is not a design, but an invention.

Outwardly, there seems to have been nothing in his personality which set him apart: he was a colorless individual, pure middle class in his clothing, habits, activities, and associations. He was once introduced to George Bernard Shaw after he had become famous; Shaw's puzzled reaction was, "But he seems like an elderly nobody!"

The milieu in which this "elderly nobody" carried on his inconspicuous activities was England in the late 1800s, a time when it was finally getting the full blast of the Industrial Revolution. Along with new wealth and imperial power, both cities and countryside had deteriorated to an appalling extent, and millions lived in desperate poverty.

When polarization in a society reaches a point where misery and indignation begin to boil over, both liberals and conservatives always join forces in a mutual concern for the stability of the established order. Then there are speeches in Parliament, letters to the *Times*, commissions to look into this or that, all the hoary political devices for smothering incipient revolution. There was a great deal of this in the 1890s in England. At one demographic conference held in 1891, the cities were described as "the graves of the physique of our race." The rural areas were no better: "Many of the cottages were so abominable that they could not call them houses, and the people were so deteriorated in physique that they were not able to do the amount of work which able-bodied persons should do."

Despite the brouhaha, despite all the public breast-beatings by the well-fed, no solutions were forthcoming. The slums remained lethal, conditions of work remained abominable, the air carried its regular burden of soot and poison gases, and malnutrition continued as a way of life for millions. The general public was bombarded daily by splendid statements combining impeccable rhetoric and conceptual vacuums, and the London Cockney remained, on the average, a head shorter than the landed aristocrats and the merchant princes.

There is no mystery in the inability of the great minds of Victorian England to find remedies for the exploding cities and the decaying countryside: they did not want to pay the price. All they were after, then as now, was some cheap way to cool the situation and pacify the restless masses. It was Ebenezer Howard's extraordinary luck—or genius—to find a solution which did not interfere with established social priorities and left the pillars of 19th-century capitalism unshaken. As we shall see, it was an exceedingly limited solution, but it was something.

Howard's invention was what we call today the "satellite city," a community surrounded by a greenbelt used for agriculture and recreation. After nearly a century it all sounds pretty obvious and harmless, but the thinking it took to arrive at this concept was original, bold, and brilliant.

The thinking began, if we are to follow the sequence in the book he published in 1898, with speculation on the relative virtues of urban and rural life. In the city, he decided, there were social opportunities, entertainment of all kinds, and chances to get work at good pay. The country offered the beauties of Nature, clean air, cheap rents, and a healthful outdoor life. The disadvantages were also recorded: foul air, noise, high rents, grim housing, long trips to work, etc., in the city. Low pay, few job opportunities, a boring social life were some of the handicaps of life in the country. It was all put together like a balance sheet.

Having assembled this primitive data, Howard then addressed himself to the question of how to merge the positive elements in each kind of existence.

While this exercise was going on, he was also asking why decent housing and other amenities could not be provided in the big cities, and he concluded that the cost of land was the chief obstacle. Investigating the matter of land costs in London, he discovered that the price of an acre in the city was roughly 250 times as much as an acre 25 to 30 miles away. Putting this information together, he jumped to the idea of a new city, to be built on rural land, less than an hour by train from London. His calculations took him to 1,000 acres for the city (the price of 4 acres in London) and to a farm greenbelt of 5,000 acres as permanent insurance against sprawl.

Once he had the concept in order, ideas began to come in a flood. Land values, he reasoned, rise in relation to density, or traffic. A landowner can become rich without doing a thing if enough people crowd around his property. If this is so, why should not the land in Garden City be owned by the community? Then, as people moved in and values went up, the community as a whole would profit. The idea sounds socialistic, but in actuality there was nothing frightening about it. Crown lands in England are not sold, but leased to would-be developers, and Garden City, as a permanent trust, was proposed as the same

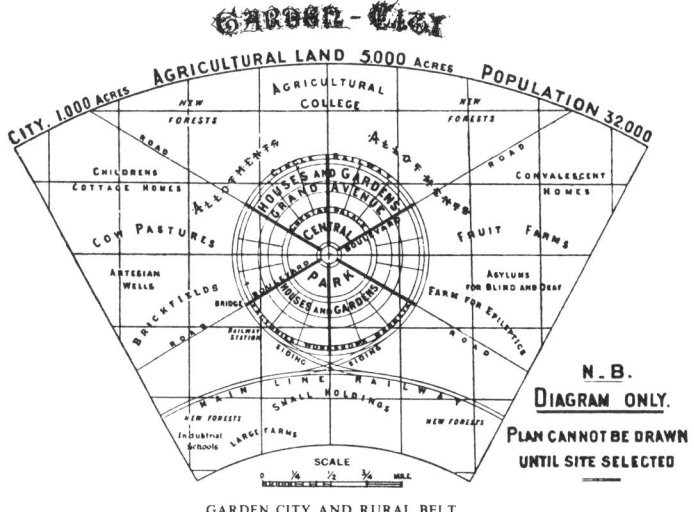

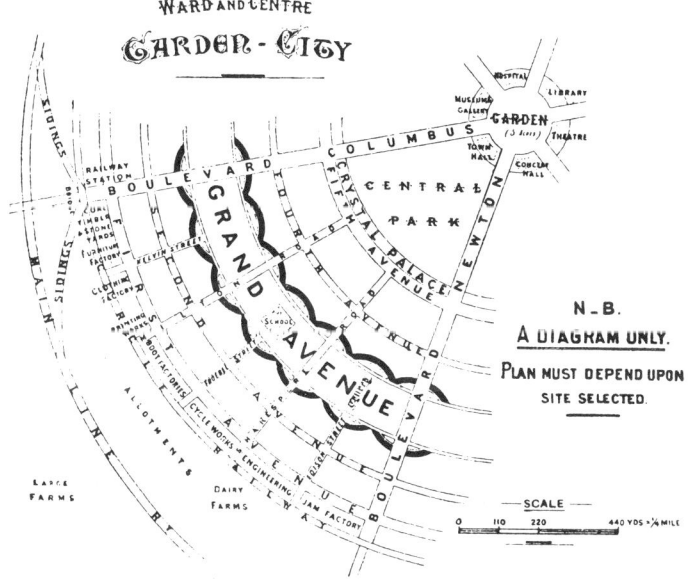

Schemes by Ebenezer Howard for a Garden City, 1898: not being an architect, Howard put all his ideas in diagram form. It is odd indeed that his concept, which was actually built, had no other illustrations; this may have been one of the secrets of its success, for the omission left everyone free to create his own mental image. From Ebenezer Howard's book, Garden City.

thing. The difference was that the income could be used for municipal services, with the possibility of keeping taxes close to the vanishing point.

Another notion that suggested itself was that a town of 30,000, surrounded by farmland, could get its food more cheaply while at the same time the farmers would prosper. What Howard envisaged here was simply a situation in which there were no transportation costs and no middlemen. All the town had to do was provide a marketplace.

Behind much of Howard's thinking was another idea, very important to him, which failed for reasons he was unable to foresee. If London land prices were so high that economical building was impossible, he reasoned, draining population out to his satellites would presently bring these prices down to a point where the city could afford to renovate itself. He failed to realize that the influx was going to be greater than any possible drain. Even after World War II, when many new towns were built in England, draining some 250,000 people from London alone, the city continued to grow.

Not the least of the attractions of Howard's presentation of his Garden City concept was that it was not a design. His book had a few plans and diagrams in it, but there was nothing to show exactly how it would look. There were appetizing descriptions of grand avenues, playing fields, plots for houses, places for business and industry. Thus his dream image could become a personal image: each prospective inhabitant could see his future house as he wanted to see it, he could imagine walking to work, look forward to evenings in the town center and perhaps pleasant weekend visits to the surrounding farms. There was nothing to dislike. Even the arithmetic was soothing: no cash down payment for land, low taxes, and literally free urban amenities.

Given all these attractions, the idea caught on instantly. Only seven years after his book appeared, Letchworth, the first Garden City, was built. True to his convictions, Howard left London and moved in.

It was not design, but the promise of a decent life, based on solid financial planning, that made Howard's project a reality. Associations to promote his ideas were formed in nine European countries and the U.S. "Greenbelt" has become a household word in dozens of others. There is no new town that does not owe something to Howard and his satellite concept.

Now that urban crises are upon us again, there will undoubtedly be renewed interest in the Garden City idea, but times have changed. Land within 25 to 30 miles of metropolitan centers is no longer available for .4 percent of urban prices: the automobile has taken care of that. Population is reaching levels undreamed of by Malthus and the Victorians. Manufacturing is no longer the base of city development: it is the tertiary industries which now feed metropolitan growth. Even so, we have by no means come to the end of building new towns, and as long as this continues, each one will to some degree be a monument to the colorless court stenographer who did his homework with such inspired patience.

The inventor of Garden City died in 1928, laden with honors. But six years before he died, another powerful image of the new city had been launched, this time in France. The differences between the two proposals were in themselves an indicator of the speed with which times were changing.

The Radiant City
This time it was no plodding student of real estate values, but a maverick, a fiery young Swiss evangelist with the family name of Jeanneret who had moved to Paris, where he adopted the name of Le Corbusier. Architect, painter, sculptor, propagandist, he combined a Calvinist sense of righteousness with the talents of a circus pitchman. His book *Towards a New Architecture* of 1923 had gone all over the world, with the message that traditional design was dead and that technology had produced enough new materials, textures, and forms for any imaginable contemporary design vocabulary.

A resident of Paris for virtually his entire working life, he lived in old apartments in old buildings, violently disapproving of them, of the city, of everything that was out of step with modern life. But instead of moving out into a place of his own design, his condemnation exploded into a plan for a new city of 3 million inhabitants, laid out in superblocks ½ mile on each side, with skyscrapers in enormous parks, and elevated superhighways laid out along the grid lines. "No pedestrian," he stated proudly, "will ever again meet a high-speed vehicle."

La Ville Radieuse (Radiant City), first presented to a shocked citizenry in 1922, was also one of the first urban designs in which the automobile and its requirements were given top priority.

Le Corbusier was in every way the polar opposite of Ebenezer Howard. He could draw brilliantly: we can see very clearly what it was he proposed to build. Howard was very concerned with the *how* of his proposal; Le Corbusier couldn't have cared less: the *what* was the only thing that interested him. Howard tried to plan for

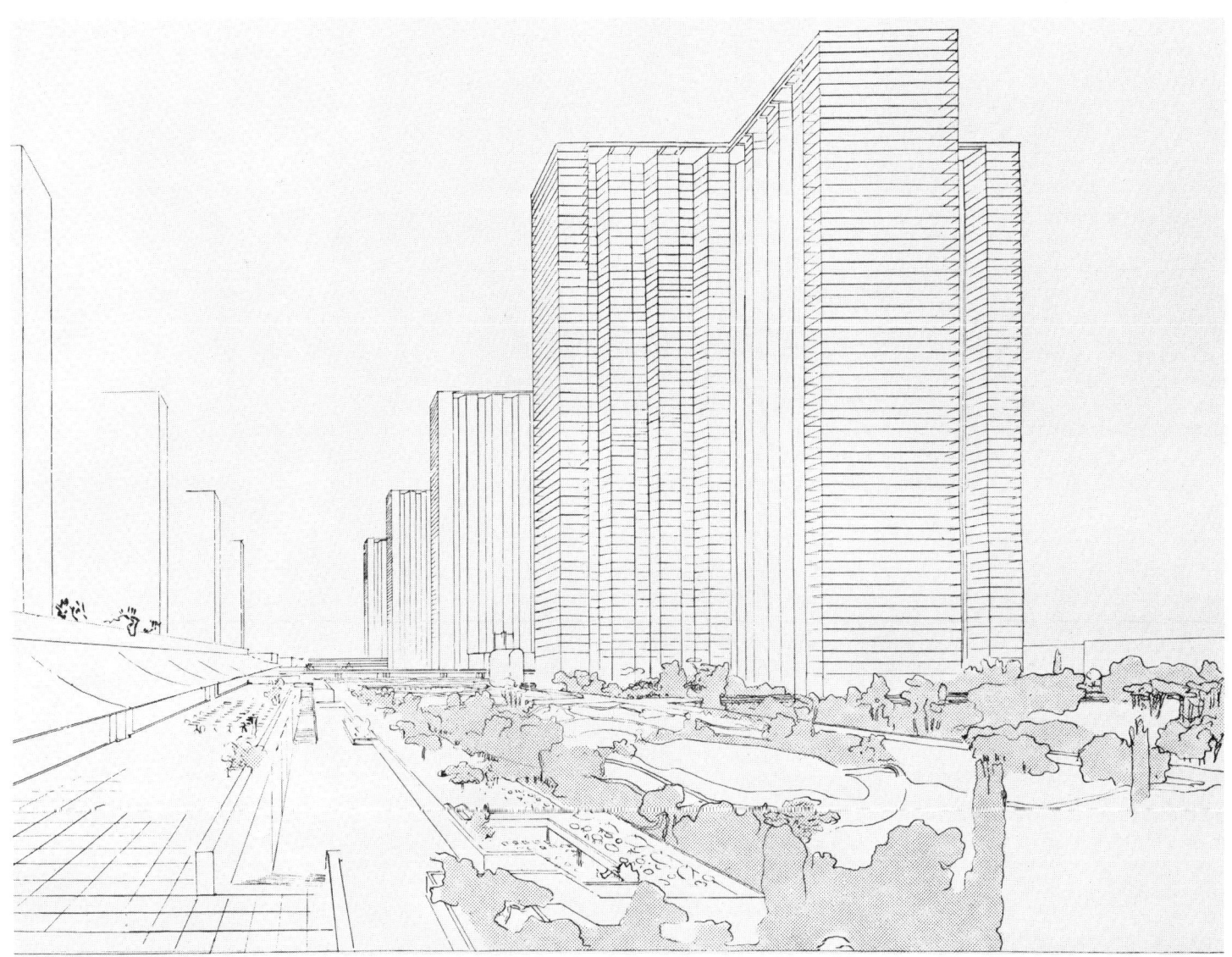

Plan Voisin for Paris by Le Corbusier, 1925: Le Corbusier's concept was decades ahead of its time and no city of any size has since escaped its influence. But now that we have it—in bits and pieces—we are no longer sure that we want it. From Le Corbusier und Pierre Jeanneret, ihr Gesamtes Werk von 1910–1929 (Zurich: Verlag Dr. H. Girsberger & Cie., 1930).

30,000; Le Corbusier could see no point in anything less than 3,000,000. The only point at which the two came together was in their expressed intention to project a humane city, conceived in the spirit of service to humanity, a place abounding in green parks, a city where people could live and work in refreshing surroundings and thus cultivate body and spirit. These were the words. But, in the case of Le Corbusier, this is not what we see.

I do not know what Howard thought of the Radiant City proposal, but Le Corbusier was fully articulate on the subject of the Garden City, which was being actively discussed in professional circles all over Europe. "The garden city," he said, "leads to individualism and brings with it the destruction of the social spirit. But by increases in densities, communal services can be multiplied, allowing genuine freedom."

One thing you have to watch out for with architects is that they will say almost anything to promote the success of their pet projects, including the most egregious nonsense. Any apartment house dweller, unacquainted with a single neighbor, knows that high density has little to do with promoting the social spirit, and the suburbs are no better. Le Corbusier was also the victim of a current fad, which was the belief that communal kitchens and cafeterias promoted "freedom." The Russians also made a big thing of communal feeding, not from any interest in freedom, but because it was supposedly more "efficient." Since there is no enterprise on the face of the planet less efficient than a Russian restaurant, one wonders what they might have been thinking about.

One wonders why Le Corbusier was so vehement on the subject of Howard's creation. I suspect that as a young and ambitious architect it annoyed him to see a rival concept getting so much publicity. Even more basic was the fact that the Garden City was so clear an expression of the British spirit of compromise and sweet reasonableness. Howard's project was only meant to be a nice place to live, as acceptable to socialists and anarchists as to capitalists and the landed gentry. There was no esthetic discipline implied in the concept, no control of the vulgar majority, none of the French idea of "grandeur" that runs from Louis XIV to De Gaulle. For an orderly Swiss brainwashed by an immersion in French culture, all this must have been intolerable. Just how intolerable is made quite clear by his own design, so completely dictated in every aspect that there is no room for a single Venetian blind out of place, a single added bedroom or even a small, unplanned garden shed.

Le Corbusier was an absolute dictator when it came to architecture and planning, one of the last of the "Father knows best" school. Quite possibly he had to play it this way: knowing all the answers, he had to be severe with those foolish enough to disagree. One can get away with this on a single building, but this was a proposed city of 3 million.

Let us look at the drawings. What I find is a hymn to 1920 technology parading as concern for the human spirit. The air view shows a town where all that air and sunlight might be great for the shrubbery, but hardly a place one would dream of coming home to. It is monotonous, rigid, authoritarian. "The materials of city planning," Le Corbusier once declared, "are sun, sky, trees, steel, cement, in that order of importance." The statement probably sounded very brave and far-out in the twenties but, leaving out the steel and cement, it is hard to see the difference between his creation and regal monsters like Versailles and the Escorial. In fact, it has more than a little in common with those megalomaniac enterprises, where every rosebush and fountain was laid with an accuracy to four decimal places. And there is more than a suggestion of something Big Brother might whip up for the occupants of his Brave New World. However we look at it, the concept is totalitarian.

This rather dim view of a great architect's youthful excesses changes on closer inspection. The decision to handle automotive traffic on a large scale was right. The use of huge towers to cope with high densities and the demonstration that the truly modern city would have very little in common with the old ones—these insights have held up. After publication of this project, things were never quite the same again. The spaced towers are to be found everywhere from Middletown to Moscow. New cities like Brasilia are laid out in superblocks. Even New York and Chicago now put little plazas and fountains at the feet of their 100-story monuments to bureaucracy.

Broadacre City

Frank Lloyd Wright, another giant of the early 20th century, had no use for Le Corbusier and whatever he stood for. There was nothing personal in this: he also despised everything that came out under the Bauhaus banner and whatever else he saw as the International Style. For him it was all flimsy paper cut-outs, not "real" architecture.

Wright, like Le Corbusier, was very much of his time and place except that the times and places could hardly be more different. He was brought up on a large Wisconsin farm; his ancestors were sturdy Welsh farmers and his heroes were Whitman, Thoreau, and Emerson. He was

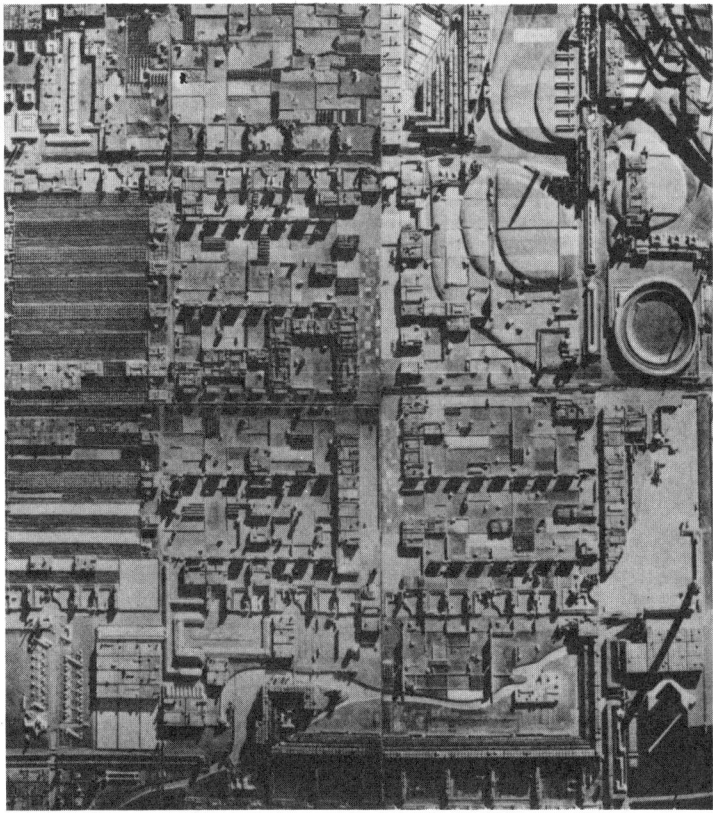

Model for Broadacre City, Frank Lloyd Wright, 1934: Wright's dream of the modern city turns out to be a preview of modern suburbia on 5-acre plots. The concept is attractive in a period of urban decay but ignores the current reality, that we are running out of land. Courtesy Frank Lloyd Wright Foundation and Horizon Press; Frank Lloyd Wright, The Living City (New York: Horizon Press, 1958).

nourished on an optimistic faith in American democracy, and his neighbors were rugged individuals, isolationists politically and deeply suspicious of big government. His early work had taken him to Chicago, where he worked for another great, Louis Sullivan, and later he was exposed to Japan through his commission to design the Imperial Hotel. He never learned to like any of the big cities. Chicago always remained for him the "hog butcher for the world" of Carl Sandburg, and New York was "a cinder strip on the East Coast." Like many of his contemporaries he saw the modern city largely in terms of its destruction of real values, which for him were inextricably tied in with the land. In his old age, when he designed his "mile-high" skyscraper for Chicago, it was with tongue in cheek: if those upstart architects were going to litter the city with 50- and 100-story buildings, he would show them how to go to 500.

Not that he was against towers: his lovely designs for St. Marks-in-the-Bouwerie, later executed in Bartlesville, Oklahoma, are evidence. He also introduced a number of tall buildings into his Broadacre City plan, using them as accents in an otherwise one-story landscape. Towers, said Wright, were all right as long as they were set apart in parks.

It is hard to think of Broadacre City as a fresh concept. In one sense, it is a development of what was going on in the Middle West anyway: houses set out on plots lining both sides of a street. At the same time, one finds Howard's idea of merging the virtues of town and country. Unlike Garden City, Broadacre is endless: there is no greenbelt to limit its growth. Wright's thought was that each individual should have 1 acre of land, a notion unthinkable in any part of the modern world, with the possible exceptions of Brazil and Siberia.

Broadacre, as an expression of Wright's vision of the Good Life, has a few flaws. Naturally, its generous land allocations reflected his own experiences and tastes, but it is not at all certain that a part-time family farm would suit the typical office functionary or factory worker. A family of five would automatically get 5 acres and even this, operated as a family farm, would not be the easiest part-time job in the world for people without the experience or taste for such activity. His other idea—that many of the inhabitants would run small businesses or industries on their property—also brings up questions of suitability, capability, and interest. The whole thing smacks of small, dispersed populations and a social and economic organization which no longer exists except in a scattering of villages and small towns.

None of this kept Wright from staying fascinated with it. The project was shown in 1932 and it was described in a book, *The Disappearing City*. The model his apprentices built was enormous, and for a long time it kept growing. He fiddled with it from time to time, designing schools, gas stations, model farms, and other buildings for it. It was like the world's largest doll house.

It is a pity, in a way, that the attitudes and social values expressed in Broadacre no longer exist in a world largely composed of apartment dwellers and suburbanites, for they were healthy and constructive. But population growth and automotive mobility pretty much destroyed the life styles with which Wright grew up. However, one cannot say that the project "failed" because what we see in the model is a picture of what has actually been happening. Suburbia is the fastest-growing segment of the American scene, and the difference between it and Broadacre is the difference between unrestricted commercially oriented development and a planned environment of the same open type conceived by a man of genius.

At this point we begin to get a sniff of what is wrong with so many of the architect's utopias: each is a strong expression of a personal life style and each treats the city not so much as a constantly growing and changing organism, but as a fixed design which has very little room for the unexpected. In this sense, Broadacre is far more adaptable than Radiant City, for in the latter there is no room for change of any kind. Architecture, in the sense of a single building, can be treated in this way, but this procedure does not work for cities at all. We might even conclude from this that the architect, as he has been trained, is not the person to redo cities or to create new ones, simply because he is not at home with the design of fluid systems. Since trends in urban development are not going to change, it looks as if the architect were going to have to relearn his trade. Good intentions, as expressed by the men whose work is shown here, are no longer enough.

Roadtown

The practice of building a community along a route is as old as communities or routes. One can still see villages in eastern Roumania which consist of nothing more than houses strung out for a mile or more on each side of the road, with nothing behind them except farmland. The persistence of many Main Street merchants, even today, in resisting proposals for bypass roads is another expression of the ancient feeling that roads and towns belong together. This logical relationship persisted for thousands of years, and it only began to be questioned when traffic

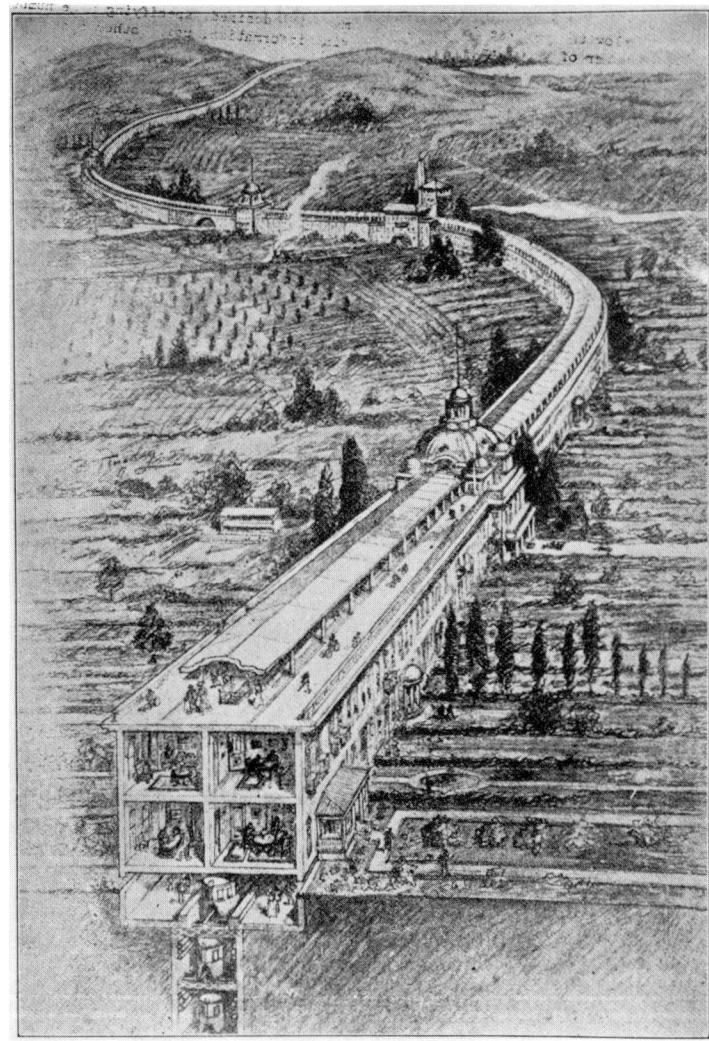

Project from Roadtown by Edgar Chambless, designer 1910: the emergence of railroads, and later highways, prodded the concept of the linear city into existence. The scheme of Edgar Chambless, already hopelessly unworkable, is one of the boldest, most explicit and nostalgic of the early proposals. Sunset, The Pacific Monthly, *vol. 32 (January 1914), p. 110.*

reached levels which made it unworkable. Nevertheless, the idea keeps coming up in new forms, and in the 1960 project for Tokyo by Kenzo Tange (see later discussion), it reaches an extraordinary level of complexity and technical virtuosity.

The first modern Roadtown, to my knowledge, was proposed by a man named Edgar Chambless in 1910. His notion was odd, but it was not entirely illogical. The scheme, shown here in a rather naive drawing, was to cover the tracks of commuter railroads with housing. The town resulting from this has no lateral spread at all and in this sense is exactly like the Roumanian villages. It is a line, theoretically infinite in extent, consisting of a basement where the trains run, a two-story (!!) apartment house, and a promenade on the roof. Nothing gives a clearer picture of the difference between population pressures then and now than the estimate of the number of dwellings needed. A mile of such housing might accommodate 400 families, and it would take 5,000 miles of track to house the 2 million commuters who move in and out of the giant cities every day.

Chambless's intentions, as one might expect, were of the best: his Roadtown was going to reduce commuting time, relieve population pressures on the big cities (here we have Ebenezer Howard's old dream again), provide savings in utilities, and protect the countryside from sprawl. It was a brave try, but rather silly in that it assumed that a town consists only of housing, and prophetic in terms of what came later.

The next pass at Roadtown came from Le Corbusier, and like so many of his other projects, it is huge in scale and spectacular in concept. This was no utopia, but a design to be built in the city of Rio do Janeiro. The date is 1929.

Again we have housing rather than a complete city, but the communication link is the automobile rather than the railroad. The basis of the scheme was a rather acute observation, and as usual with Le Corbusier, it was well ahead of its time. He had observed in the course of many efforts to get his designs built that governments invariably had great difficulty in assembling land for urban projects, while they seemed to have no trouble at all in clearing the way for new roads. This observation led to the idea that if one combined the two operations, the housing authorities might be able to get a free ride, using land already condemned for public use. What this meant in practice was that the housing either had to go over the road, which might have put motorists in tunnels of excessive length, or under it. There is precedent for the idea. In Spain, for instance, one finds housing tucked in between the high arches of Roman aqueducts. In relation to a high volume of automobile traffic, it was pretty spectacular.

Given this preliminary thinking, the solution proposed was an apartment house 14 miles long and 14 stories high. One can fault this man on many points, but he can never be accused of tackling large problems in small bites.

The fourteen floors were conceived as duplex-type spaces, and his idea, now beginning to gain currency some 40 years later, was that the floor platforms be treated as lots in the sky. Each tenant, in other words, would buy or lease a piece of synthetic land which he would then enclose as he saw fit. There were other subtle values in the scheme: 14 miles of conventional apartment houses could be absolutely deadly in its visual impact, but this long, undulating ribbon under a highway would be something entirely different. The effect would be much less chaotic and, paradoxically, much less monotonous. The hilly terrain, of course, would also have been a great help. The project was not executed, which should come as no surprise, for it was decades ahead of prevailing thinking. But it stands out as one of the first megastructure proposals, and there is little doubt that as urban land prices and city congestion go up, the idea will find takers. There are already proposals being made for the use of the air under elevated roads, whether for housing or light manufacturing would depend on location.

Roadtowns are not as a rule complete cities, but rather components, such as housing. Frank Lloyd Wright made a proposal in 1947 for a civic center in Pittsburgh which involved coiling a road and parking around the center, rather like a giant spring. The ill-fated Helicoide in Caracas, never finished, was an attempt to convert a mountain into a shopping center, again with a spiral road and parking on the exterior, with shops strung out on the inside.

All such examples, whether they suggest complete towns or fragments, whether practical or fantastic, emphasize the growing ascendency of transportation networks and the persistent desire to merge occupied space with road systems.

In some instances the Roadtown idea is merely an expression of the inability of capitalist economies to provide needed land at affordable prices. The Linear City (1967) designed by McMillan, Griffin and Mileto was a study project for New York City, planned to go over commuter tracks simply because there was no feasible way of acquiring interim housing for displaced tenants. It was to extend for some 5 miles, and the hope was that as people moved in, the slums lining the right of way would be torn down and converted into linear parks. Since the city is constantly on the edge of bankruptcy, it is unlikely that the scheme will be built, but even if it were, it is questionable that the slums could be torn down. The story in the megacities seems to be that everything gets filled up as fast as it is emptied out.

The Buried City
The implication of Roadtown—that a system as complex as a city could be broken down into elements for study and experimentation—suggests that other ventures could be set up, examined, designed, and tested in a real-life situation.

One possibility is the unhappy fact that the largest single contribution to visual pollution in the urban scene is not billboards or telephone wires, but architecture. This may sound paradoxical, since cities are places where there are a lot of buildings. If the buildings are handsome, harmonious in their relationships, and well-placed, the effect can be pleasing, but what we get in most of our communities is a nasty visual mess, a constant irritant to the eyes.

Given the proposition that the bulk of urban architecture is worse than mediocre, then it follows that the less of it we have to look at, the better. We can then consider the problem: how might we reduce the architectural blight in cities by, say, 50 percent? At first it seems insoluble, since city functions have to be housed in structures of some sort. However, if we can't eliminate the buildings in actuality, could we at least make them invisible? (For further discussion on this subject, see "The Hidden City," pages 25–33.) Strange as it may seem, this is possible. The Indians of Colonial Mexico did exactly that when the Spaniards invaded: they covered their pyramidical temples with earth, hoping that they would be mistaken for hills. A building that looked like a hill would be, for all practical purposes, invisible.

Given the increasing unhappiness with congestion, artificial mountains would offer interesting advantages. For one thing, a city of 1,000,000 might end up looking like a town of 500,000. This alone would reduce the sense of overcrowding. For another, those buildings requiring windows, such as housing, offices, schools, hotels, hospitals, and so on, would have a more pleasant outlook.

The moral of this example is that thinking about the renewal of old cities and the planning of new towns does not have to proceed in terms of exclusively familiar traditional patterns. There is very little that is traditional in the forms of metropolitan life now emerging.

Tange's Tokyo
The last two scenarios show how dramatic the new expressions of metropolitan life can be. Kenzo Tange's

Helicoide de la Roca Tarpeya, Caracas, Venezuela, 1956: the idea of bending a road (with parking) around a facility of some sort was proposed for Pittsburgh by Frank Lloyd Wright and built in Caracas for a shopping center but never completed. Whatever its defects, the scheme does less violence to the townscape than most megastructures. Architects: J.R. Gutierrez, P. Neuberger, Dick Bornhorst. Photo by Studios Jacky, Caracas.

Tokyo project, presented in 1960, is a solution offered for the biggest city in the world, with a price tag (then) of $50 billion. The scheme is professional in every sense: there is none of the fuzziness of detail in the Radiant City, none of the sweeping generalizations that accompanied Broadacre City. The technological demands can be met, costs have been estimated, the structural engineers have already done their preliminary work. This is no broad picture of some city of the future, but a specific design intended to "save Tokyo."

More than a dozen years have passed and Tokyo is still not about to be saved by Tange's design. It must have impressed many as being far too radical. But Tange saw other, more serious obstacles: "Many people will ask whether the construction as proposed can actually be carried out under the present political system. Here . . . the doubt is legitimate, for the sectionalism that prevails in the government and in the bureaucracy prevents the birth of any comprehensive policy. Under this system and organization no total plan is capable of realization."

The Tokyo plan is very total indeed, and it reflects its author's view that Tokyo's problems, like those of other giant cities, cannot be coped with by palliatives such as urban renewal projects.

The first thing we notice in the model photographs is that the view is dominated by highways. These are laid out as a series of enormous square loops which begin at the administrative center of Tokyo and then march across the bay for about 5 miles until they reach the opposite shore.

We have seen the loops before, much more simply expressed in Le Corbusier's city for 3 million people. Here, the scale of the highways, which are arranged on three levels, is staggering. As these immense structures recede from the old city, they sprout transverse arms dotted with huge tentlike structures containing dwellings, schools, and shopping centers. Scattered through the branches are parks, stadia, and other recreational facilities. Some of these are on platforms; others are placed on reclaimed land.

Despite its immensity, the underlying concept is relatively simple: a linear structure, much like the spine of a vertebrate. It is Roadtown, but now finely articulated with a wealth of interfacing systems, developed and enriched to a degree which makes its ancestry barely discernible.

As we move in closer we begin to see that the highway loops do not spin off into the familiar cloverleaf patterns: here each lane has its own ramp. Our superhighways can handle about 12,000 cars per hour in three lanes at 60 miles per hour. Tange was looking for a system that would carry at least 100,000, and his answer is a system where traffic at the top level moves at 70, about 55 in the middle, and 35 at the bottom. The slow road leads directly to parking platforms which in turn connect with the buildings.

When we get this far in our inspection of an intellectual and architectural tour de force we suddenly realize that all we are dealing with, really, is traffic. The city of 5 million is somewhere, of course, but what dominates is the circulation system. This is not accidental. As the designer points out, modern man is highly mobile, and in a city largely devoted to the tertiary industries—those devoted to communication and control, rather than manufacturing—the population is in motion a good part of the working day. In contrast with older cities, the "ideal trip" which took one from starting point to destination on a door-to-door basis, worked out well enough as long as traffic was largely pedestrian or moved at a pedestrian pace. Once there is movement of hundreds of thousands of cars, the possibility of parking or even stopping at the destination becomes impossible, and new solutions have to be found to meet the door-to-door criterion. The answers, in a megacity, become so radical in scale and complexity that the old city would simply be blown apart by the pressures for adequate roadways. Thus we come to Tange's view that the city of 10 million or more is an entirely new animal.

We may ask why are cities of such size necessary, and Tange's answer is that the postindustrial city is essentially a cybernetic city, a place where the activities of an entire nation are regulated and directed. It requires larger numbers of people than industry, and these people must be able to get in touch with each other, not only by phone, but in direct contact. Thus the rush hours of the industrial city tend to be replaced by constant and random movement. Hence the anticipated need, in a project of this size, to handle traffic counts as high as 200,000 cars per hour in two directions. This figure, incidentally, is on top of whatever numbers are carried by the mass transportation system.

Tokyo, like Paris, Moscow, and Vienna, is a radial or "centripetal" city, a type which emerged with the fortified towns of the Middle Ages. In such places, the seats of power (cathedral, palace, castle) were concentrated at the hub, with streets radiating out like spokes to the rim. Such cities, which can also be described as "closed" systems, worked well as long as they were relatively small.

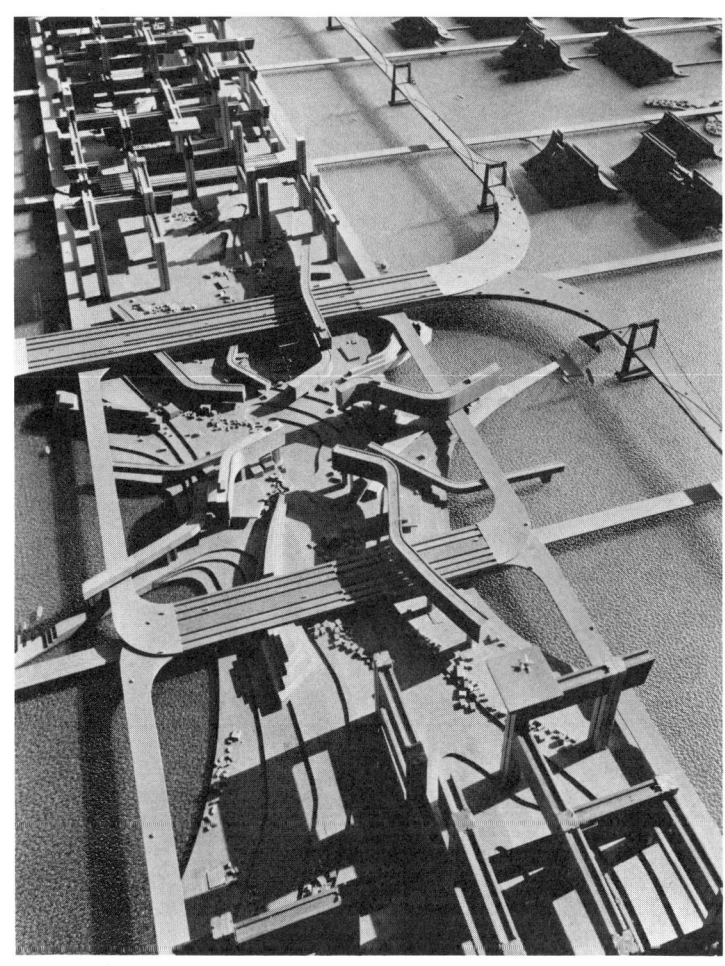

Model of Kenzo Tange's plan for Tokyo, 1960: one of the most massive urban proposals ever made. Tange's fully detailed scheme for an extension of Tokyo across the bay is a dramatic presentation of a possible form for the city if needs for mobility are fully met. Photos by Oasamu Murai.

With the coming of manufacturing in the 19th century, they began to disintegrate and to spawn factory and slum districts which simply could not be contained within the old limits. The railroads made the beginnings of sprawl possible, and in the postindustrial phase, such cities become traffic bottlenecks, smog-filled cesspools, audiovisual nightmares.

Tange's view is that trying to renew such cities, whether radial types or the grid patterns which became popular later, is hopeless. Slum clearance, street widening, and highway construction—all the tricks of urban renewal—merely hasten the day of total paralysis for traffic, bankruptcy for the cities, and the screaming meemies for the populace. The scale of existence and traffic in the giant cities simply has no connection with their now-obsolete designs. To "modernize" such places is comparable to putting a 350-horsepower motor on a Conestoga wagon.

Tange was by no means the first planner to observe the total inadequacy of existing city design. About 20 years ago a group of French architects proposed that Paris be "saved" by building a postindustrial city a few miles away. This would have taken some of the pressures off the old city, and with fast shuttle trains and good roads a separation of 5 or 10 miles would not have been a serious deterrent to communication. Le Corbusier made a similar proposal for Moscow even earlier. By selecting Tokyo Bay as his building site, Tange has done the same thing. All three schemes were found to be too radical and too difficult to implement, a disastrous miscalculation. By adding to the rings of the old giants, the price of movement has become exorbitant in both money and human terms. Hundreds of thousands of commuters, coming from farther and farther out, jam the roads, trains, buses, and subways in their efforts to get to the centers. Moscow, with a metropolitan population around 10 million, is better off than Paris and Tokyo largely because there are still relatively few cars.

One cannot help wondering what might happen to Tokyo's already poisoned atmosphere if 200,000 cars per hour were to start squirreling around Tange's giant highway loops. It would be easy to look to mass transportation for the answer, but the fact seems to be that only a complex of coordinated systems can handle total transportation requirements. The Japanese expectations of population pressures over the next two decades are staggering: today, some 2.5 million people move in and out of central Tokyo each day, and it is expected that this figure will go to 5 million or 6 million. The population of the proposed linear core over the bay is estimated at 5 million, with parking spaces for 920,000 cars.

We have come a long way indeed from Wright's Broadacre City with its acre of land for every man, woman, and child. A Tokyo of the year 2000, laid out on this basis, would be larger than the state of Indiana.

Tange, like the other planners whose projects are shown here, claims to be deeply concerned with the need to create a humane environment. It takes a bit of doing to see his spectacular model as an answer. Yet under the extreme conditions with which he is trying to cope, it cannot be dismissed as antihuman. The highways are well isolated. There are huge pedestrian areas everywhere. Many of the housing blocks, rather than hugging the ground, are slung between towers like bridges which start at 120 feet from the ground. We could see here, with a bit of effort, a new kind of three-dimensional spaciousness, the polar opposite of the noisy, claustrophobic clutter of the old cities. One could even imagine it as a kind of superscale Venice. "By building on the bay," says Tange, "Japan would rediscover the sea." Maybe it would, but giving each family a sailboat would be cheaper.

Why did he choose the bay? Is the city really so hopelessly overcrowded that no land is left?

The real problem is not the land supply: the city today is covered with hundreds of thousands of small wood dwellings, any number of which, one would think, could be advantageously replaced. The problem is what Tange euphemistically describes as "land speculation," a polite phrase for the infinitely fragmented system of land ownership which effectively prevents the city from renewing itself in a simpler and less costly way. Tokyo land, in utterly nondescript sections a good 45 minutes from the center, sells for $800,000 an acre and more. It is this which pushed the project out into the bay. It also pushed Ebenezer Howard out of London.

No one can argue that the concept and its development are less than brilliant, but it does take drastic adjustment to see it as the image of a new and better life. Living on concrete platforms is not exactly the contact with Nature we sometimes think we need.

Driving back and forth on 25-lane roads at 70 miles per hour is not relaxing. But as long as land prices stay where they are, as long as urban populations continue to swell, as long as we cannot find an alternative to our love affair with constant movement, the building of superscale monsters like this will be necessary. The answer is monstrous because the problem, as we have set it up, is monstrous.

The most alarming thing about this approach is not the solution, but the new problems it might generate. One of the most visible characteristics of technology as we use it is the way solutions escalate into new problems. The elevator was invented so that we could build higher buildings. Presently buildings go from 4 or 5 stories to 50 or more. When the occupants pour out into the streets the traffic jams and the subways overflow. It is too late to widen the streets, and even if this could be done, it would only encourage more traffic.

In the case of the Tokyo project, the enormous scale and the harshness of the surroundings could well breed a desire to escape, at least on weekends, to a softer, more natural, and less crowded environment. We have already experienced this weekly flight and know what it does to the roads and the countryside. The result of a mass exodus from the giants could then be a new rash of "free-time cities," a duplication, in other words, of existing facilities. This escalation could continue, in theory, to infinity, and when the overburdened earth was finally covered with concrete, asphalt, and buildings, the remaining shrubs and trees could then be put into botanical gardens.

None of this should be taken as a criticism of a brilliant project. Design is a reflection of society's shape and values. Tange and his team designed for what is, not what might be. Perhaps the greatest contribution of this unrealized project is the message that unless prevailing values change, the price to be paid for a viable city will be nothing less than the quality of life itself.

Soleri's Arcologies
With Soleri's visions of a new world we come back to the utopias. Soleri is a man who sees the problems of population, cities, and the natural environment in terms so extreme that even Tange's bold leap into the immediate future seems conservative by comparison. Soleri's ferocious energy and burning prophetic visions have driven him to a point where he needs a whole new vocabulary to describe them. We find words like "neonature," "aesthetogenesis," and "arcology," the last apparently being a merger of architecture and ecology. His town names are equally special: Novanoah, Arcube, Babel IID, Theodiga, Infrababel. His message is unfolded in a book so large (4 feet wide when open) that it can only be scanned like a tennis match. Perhaps it doesn't matter: the prodigious drawings need space, and the text, at least for me, is frequently obscure to the point of unintelligibility.

What we see in Soleri's extraordinary output is a series of closed communities which take a variety of geometric forms, mostly circular. It is hard to think of a precedent for these astonishing creations, most of which suggest cross sections of huge machines from an alien planet. The designer has thoughtfully placed a drawing of the Empire State Building on most of his projects to show their size at a glance, and in many instances it is dwarfed by the proposed new construction. Populations in these arcologies runs as high as 6 million in at least one, with the majority somewhere between 500,000 and 1,000,000. The densities run as high as 1,100 people per acre, although most seem to level off between 300 and 500. To understand how tightly Soleri proposes to pack his populations, Chicago has 25 people to the acre; Tokyo, 50; New York, 33; and Paris, 107.

It is hard for anyone conditioned like most of us, by life in cities which are loose, open, and sparsely populated by comparison with Soleri's, to view these creations with anything other than a sense of absolute horror, and yet they cannot be dismissed with an exasperated "he must be crazy." In a way, the arcologies may relate to what has happened to the utopian novel over four centuries. These start with delightful visions of life in a civilized society where all contemporary problems, from war to poverty to the productive use of leisure time, are solved. The books go on in this vein all the way to H.G. Wells' *Men Like Gods*. Optimism and beautiful images of the Good Life prevail. Then around the middle of this century, we get books like *Brave New World* and *Animal Farm* which suddenly project a perfectly plausible but utterly nightmarish future. I get the same feeling from most of Soleri's arcologies, although his professed intention, like that of his predecessors, is to take us to a richer and more humane existence.

Even the sites he has imagined are mostly special: canyons hidden in desert mountain ranges, lunar cliffs, huge dams, pile-ups like the cliff dwellings of Mesa Verde magnified a thousand times. These cities, often suggesting concrete beehives for populations blinded by too close a view of H-bomb explosions, were presumably designed for Planet Earth, but one gets the sense of a planet so devastated by war, or overwhelming man-made catastrophes, that nothing is left but densely packed hideaways where huddled billions subsist on vitamin pills and wait for time to come to an end.

One of the curious things about Soleri's science fic-

Babel IIA, Paolo Soleri, 1969: like Kenzo Tange, Soleri sees a future of megastructures for a planet weighed down by billions of human bodies, but goes on from these into technological fantasies of unprecedented dimensions. Note Empire State Building at lower right. Paolo Soleri, Arcology (Cambridge, Mass.: MIT Press, 1969).

tion megastructures is that they are riddled with lightwells, many of them with a depth of 100 stories or more. Since even a superdense city could presumably be laid out so that all dwellings and offices could get a view of the sky, he must have a reason for this. A lightwell 1,000 feet deep is hardly something that would cheer up the inhabitants unless they had been conditioned in the fetal stage. I suspect that what is dominating in Soleri's anti-utopias is not so much the expressed intention to create a framework for urban existence, but rather an obsession with the creation of extraordinary geometrical abstractions. The French architect Claude Ledoux fell into the grip of similar preoccupations almost 200 years ago.

Behind all these arcologies, there is clearly a preoccupation with both growing populations and the dangers to the natural environment. If one jams the teeming billions into clearly delimited megastructures, then this theoretically leaves the rest of the planet in its natural state. But the price, comparable with drastic control of population, is beyond calculation. It is hard to imagine a race of people who would find this kind of existence tolerable.

Soleri is a man of uncommon talent, and the fact that I take a dim view of what he has been proposing does not mean that these images are without value, for at the very worst they present a clear picture of something that might possibly happen. However, I do find a sharp contradiction between Soleri's professed concern for humanity and his obvious delight in the concoction of dazzling industrial geometry. It is even possible that these synthetic environments could in some mysterious way allow the spirit of humanity to flourish again, but I have an uneasy suspicion that it will take a lot of tranquilizers. That, if you will recall, was the solution provided by Aldous Huxley for the citizens of his Brave New World.

The City and the Mayor

This article, written for *Holiday* magazine in 1966, was to have been about a rash of exciting modern buildings which were going up in New Haven, largely under the sponsorship of Yale University. It would have turned out that way, too, but I met the city's Mayor, Richard Lee, and that changed everything.

Lee, who was reelected six times, was a real pro politician who knew all about kissing babies and appearing at wakes, barmitzvahs, and confirmations; he turned out, to my utter amazement, to be a genuine folk hero on a modest scale, which means that he was brave, wise, and humble and that he was totally dedicated to something that was not his own career: the city and its people. Lee was not widely known, partly because what he did for the city was never spectacular, and he had no stomach for the publicity machinery needed to manufacture instant immortality. I think he was about as selfless as a politician could get and still survive.

Court Street, a short block with thirteen dilapidated houses from the 19th century, was redeveloped in 1962 by the city. The restored and modernized houses were sold in one morning, and with good maintenance by owners and the growth of planting, the neighborhood has become one of the most desirable places to live in the downtown area.

Going between New York and New Haven isn't like it was in the old days when as students we used to leave after the last Saturday class and head for New York to taste the illegal delights of the speakeasies and, on occasion, the puritanical commercialism of the taxi dance halls. On Sunday, after a refreshing night in the Turkish bath of the old Hotel Pennsylvania and some mild social activity, we would set out for New Haven again, usually in the small hours. The car, a souped-up Dodge roadster, would roar through a quiet Manhattan and along the twisting Boston Post Road, getting us back to the Yale campus in two hours and fifteen minutes flat. Now one can make the trip in less time without a trick car, and the only problem is to stay awake while following the hypnotic ribbon of the expressway.

The new highway, in conformity with the emerging national pattern, goes directly to the heart of the city; but I turned off before that to take the last nostalgic stretch of old road, past West Rock and the Yale Bowl, over to Whalley Avenue, and towards the university and the New Haven Green. This city of 160,000, founded in the early 17th century and 300 years later described as a "big slum around a big school," has recently been singled out as the most successful example of urban renewal in the U.S., and its Mayor has become something of a legend. What makes the claim interesting at the moment is the fact that urban renewal is under heavy fire from both the far right and far left. The statistics on New Haven's achievements are impressive ("largest per capita investment in overall rehabilitation and new building," etc., etc.,) and the cup of superlatives runs over in a recent local newspaper article which describes the city as an "Athens of Modern Architecture."

I entered the New Athens on Whalley Avenue behind a truck stuffed with loaves of "batter-whipped" bread. It carried a second sign, which may or may not have been the bakery's idea: "Don't litter Connecticut," it implored. "It's a beautiful state."

The section of beautiful Connecticut through which we were moving at that moment contained a batter-whipped assortment of motels, second-hand car lots, overburdened telephone poles, and block after block of two-family wood houses bulging with shingled cupolas, fat bay windows, and sagging porches. Into many of these, glassy stores and automobile showrooms had been forcibly inserted, rather like the clocks an earlier generation installed in the bellies of naked bronze ladies. On both sides of the street it was open war, waged by battalions of shop fronts and illuminated signs, all executed with a polychrome violence comparable only with the uninhibited primitive sculpture of the South Pacific. Delicatessens charged supermarkets, littering the streets with bleeding posters, menus, and price lists; drug stores strafed gas stations; instant dry cleaners dropped neon bombs on bar-grilles, candy stores, and housewares establishments. Kamikaze salesmen shot themselves out of car salesrooms to expire on enemy positions. Barrages of words fell everywhere, deafening and blinding both customers and competitors, printed words like NEW, NOW, BUY, BARGAIN, designed for easy comprehension by a TV-conditioned audience.

Lining both sides of the avenue there were other kinds of printed exhortations, a pop art jungle of sizes, shapes, lettering styles, and bright colors, all united in a hymn to civic confusion: slow down to 15 mph—take the so and so bus here but not the such and such—this mail-kinds of printed exhortations, a pop art jungle of sizes, shapes, lettering styles, and bright colors, all united in a hymn to civic confusion: slow down to 15 MPH—take the so and so bus here but not the such and such—this mailbox is not for mail—do not turn right at the next intersection—come to think of it, better not turn left either—shut up, please, this is a Quiet Zone (played to the music of air hammers mutilating a shell-shocked pavement)—park here and we'll tow your goddam car away (except, of course, on Tuesdays and Fridays between the hours of now and then and on alternate sides of the street)—park here (just try and find a place, we dare you) but don't expect us to tell you how much to put into the meter.

Whalley Avenue was not precisely the place a Chamber of Commerce would recommend starting a tour of the "new" New Haven, but there is nothing unusual about that. The same can be seen in a hundred thousand streets in all the tru-blue U.S. towns, from sea to shining sea. "God's Own Junkyard," an observer recently named it, living testimony to modern man's ability to put up with practically anything.

"Practically anything" is what New Haven's inmates have been putting up with for at least a half-century; and in this, like Whalley Avenue, there is nothing unusual either. U.S. cities have been obsolete for lo these many years—and sick to boot. There has been no shortage of voices to warn of trouble ahead, but general awareness of the extent and depth of the urban malady is very recent. New Haven's list of ailments was standard: slums, vanishing downtown trade, a gradual decline of industry, the decay of public assets. In a thirty-year period (1920 to 1950) only two schools were built and not a single public library, fire, or police station. Private initiative had neglected to produce a single new hotel or office building. Given this familiar picture of creeping disintegration, is it small wonder that every family headed for the suburbs as fast as it could afford the move. This flight of taxpayers was enormously accelerated by federal support of home mortgages. The escape of the better-heeled citizens rapidly pushed the central city into a tailspin, for with the loss of taxes came mounting municipal expenses, due to the growth of slums. Slums cost a city more than stable neighborhoods.

To make the point about the city's deterioration, it is not necessary to claim that New Haven's slums were bigger or worse than those of other communities. They were adequate, let us say, to create a full assortment of municipal headaches, fiscal and otherwise. The blacks lived in slums on and near Dixwell Avenue (the Mayor was born and brought up in this neighborhood), and the whites lived in slums on streets with other names. The gem in New Haven's crown was the Oak Street area, dozens and dozens of acres right behind the downtown shopping district, where families of six lived in two rooms, their offal littering the streets and alleys. Shortly before he was elected, the Mayor paid a visit to Oak Street. After an exposure of minutes, he came out again and was sick in the gutter. Considering that his upbringing had been far from soft or sheltered, his involuntary comment left little to be added. Oak Street's occupants, in addition to derelict people and garbage, included some 10,000 rats, which must have created interesting problems for people with infants. The chief products of the district were prostitution and petty crime. These in turn produced an average of six arrests a day and fire calls some 600 percent higher than anywhere else in the city.

This decaying community was atypical only in that it was the setting for one of the nation's proudest and best-endowed seats of learning. The Yale payroll of some $25 million per year was one of the few steady props of the city's enfeebled economy, but this flow of badly needed money did not endear the university to the town any more than U.S. aid to Latin America has sweetened relations with our neighbors to the south. In general, the university stayed aloof from the city's problems—an attitude for which it can hardly be criticized, since New Haven's leading citizens were doing the same thing. A notable exception was John Day Jackson, owner of the city's two newspapers. Jackson's antipathy to anything which might ameliorate the city's miseries was ferocious, and his considerable power was devoted to destroying or denigrating

Church Street before redevelopment, shown on page 86.

Knights of Columbus: this office tower by Roche & Dinkeloo would have gone the way of most small city projects but for the Mayor's insistence on architects of outstanding ability. The Coliseum, next door, was done later by the same firm and added substantially to the city's downtown parking space.

anyone who tried to do anything about them. When Richard Lee was running for the Mayor's office, his strongest opposition came from the *New Haven Register*, and it has continued unabated until rather recently. The paper now expresses solid pride in the revitalized city—a gratifying change of heart attributed by some cynics to the sharp increases in advertising revenue from the new downtown shopping area, including an estimated $500,000 per year from the new Macy's store alone.

I caught a glimpse of Macy's and the new parking garage in the rebuilt downtown area after escaping from the chaos of Whalley Avenue. There was an enormous excavation between this cluster and the Green, and it was clearly apparent that this beautiful open space which had been the pride of the city since it was founded in 1638 was going to have the first significant change in its setting in more than a generation. I remembered the low buildings which had been torn down as a block-long assembly of architectural rubbish, and it seemed safe to assume that whatever rose out of the excavation to replace them would be an improvement. I put aside the temptation to take a closer look, for I was already late for my first appointment with the Mayor.

As things turned out, it didn't matter. The Mayor, on the most recent of his restless forays into the town, had stepped into a hole on a construction project and had broken his leg. I was passed on to Thomas Appleby, Director of Development. Appleby, a quiet, intelligent man in his thirties, occupies a nondescript office in a shabby office building a few steps from City Hall. When we met it was apparent that he was torn between regret that I had not been sent to someone else and the desire to let a new listener in on all the exciting things going on in New Haven. The latter won, and he plunged into the tangle of complexities which make up the story of a city's experience with urban renewal. His enthusiasm was contagious, and we both got lost in the tale. After perhaps an hour he stopped and said, "Look. You've got to see the Mayor. You won't make any sense at all out of this story unless you see the Mayor."

"It doesn't really matter," I replied. "I'm writing about the city, and I can get all I need from you."

"You're talking through your hat," he retorted politely. "The city *is* the Mayor. Or if you prefer, the Mayor is the city. There is no way to disentangle them. Let me phone."

"They said the Mayor is out of commission."

Appleby laughed and reached for the telephone. "That'll be the day," he said, dialing. Twenty minutes later he got past the busy signals, and then we went out.

The Mayor lives in a well-kept middle class neighborhood in one of those romantic half-timber houses so dear to the hearts of architects and builders a generation back. His wife let us in and took us upstairs to a large sunny bedroom where her husband was stretched out on a chaise, one leg encased in plaster. Appleby and I sat in straight chairs while the Mayor cheerfully lamented his broken leg and ruined health. Before we could get on with the business at hand, the Fire Chief came in, silent, a ruddy-faced man who filled his immaculate uniform so tightly one became nervous about the buttons. He wandered onto the sun porch in the manner of someone completely at home, found a chair, and brought it in.

The Mayor began with what must have been a set piece. New Haven has outstripped every city in the country in its accomplishments. Twenty percent of all land in the city is currently involved in rehabilitation schemes or new building. Two thousand construction projects since 1959. A quarter of a billion dollars in building completed or under way. A full highway network nearly completed, and so on. I sat and listened hard, not so much to the statistics, which were available in print, but to the Mayor himself. I had brought a businesslike notebook, mostly as a journalistic prop, for I have difficulty in reading my handwriting. The Mayor has a homely, attractive face which radiates harmless good will and easy, cheerful friendliness; and I wondered how many people, in addition to myself, had been taken in by the facade. If there is a drop of truth in all the stories told by his associates, this is a man made deeply angry and indignant by the sight of misery, a stubborn fighter with burning ideals and absolute integrity. What shows is a relaxed professional politician with full understanding of the blessings of good public relations, and it is quite impossible not to like him. Later, when it turns out that there *is* more than a drop of truth in the reports of his dedicated entourage, you like him better. If, of course, you happen to share his feelings and attitudes. In New Haven, as in any city, there are those who do not.

It is impossible, in talking about anything as involved as overall rehabilitation of an entire city, to move in a straight line. A city is a web, a network. Touch any point, and immediately a dozen lines radiate to other points. Furthermore, it is in motion. Neighborhoods change and go up or down. People and businesses move. As age groups shift, schools become overcrowded or half empty. Industries move in or go away.

The Mayor talked about all these things and kept

jumping from building programs to tax money to social problems in a kind of high-speed multichannel communication which made one wonder how long the language would remain adequate in a world where complex relationships rather than simple things and events have to be described. It was clear that he enjoyed juggling a dozen balls at once, and in this he suggested the planner-type executive more than the conventional politician. Add to this the fact that the conventional politician is not a dedicated man, and you arrive at an interesting hybrid.

Lee cannot open his mouth without revealing that he cares terribly about everything that happens to his city, and in a very personal way. "At times Dick annoys people by talking about New Haven as if he owned the joint and were personally responsible for every brick taken down or put up," one of his associates remarked, "but I suspect that the reverse is closer to the truth: he is possessed by it."

Dedication has rarely been listed as an asset by politicians, and in the case of the Mayor it nearly wrecked his career before it got under way. In 1949 he ran for office on a platform of city rehabilitation, despite the warnings of friends, and he got licked. Trying in 1951 he lost again, by an agonizing two votes. In 1953 he had all but decided to drop the whole thing when a petition with 4,000 names of independent voters came in, so he ran again and made it by a microscopic margin. In 1955 he was reelected in a near landslide, and he has been doing it ever since.

The biography of Richard Lee comes close to being a recapitulation of the Horatio Alger stories which so delighted our parents. An authentic slum kid, the only white player on his neighborhood's baseball team, he left school in his teens to help support his family, worked as a clerk in the A & P, and went through a series of the jobs available to boys of his age. He recalls with glee meeting one of his early employers shortly after he had been elected Mayor. "It's nice to see you after so many years, Richard," said the old man. "What are you doing these days?"

"I'm down at City Hall at the moment," replied Lee. "I've got a temporary job there."

At some point while he was still in his teens, Lee pushed his career to the next plateau: he gave up clerking and became a reporter. This led to an invitation to work in the university's press bureau, and he remained there for eleven years. Just as in the Alger stories, he came to the attention of a power in the university, the late Carl Lohman, who befriended him and no doubt filled in many of the gaps in his education. Lee has become one of Yale's most loyal nonalumni, eats whenever he can at Mory's, and feels at home in Ivy League clothes. If, in the fullness of time, his non-alma mater sees fit to recognize his prodigious labors in a critical part of the American scene with an honorary degree, nobody will be very surprised.

Never a man to feel fulfilled by one job, Lee became a moonlighter in politics and was appointed Alderman shortly after reaching voting age. When a City Planning Commission was formed in 1941, he was put on it by his own request. He was the Democratic nominee for Mayor when he was thirty-three; but as we have seen, he failed to make it before reaching the ripe old age of thirty-eight.

This is a 60-second snapshot of a tired man in a sunny bedroom, nursing a broken leg. He was talking, at the moment, about public housing, illiteracy, and fire engines.

"We learned something from all this tearing down and rebuilding," he said. "It is that building isn't enough. The great cry today is 'tear down the slums and replace them with decent housing.' A noble sentiment, but it doesn't work. People make slums; and unless you can teach them not to make slums, they will go on doing it wherever you put them. Urban renewal thus has to include people renewal, and this means all the things which condition people for responsible citizenship. It is a terrible job. Do you know that after nearly ten years of work this city still has several thousand functional illiterates?"

I had not heard of a "functional" illiterate. It seems that this is an individual who never got beyond fourth-grade reading ability.

"So, what do you do about housing?" I asked. "Wait until the entire slum population has been reconditioned?"

"Of course not," he snorted. "You have to do everything at once. This is impossible. So you do what you can. It's very discouraging, but you have to keep on trying. He turned to the Fire Chief.

"Tom," he said. "The pumper stopped when it went by this morning." The Chief looked at him without comment.

"They *stopped*," the Mayor repeated and turned to me to explain. "They probably figured I'd be looking out of the window. It's a real job to persuade those boys to hold back at the 'stop' streets. As a result we've had more firemen killed in accidents than in fires. Civilians, too. The trouble is, some driver comes to the intersection, he knows he has the right of way, his car windows are closed and the radio is on, so he doesn't hear the fire truck. Forty thousand pounds at 35 miles an hour can make quite a mess. I think I'm finally getting the idea across, but it has been a battle."

The Mayor fusses endlessly about everything, and it is probably one of the reasons his old ulcer flares up from time to time. Lee prowls the city constantly, reminding one strongly of New York's late, still-lamented Fiorello LaGuardia. On one of his forays he dashed unannounced into the police station and made his way to a room where a group of young blacks, picked up on some charge or other, was being questioned.

"Hi, fellas," said the Mayor to the alleged culprits. A surprised mumble returned the greeting.

"How're the cops treating you?" he asked.

"They're treatin' us okay, Your Honor," said one of the boys.

"Fine," said the Mayor, "I figured they would."

The news of the visit probably reached a fair percentage of the black voters some time that evening; but while one could never accuse Lee of passing up the chance to make a profitable political gesture, he would have gone to the police station anyway. He worries about his flock. At a recent ceremony involving several hundred crippled and retarded children, he shook hands with every one of them, talked with as many as he could—and kept the press photographers out. "Sure I did," he said when I checked with him. "These were unfortunate people, underprivileged in the most basic and irremedial way. You don't make political capital of unfortunate people. You can't imagine what it was like to see so many kids like that all at once. I don't think I was ever so tired in all my life as when it was over."

At the last election a black man was put up as an opposition candidate. He got 700 out of a possible 7,000 votes in the district. The Mayor's position on racial problems has never been left in doubt, and one has the impression that during the years when he grew up as a minority member in a predominantly black neighborhood, he never had a chance to learn that blacks weren't really people, as most other white Americans were taught, and as a result he never learned to treat them as anything but people. The simplicity of this method for achieving racial harmony apparently arouses some skepticism, but it seems to work in New Haven.

As I came to see more of Lee, I began to notice that a lot of people assume an affectionate and somehow protective attitude towards him, as if he were a kind of *wunderkind*, always a source of worry as he sped about town without regard for his own health or safety. One morning he insisted that we visit the big excavation south of the Green where there is to be a $15 million project with a hotel, office tower, a two-story shopping mall, and an underground area for parking and deliveries. The project is more significant than its size or dollar value, for this was the place where the whole downtown planning effort almost went on the rocks, and its completion will mark the success of the drive to revitalize the central shopping district. The official Cadillac rolled down through the Church Street tunnel and came to a stop in the excavation. A large crane stopped operations as the Mayor limped out into the open (he had been allowed to shed his cane a few days before), and a burly character in a hard hat stuck his head out of the cab.

"Hey, Dick!" he yelled. Practically everyone seems to call the Mayor Dick or Richard. "How's the leg?" The Mayor's latest mishap had been given a lot of local publicity, almost as if to prove that he would get into trouble if someone didn't keep an eye on him.

"Fine!" shouted the Mayor. "See? No cane!"

"Serve you goddam well right if you busted the other one!" retorted his worried constituent. "Time you got sense enough to keep off construction jobs!"

They grinned at each other, the crane started up again, and Skipper—the Mayor's driver—turned the car around.

Skipper, like all the people in the Mayor's entourage, is a superior individual. An impeccable driver, with the dress and bearing of a first-class Secret Service agent, he also doubles as an executive assistant-in-motion, able to fill in for the Mayor on those rare occasions when he forgets a name or a statistic. The high-quality personnel go all the way up the line, from the secretaries in the front office to the top planners, like Edward Logue who was drafted by Boston to head its planning activity and Thomas Appleby who followed him in New Haven and has now been lured away to take the same job in Washington.

"He was lucky, in a way," said one of the Mayor's aides, when I remarked on the quality of the people I had met. "Don't forget that he came in in 1954. Eisenhower was in Washington, and the bright young men didn't have to be told that this was no place for them. So where? Word began to get around that something was happening in New Haven, and the quiz kids with ideals began to drift in. Ed Logue smelled it all the way to India, Mike Sviridoff came in from the labor movement to help whip the school system into shape—lots of absolutely first-rate guys. I call Dick Lee lucky because he got in before Kennedy, who had the same appeal to the same kinds of people. Kennedy had greater pulling power, of course, and putting this crew together might not have been so easy a few years later. Now the raiding has started. Cities offering bigger jobs with bigger pay naturally want the best people they can get, and New Haven is one of the places to find them. It's rough to lose our best people; but as you have no doubt noticed, the Mayor is a pretty effective publicist, and it will be a long time before New Haven loses its appeal for bright young people who want a career in public service. And a number of them are just bright enough to read between the lines and realize that what the Mayor is conducting, behind a facade of urban renewal, is a moral crusade."

"A moral crusade against what?," I asked.

"Against the slum—in the broadest sense of the word—and against everything which produces it. New Haven, in case nobody has told you, is where the antipoverty program started before there was a program. Having been brought up in a slum himself, the Mayor doesn't have to be told where the troubles are, and he knows how difficult the remedies are. He also knows which of the cures are politically dangerous, such as the dislocation of businesses, say, and this is why we think of him as a man of great courage as well as political know-how."

I was reminded of the moral aspect of the Mayor's politicking on one of our drives through the city. We had just passed a large abandoned brick house, with almost all its windows broken. "Hey, Skip!" shouted the Mayor. "Stop the car, will you? That house," he said to me, "was bought by the Highway Department in preparation for an extension of the Oak Street Connector. Then they let it sit there. Now the windows are smashed and there might be more vandalism, children might go in there and get hurt, a pervert could drag in a child who was going by some night. . . . I have a horror of things like that. I have an orderly mind, and I don't like to see such things."

"I repeat this over and over again, 'avoid the occasions of sin.' That house is an occasion for sin. We can control such things, and we must not allow them to happen."

Nobody in the car seemed surprised by the sudden reversion to parochial school language, and Tom Appleby took out a notebook and wrote something down. The car went past a church, never much good to begin with and now clearly in very bad condition. "We're buying that church and tearing it down," remarked the Mayor. "You know, I've bought more beat-up churches in this town—lucky they keep building new ones. . . . Tom, have we overlooked any of the denominations? Can't show favoritism when you tear down churches. . . ." We went down to the waterfront to see the city's new fireboat, named *Sally Lee* after the Mayor's daughter. He rattled off all the facts on size, tonnage, horsepower, gallons pumped per minute, and the rest, and Skipper only had to correct him once.

After the ride I went off with Tom Appleby. "How are chances for eliminating all the slums?" I asked. "What do you really think?"

Appleby sighed. It was not the first time, obviously, he had been asked that question.

"Look" he said, "the city has about 150,000 population, about 50,000 dwelling units of all kinds. To date it has purchased 5,000 of these dwellings and 1,000 business properties. About $60 million, roughly. Or put another way, about 10 percent of the existing housing supply. On top of this, we have induced owners to bring 7,500 houses up to minimum standards. That makes 25 percent, and it leaves us with another 10 percent—or 5,000 dwellings—classified as substandard. This 10 percent, in other words, is the job remaining to be done. I am confident that we are now closer to eliminating *all* slums in the city than any other community in the country.

"Now," he continued, "That's as close as I can come to answering your question, and I have to add something. We are not at all sure that it is desirable to talk about eliminating slums, as a goal. It puts a deceptively simple face on a very difficult problem and creates the impression that urban renewal is a matter of real estate manipulation and architectural upgrading. The root of the problem is people, not buildings."

Urban renewal, which is what I would have been writing about before this had the Mayor not turned out to be such a distracting character, is a nationwide response to a series of local problems too long ignored. Like the antipoverty program, it fits in with a series of moves towards the "Great Society," whatever that may turn out to be. Behind these grandiose posturings there is real trouble. The list of civic ailments is so long and is now being so widely publicized that it is hardly necessary to do more than tick them off: downtown retail areas are being badly hurt by competition from the outlying shopping centers, where parking is no problem. Industry is moving out to rural sites near the new express roads. The population mix is changing, and many cities—New Haven among them—are anticipating a nonwhite majority in the 70s. Urban traffic problems have become acute, and in many cases they are being made worse by the new highways which dump increasing numbers of cars into congested downtown areas.

Slums, always costly, are still everywhere in evidence; automation and new standards of education are rendering sizable worker groups unemployable, even if only temporarily; and the mounting rate of crime and delinquency weighs ever more heavily on city budgets.

As I listened to accounts of the various programs in New Haven, certain themes were constantly reiterated: the importance of revitalizing the downtown retail areas (prosperous business districts pay high taxes), the importance of curbing the flight of industry (taxes, again, and employment), the importance of getting middle and upper-middle income people back into the city through good schools and suitable housing (taxes, again, and buying power). Any city trying to stabilize its economy has to give high priority to these efforts. Some are already too far gone to make the grade.

No matter how one tries to simplify description of the urban problem, it remains desperately complicated. No city is any longer able to finance rehabilitation activity without state and federal assists. Many will not be able to balance their budgets, even without renewal programs. Hence the most visible element in the urban landscape is creeping decay. Conflicting interests of all kinds make constructive action difficult. A lack of awareness of the appalling ugliness everywhere is another factor; call attention to it and intense hostility is the common response. I still have vivid memories of a winter lecture in Kalamazoo, Michigan, where I was supposed to hold forth on the beauties of modern design, or something. I had been so shattered by the visual assaults between the railroad station and the hotel, by the abysmal dreariness of what was then the "best" hotel in town, by the indescribable vulgarity of the municipal Christmas decorations that when I got onto the lecture platform it was impossible to talk about anything else. The detailed descriptions of what I had seen during the past two hours did not sit at all well with the audience, which had come to the lecture to be tranquilized by pictures of all the wonderful things happening in the worlds of art, architecture, and design and not to be informed that it was living in a cesspool.

This near-universal blindness is showing signs of clearing up a bit. Kalamazoo, like other cities, has done some interesting and attractive things to upgrade itself. But now there is something else: apathy. This new national attribute is most dramatically expressed in the recent murders where two or three dozen people looked on and did nothing. The killing of cities is less spectacular, since it takes longer; but the underlying attitude is not very different. I asked Edward Logue, New Haven's chief planner during the agonizing early years, what assists the Mayor had gotten from influential civic groups. "Oh them," said Logue. "They only came out when the sun was shining." An overstatement, obviously, for the Mayor could hardly have done what he did without support. Nevertheless, it cannot be denied either that much old-fashioned civic pride has been replaced by a very modern fear of involvement.

The most special of the organizations created to help New Haven get back on its feet is called Community Progress, Inc. (CPI). It came into existence shortly after the Mayor's election in 1954 because, in the words of its executive director, Mitchell Sviridoff, "what seems to be needed is a massive, coordinated, comprehensive, and simultaneous attack on the causes of poverty...." CPI is a kind of antipoverty program in miniature, addressing itself to such problems as dropouts, retraining for employment, education for slum children, community health, and a variety of others. It is essentially a planning and implementing organization which gives both direction and funds to all sorts of city agencies. Its money comes from two very substantial Ford Foundation grants, and for many of its projects it gets federal assists as well. The great power wielded by CPI stems from the fact that it can attack problems on a broad basis, since it has none of the restrictions which limit a city department, and that it has money to give away for projects it considers important. The result in New Haven has been cooperation between municipal agencies which never talked to each other before and some very effective action.

As one goes behind the scenes in this busy town, it soon becomes apparent that its success in overall urban rehabilitation consists of thousands of small coordinated acts, any one of which is rather unimpressive taken by itself. This picture was quite different from the rather naive (and I suspect, common) idea I arrived with: that urban renewal was primarily a process of bulldozing vast acreages of slums and replacing them with shiny highrise apartments and office buildings set in tastefully landscaped surroundings. This may indeed be the way things are in some cities, but it has nothing to do with the Mayor's view of the situation.

To pick at random one of the small activities now going on, there is something called a Work Crew program. It was described to me one afternoon by a young CPI administrator named Talbot: "We take the real hard-core kids, dropouts, kids with police records, and we group them in work crews of six or seven. They are put under the direct supervision of someone, not a social worker, who is perhaps an ordinary Joe from the neighborhood who has begun to make it, we have a couple of pro football players, sometimes it is a guy who doesn't have a very good job himself but he has experience and common sense and knows what to look out for with the kids. Then we put them to work on projects around the city, either for the city itself or for nonprofit agencies. For instance, the kids are now helping build a new zoo in the West Rock area. We pay $20 for twenty hours a week, which isn't much, but a lot better than running loose around the streets, and then they study. They get intensive remedial training in only two fields: reading and math. We hit them again and again in these two subjects, so that perhaps they can learn enough to hold down a beginning job. The program is only eight months old, and so far we have dealt with 110 kids. The record to date is one-third back in school, one-third in jobs with some hope for the future. Twenty-five percent have gone into the military (this is an accomplishment in itself for kids like these), and the rest we lost. We line up employers willing to try out our 'graduates' and we reimburse the training costs up to $30 per week out of funds allocated by the U.S. Department of Labor.''

One hundred and ten kids. Not many. About nine-tenths of them take the new chance offered. Not bad. New Haven is loaded with projects of this size, and nobody apologizes because each one is statistically so unglamorous.

Nobody apologizes because this is the way they want it. Most particularly, this is the way the Mayor wants it. He becomes very impatient with people who think of cities as abstract entities with problems which can be solved on paper. For the Mayor, a city is an aggregation of human problems, which must be dealt with on an individual or a small-scale basis.

One result of this attitude is that it is rather hard to find any public housing in New Haven without a guide. I remember my first exposure to this peculiarity. We were driving through a neighborhood of little one- and two-family houses, and suddenly I noticed something and asked the driver to stop. The "something" was a miniscule housing development with only 20 or 30 family units. Then we began running into similar clusters all over town, and I got the impression that the smaller they were, the better the Mayor and Tom Appleby liked them.

"How do you solve the housing problem," I demanded, "with all these tiny pokes at it? What's the matter, can't you get at the big federal money?"

Appleby grinned. "Why don't you ask Dick when we get back?," he suggested. "By the way, how do you like this parking lot?"

We had just passed another of the Mayor's invisible accomplishments, a corner parking area, with a woven wood fence about four feet high and some planting. There was space for eleven cars, Appleby said. They had bought a derelict building and had torn it down.

"We had it down on the neighborhood plans as a tot lot," he said. "Tot lot" was new to me, but it hardly seemed necessary to ask for a translation. "Then we checked with the people who live in the area, and they seemed to think there was plenty of backyard space for the kids, and they did want more off-street parking. So we made a parking lot. They pay $3 a month for keeping a car there."

"You mean you checked out the neighborhood on what to do with that corner lot?" I asked. He seemed surprised. "Why not? It's their neighborhood."

When I got around to asking the Mayor what he thought he was doing with his program of undersized housing and parking, what I got back was a lecture. We had just arrived for a look at the new central firehouse.

"This," said Lee, "is an absolute phobia I have. It is simply stated: when you wipe out a ghetto and replace it with concentrated low-cost housing you are doing little more than continuing the ghetto with modern buildings. Because you move back in the low-income families, families with all kinds of social problems, and in concentrating them you will create more social problems. You're not uplifting the neighborhood at all. If there's a school in that neighborhood, you're filling that school with one kind of basic problem, you're not spreading the problem around so that it can be made manageable. Only in recent months, after twenty years of public housing, has the country begun to focus on the human problems in public housing.

"It is bad; it is damaging to people to dump them into a neighborhood stamped as a public housing neighborhood. It is bad to have a school stamped in this way, as a concentration of misery, poverty, and emotional problems, to put on children the stigma, which will remain with them if they stay in the community, of being public housing children from problem families."

He drew a long breath. The firemen were looking curiously through the big glass garage doors.

"If you have to have public housing, and there is a need for it, you should integrate it with regular housing in ordinary neighborhoods, sometimes to the point where you subsidize the rents they pay in existing structures. In such a case you don't bother to build. The important thing is to remove the stigma of life in a public housing project. Now I don't want you to think that we figured all this out right away. We also thought, at the beginning, that if you pulled slum families out of the slums and put them in nice clean housing your problems would be over. The hangover from that one is still with us."

He glared at the back of the driver. The firemen by this time had drifted away, back to whatever they had been doing. "Our worst slum," he continued, "was Oak Street. Okay, so we tore it down. Then we took 150 of the hard-core families there and put them into public housing, and we've had plenty trouble. Many of these families have been sullen, hostile, withdrawn; some are low IQs, and they are not susceptible to group therapy. You have to reach them in other ways. Now we have a concentrated social services program, a community school program going, and we have an employment office working there, as well as a neighborhood office for redevelopment.

"Now we've got the beginning of a kind of community spirit going for the first time, although the project has been there for years. The point is in order to make a program like this succeed, and I'm talking about a massive program of renewal, you have to approach it not only in terms of your core city and replacing the gin mills and pool halls with new structures which produce a maximum tax yield; you've got to worry about housing of all kinds, about new uses for old areas, like getting quality tenants back into the center. At the same time, as you begin to move these other families into established neighborhoods, you've got to give them the kind of assistance they need to solve the problems which plague the family from a blighted neighborhood. This is where we began to see the light. We went in with one kind of approach, and we came out with another. We finally began to realize that it wasn't enough to simply tear down the slums and rebuild. We had to rewrite our laws: provide new building codes, housing codes, sanitary, fire, and electrical codes. Then we had to tighten up inspection and make sure that these laws were enforced. We had to create a division of neighborhood improvement, a code enforcement committee; we had to hire a lawyer to follow cases of code violation and make sure the courts didn't fool around too long. . . . So many of these families we have been displacing are marginal families, marginal in income, education, and desire. It's the old problem of background. This is where your poverty program comes in. You have to begin with prekindergarten, and you go on, one slow step after another, until you arrive at job training." He sighed and was silent.

The Mayor stared unseeingly at his favorite firehouse. "Tom told me what you said this morning about our housing projects and parking lots. Invisible. . . wasn't that what you called them?"

"That's right," I replied. "Invisible."

He chuckled. "I don't know how you meant that, but I'm taking it as a compliment. Invisible. . . I like that. You know, too much urban renewal architecture is being done for the newspapers and the magazines instead of the poor devils who have to live with it."

Given this orientation, it comes as no surprise to learn that the Mayor's first major move, after assuming office in 1954, was not urban renewal but school renewal. As I mentioned earlier, the city's record on schools was disgraceful: two schools had been built in thirty years, and the curricula and staff morale were as bad as the physical plant. Other public services were equally bad: not a single library, fire station, or police station had been built since 1920. The school situation was tackled first, and in no time at all the startled city found itself committed to $13 million in bonds for new construction.

Along with the building program, a number of first-rate people who had been languishing under earlier administrations found a sympathetic ear. What they had to say was that they had known for a long time that a curric-

Wooster Square Project, residential parking: Mayor Lee and his planners were responsible for a number of miniature parking lots (about twelve cars as a rule) in older residential neighborhoods. Low walls and planting transform what would normally be an eyesore into an amenity.

ulum designed for the children of middle-class families was virtually useless when inflicted on youngsters from the slums. Changes were made. Then the "community school" was invented. Whether this was the brain child of Abraham Wechsler, principal of the Winchester School, of the Mayor, of a group, or nothing more than the implementation of a much older idea, I never did discover. All were unanimous, however, in stating that New Haven was the first U.S. city where the community school achieved physical expression. On the handsomely refurbished Wooster Square, one can now visit the Conte School, designed by Skidmore, Owings and Merrill—an elegant, sophisticated, and durable affair which would do credit to any community. Another, by the firm of Eero Saarinen and Associates, is under construction. Eventually there will be such a school in each of the city's six neighborhoods.

The idea of the community school is simply that it provide a broad range of neighborhood services. Thus the school includes a gathering place for older citizens, a public library branch, and outdoor adult recreation facilities. In addition, the school auditorium, gymnasium, and swimming pool are oversize, so that they can be used out of hours for neighborhood activities. The result is a school which costs more but which works quite literally around the clock and becomes a focus of civic awareness for a neighborhood. It also exerts an insidious influence on municipal agencies (which traditionally pay no attention to each other) by forcing them to cooperate.

The community school could theoretically house all neighborhood facilities, but in practice many are placed elsewhere. The planning offices, for instance, usually occupy cheap store space and devote themselves to local matters of planning, rehabilitation, employment, and so on. (In the main black district, for instance, the neighborhood office contains a model of the "Dixwell Plaza" project, a complex of shops, public buildings, and housing which when completed will be very far from "invisible.") Decentralization of planning means that literally every family in the city can be reached. As a result, one can find entire streets where every house has been painted and its grounds put in order. The Mayor relates with great satisfaction that the neighborhood planners discovered dozens or hundreds of home owners who had been paying 12 percent on mortgages for years. These owners were aided in refinancing at more reasonable rates, often increasing the loans to provide cash for remodeling without raising the interest payments. In this instance, the direct concern with the problems of individuals paid off well for the city, for many properties were brought up to standard minimums without use of municipal funds.

In the heart of the black area, one of the larger projects is being completed. With over 100 units spaced out in little clusters of two-story row houses, it will provide a modest assist to families in need of better accommodations. On one of our tours we stopped in at the office, which had also been fixed up as a model apartment by a department store.

"How are they renting?," demanded the Mayor when he was halfway out of the car. An attractive young woman who worked in the office had come outside to greet him.

"Fine," she said. "We could fill it right now with the black applications already in."

"I'm sure of it," growled the Mayor. "But we aren't having a 100 percent black project as long as I have anything to say about it. We are getting 30 percent whites, or I don't open it." There were a number of blacks standing around as he delivered this ultimatum, and all I could read on their faces was sober approval. We got back into the car. The Mayor was still growling, but nobody seemed nervous.

"Integration!" he said. "There is too much talk about integration. They "integrate" the schools, but what it means in reality is that the city has to cart kids all over town in buses. It's expensive and senseless. Integration has to begin with housing, with the neighborhoods. Then everything takes care of itself. We talk integration but silently obstruct it. That's why Florence Virtue Houses won't open until 30 percent of the tenants signed up are white."

The Mayor, one gathers, is antisegregation in whatever form it takes. His attitudes on the black-white situation are identical with his opinions on segregating problem children in problem neighborhoods.

So the 60-second snapshot expands from the image of a skilled and likable professional politician to that of a dedicated and deeply moral man using his skills in manipulation for ends rarely considered seriously by people in elective office. Angry and indignant, cheerful and relaxed, nervous, worried, optimistic, dedicated, stubborn, a flexible compromiser, a super-salesman, publicist, and pastor. All the words, contradictory as they are, fit. Shocking as the description may be, the only single word which appears to sum up the Mayor's attitude towards his job, his life, and his people is—if you will excuse the expression—Christian.

The only suitable, traditional role for authentic

Conte Community School is claimed to be the first of its kind in the country; the facility combines a school with other community functions. Architects: Skidmore, Owings, & Merrill.

Christians is to be thrown to the lions, and it has been played out in political arenas long after those of the Romans fell into disrepair. The Mayor, thanks to his formidable non-Christian skills, has managed to avoid the standard fate of more naive people of good will. To take a declining city of 150,000, however, and to engineer so massive and delicate and complex a process as total rehabilitation (not total yet—there is still Whalley Avenue—but now demonstrably possible) requires more than good intentions and political know-how. City planning, or re-planning, is also a difficult technical problem; and here again Lee did a great deal of homework. As far back as 1936, for instance, he familiarized himself with the "insane" proposal of Arnold Dana: that the city provide downtown off-street parking for 10,000 to 20,000 cars. As a member of the planning commission in 1941, he studied the comprehensive plan made by Maurice Rotival, then a professor at Yale.

The Rotival plan was both farsighted and practical; and while it was premature in terms of existing understanding and capabilities, it has had great influence on what the city is doing today. At some point Lee also became familiar with architects and architecture and learned that a first-class building does not cost more in the long run than a bad one. While I was in his office one day, a man called about a building his organization wanted to put up in the new downtown area. It was a sizable project, and Lee, always on the lookout for new taxpayers, was surprisingly apathetic.

"That rascal!," he said after hanging up. "He's been after me for months. Wants to put up an office building, and you wouldn't believe the drawings if you saw them. An eyesore. I told him we would sell him the land he wants if he hires _____ to design the building. [The firm he named was one of the half-dozen best in the U.S.] He's too cheap to pay a fair fee, and he's stalling. As far as I'm concerned, he can stall until hell freezes over; he's not getting that land until he promises in writing to behave himself. There's enough junk in this city already without deliberately adding to it." This attitude, which is indeed taking the city in the direction of a "new Athens" (one has to include Yale's exciting and impressive contribution), has also been responsible for saving a good bit of New Haven's fine old residential buildings. Court Street, for instance, a short block of handsome row houses of the early 19th century, was a decayed rooming house area when the city snapped it up and restored and modernized the buildings. Offered at public auction (bidders had to guarantee personal occupancy), they were all sold the first morning. Other reminders of the city's handsome and civilized past are getting similar treatment.

The most spectacular of these salvaging operations was Wooster Square, into which Court Street leads. This parklike space, only ten minutes' walk from the town center, was slated to become the site of the northbound superhighway. It had been chosen because it was open, and hence there would be less to tear down. The Mayor and his planners managed to convince the engineers that the road would work just as well a couple hundred yards to the east. The result was the saving of an ornament to the city, the destruction of some industrial slums, and the creation of a Chinese wall between a now desirable residential area and the new light industry and warehouse district on the far side of the road.

"The highway engineers," says the Mayor, "were terribly nice about the whole thing. They just hadn't considered the possibility that Wooster Square could again become an asset to the community." The voters who have been reelecting Lee for almost ten years probably didn't consider at the outset that a Mayor with a sharp eye for architectural values could be a community asset too.

New Haven's most public servant has another set of talents he has had to put into play at critical moments. With them, in an earlier generation, he could have sold the Brooklyn Bridge at least once a week. During his incumbency he has had to use them to keep the city's finances from drifting closer to the rocks and to preserve some of the most important components of the urban renewal project.

The ones most frequently talked about are Sargent and Macy's. Sargent is a hardware company, long a part of the city's industrial history. For generations it occupied a cluster of factory buildings which could have been designed by Charles Dickens, and in recent years—like many manufacturers in New England—it was strongly tempted to pull up stakes and move South. The Mayor moved in and stopped the move. The way he did it was to find out what inducements were being offered the company in the South and to match them. The city bought the useless factories and the land they were on, offered the company cleared land on a site near the harbor, and the result is a shiny new $4 million plant, a large payroll saved, and a contented management, which had contemplated abandoning New Haven only because it felt there was no choice. The city will recondition the original Sargent land and ultimately dispose of it to new industry.

The Macy's affair was more serious. A pivot point in the New Haven renewal plan was the restoration of down-

Dixwell Avenue before redevelopment, shown below.

Florence Virtue Houses, 129 units for low- and moderate-income families: the low density and relatively small size were qualities the Mayor insisted upon, and the requirement that occupancy be a mixture of black and white tenants was his way of fighting the busing of school children.

town as a trading area. A major store was needed to put it over. The big local store, Malley's, was willing to buy some of the cleared land and to build a new store, but it wanted a next-door competitor of national stature. Odd as it may seem, there are businesses which get nervous when presented with the opportunity for a monopoly. Macy's had been approached by a number of star salesmen, but without results. Just what the Mayor did when it became necessary for him to mount his white charger and go to New York has never been satisfactorily explained; but when he came back, Macy's was in the bag, the success of the downtown project was assured, and another employer with a payroll of nearly 1,000 had been added.

One of the things which provided Lee with a considerable assist during his last campaign for the office to which he has grown accustomed was a promise to the voters that he would not raise taxes. It was quite a promise, considering that he was trying to make up for the neglect and inaction of nearly fifty years in a single decade, but he made it. That the city went as far as it did without a hike in taxes was a miracle of municipal financing in itself. But the time is now coming when New Haven, like plenty of other communities, must find direct and immediate ways to increase its revenues. All this came up in a discussion the Mayor had with his thirteen-year-old daughter Sally. The Mayor, who seems to feel about this child like other fathers feel about their daughters, is gratified by Sally's lively and intelligent interest in civic affairs.

"Daddy," asked Sally, "is it true that you are going to raise taxes?"

"Yes," said the Mayor, wondering how to change the subject. "Yes, I am."

"Daddy," asked Sally, " didn't you promise in your last campaign that you wouldn't raise taxes?"

"Yes," said the Mayor. "I promised."

"Then Daddy," asked Sally, "if you promised you wouldn't, why are you going to raise taxes?"

The Mayor looked out the window of the car in which we were riding and sighed. "One of these days," he said, "I'm going to have to tell her."

The car came to a stop at a red light, and on the vacant lot at the corner there was a strange sight. The land had been paved with slate or stone of some sort. It was flanked by a wall, also of stone. There were two park benches at the back. The paving looked as though it had been laid on the deck of a ship during a typhoon, and the wall—which appeared to be lacking mortar—presented a top surface which resembled a distant view of the Alps. One had the impression that a crack surfboarder could have made it over the paved terrace to the benches, but that once there he would have a sitting problem, for the benches, like everything else, were not level. The only explanation was a sign, hand-lettered, which announced that this project was being executed by the Freddy Fixer Club. The sign went on to urge readers to help keep the neighborhood clean.

The Mayor looked out and saw it too. "Hey Tom," he said to Appleby. "Will you look at that! Did you know about this one?" Appleby confessed that this contribution to the city's renewal program was new to him. The Mayor turned to me. "Do you know about the Freddy Fixer Club?" he demanded. I pleaded ignorance.

"It's the neighborhood kids," he said, beaming like a proud and foolish parent. "Their own idea. Kids about ten to thirteen. Can you imagine, they built that whole thing all by themselves!" The light changed. "Wait a minute, Skipper, don't move on yet." He leaned over me and continued to stare through the window. Then he settled back, still beaming.

"What do you think, George?" he demanded. "Pretty nice job, eh?"

I looked out again, at the slate and rock so lovingly misplaced by young hands, at the out-of-plumb benches, and at the sign—so clear and unself-conscious in its statement, proud as a fine banner—and then I finally saw it as it really was. The Mayor was right. It was beautiful.

All photos courtesy Office of Public Information, New Haven Redevelopment Agency.

OBJECTS

Tents

In the summer of 1978 I ran into Mark Brutton, editor of the British magazine *Design*, and he asked for a series of monthly articles, of 800 words or less, mostly on various aspects of product design. The prospect of getting stuck with a chore like that, with all the attendant deadline pressures, really turned me off. So we compromised, agreeing that if something arrived that he liked, he would use it, and that if he didn't he would refrain from overloading the transatlantic telephone network.

Then a few weeks later, a letter arrived suggesting some heavy meditation on the subject of kitchen cabinets and I responded with this essay. The perversity of authors passeth all understanding, and to this day I am unable to recollect what triggered the notion that what the world needed was more impermanent tension structures.

I think that what happened to me after forty years of looking at, and thinking about architecture, is a feeling that there is too much of it

Japanese tent, International Design Conference at Aspen: a taut structure with rigid compression members and an extensive reliance on cables. The skin is strong enough for young children to climb on. Photo by Jacqueline Nelson.

around. I know that this was behind the Hidden City project (page 25) and also the short essay on Miniaturization (page 175). I am convinced that anything we might do to reduce the tonnage of buildings, which ultimately weigh so heavily on our senses and spirits, would be worth doing.

Although a tent can be regarded as a legitimate product, I think Mark was so startled by the theme that he published it before the shock wore off. In any case, nothing has been heard about kitchen cabinets since.

The thing to keep in mind about tents is the way they sound. A decibel meter's delight, they flap, sigh, creak, groan, rustle, and when used as enclosures for revival meetings, conferences, circuses, and the like, they give the assembled public the choice of listening to speakers, or the snarls of caged beasts, or the near-subliminal symphonies created by the responses of fabric and ropes to the shifting pressures of air movement.

It is also a fine thing to see what tents do with outside light: they diffuse the sharp rays of the sun and seem to shrink with the passage of clouds. Overhead shadows of things nearby, ropes, cables, and bits of hardware, are razor sharp and these too move occasionally in the wind.

A permanent feast for the senses, tents are also—and have been for millenia—structures of unsurpassed elegance and economy, first cousins to the sail, as fluid as a full clothesline in a breeze, kinetic sculpture in its most nearly dematerialized form.

Tents are the only structures that stay fully alive as long as their materials hold together, and for me, they provide the only big spaces in which one can sit placidly for hours. People, it seems to me, thrive in tents as in no other man-made enclosure. In the great tent used for the Aspen Design Conference, people have listened to a long list of brilliant speakers over the years, but for me, in this environment which is at once tranquilizing and lively, I do believe that I could even sit happily through an entire morning of Richard Milhous Nixon reading the Manhattan telephone directory.

Only once in my life did I find myself in a hard building which seemed to match some of the qualities of a tent: this was in Chartres on a gusty fall afternoon. The sunlight was turning the glass walls into cornucopias spilling out pure prismatic color and the clouds scudding across the sky acted as feathery modulators, dimming the interior as they crossed the sun. The whole building seemed to swell and shrink with changes in the light and in the organ loft someone was playing. The fading sounds and the

Design of the Afghan yurt suggests conditions less extreme than those encountered on the Mongolian steppes. Note ribbon fastenings in detail. Courtesy American Museum of Natural History.

The Mongolian yurt, built of wood and hides, was designed for nomadic use and to provide shelter from gales and blizzards. Courtesy American Museum of Natural History.

Teepees in a Cheyenne camp, photographed in the 1860s or 1870s. The classic conical shape of the teepee, with its smoke hole and wind deflector: the design allowed fast erection and dismantling as well as transportation by sled. Courtesy The Smithsonian Institution; photo by William S. Soule.

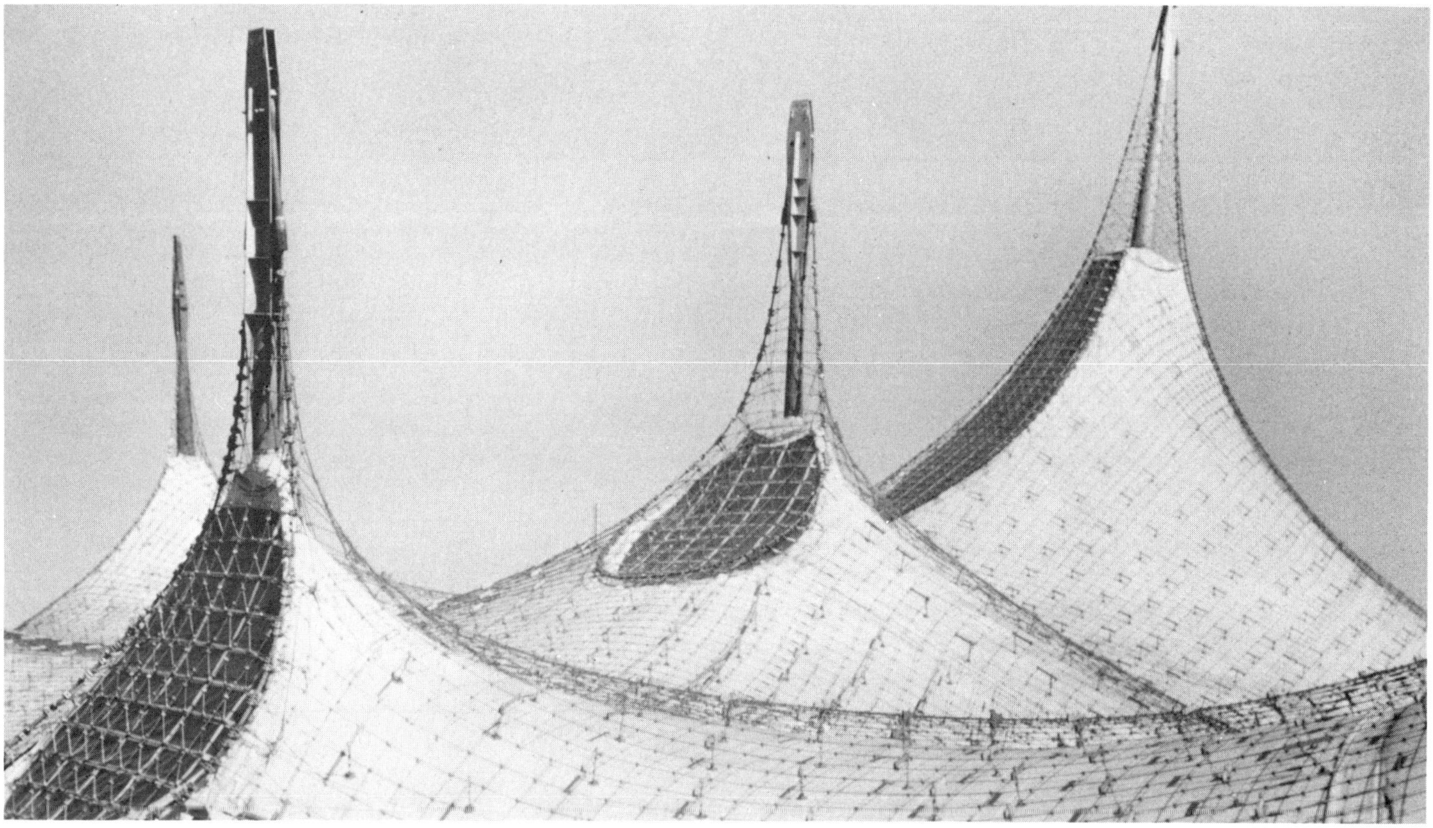

The great tents by Frei Otto, notably the installations at Montreal's Expo in 1967 and those for the Munich Olympics, are probably the most complex and expensive in existence. Otto goes far beyond the traditional tent in both his structures and materials to reach building forms that might be considered hybrids rather than tents. What remains is the drama of tension and compression strongly expressed and the hint of immense structures to come based on this technology.

Pavilion at the Lausanne Exhibition, 1964: a vivid articulation of rigid structures and fabric in tension.

In this airport project for Saudi Arabia, Skidmore, Owings, & Merrill have taken the tent concept to a new level. The detail photograph shows the basic modules, each of which is 150 feet in diameter. With some 200 such components, the air terminal reaches a size of 1 square kilometer. The tents are made of Teflon-coated fiberglass fabric, white, translucent, and about 75 percent reflective. The fabric is not merely a skin, but a vital tension element in the structure. With such examples as this, the entire concept of lightweight architecture on a large scale becomes believable.

booming crescendos were a perfect match for what the sun and stained glass were doing, creating an unexpected *son et lumière* performance of extraordinary intensity.

Not all tents act in the same way. Next to the main Aspen tent there is a smaller one, a gift from Japan, which looks like a topological model, its skin so tightly drawn that small children in rubber-soled shoes can run across it all the way to the peak, rather like small frogs jumping around on the surface of a big bass drum. And once I was taken to a Mongolian restaurant in Tokyo where an unbelievably expensive meal was served inside yurts scattered through a garden.

The yurt, which looks not unlike a half watermelon, has a framework of light wood with metal connectors, as delicate as interlaced branches, giving an impression of strength and stability. There is no creaking or flapping at all, and it evokes images of huddled clusters on some frozen Northern plain, immune to the gales howling around them. In the impeccably manicured Japanese garden they sat placidly, all their strength in reserve, creating a sense of light, warm, womblike enclosure, utterly safe and secure without the oppressive weight of steel or concrete overhead.

When the Shah of Iran threw his great party for Persia's 2,500th birthday, tents of the most varied kinds dominated the scene as meeting halls, banquet enclosures, and private apartments. The tents in this case were pure theater design, spelling out opulence, high culture, and ancient power, along with the ever-present suggestion that the new oil empire was not without respectable ancestry.

Tents can do things no building has ever done, and depending on their size, they straddle the areas of both products and architecture.

As structures, tents exhibit the same kind of interplay between tension and compression as the humble umbrella, surely one of the most perfect design-inventions the race has to its credit. Even today, in the immense air-supported domes that represent some of our most advanced enclosure technology, the same old tension–compression drama is there, although the latter, now provided by the air itself, has become invisible and impalpable.

There is talk these days of covering entire cities in the Arctic and other inhospitable places, and assuming that there are reasons for such cities, there do not appear to be insuperable technical obstacles.

An entire town under cover would be a curious place to see, for all the normal constraints imposed by rain,

Aspen Conference Tent, originally designed in the early fifties by Eero Saarinen and later modified by Herbert Bayer. A very large enclosure, holding audiences up to 1,500, used mainly for concerts.

snow, heat, and cold would be absent. Under such conditions "buildings" could be simple screen walls or, for that matter, thatched South Sea island huts. It is a pity we are so fearful of experiment these days for we might learn something about cities from them. If such domes are built it will be for other reasons, a big new oil deposit or a uranium strike. Such places, one would imagine, would be designed to become instant ghost towns.

What the tent seems to do in its more modest forms is provide an increasingly insistent hint that we may yet come to perceive buildings as lightweight products and the "modern" architecture of this time as too hard for psychic comfort, too heavy for human consumption, and too costly in terms of imbedded energy.

It is useful to think of tents as a kind of paradigm, something to remind us that vast, durable, and beautiful enclosures can be soft as well as hard, flexible as well as rigid, weightless (for all practical purposes) as well as ponderous. An interesting model for a time when the reality of materials depletion is only a few decades away. If all the dire speculations of the Club of Rome and other Cassandras do come true (should one say *when* rather than *if*?), the tent has one last quality in reserve that may yet make it infinitely precious: we can grow it.

Tractor seat, stamped metal pan used on tractors prior to 1940. Courtesy John Deere and Henry Dreyfuss Associates.

Mobile Seating

Some ventures in communication are less communicative than others. "Mobile Seating" was a scheduled exhibit in the Smithsonian's Renwick Gallery; a phone call asked for an introduction to the catalog; photographs of selected items were sent to help the writing. The introduction was written, the exhibit went on in 1974 and was, I have been told, a good one. The catalog was never printed, apparently, which is probably just as well—there are so many exhibition catalogs—and so the question is what does one call an introduction to a noncatalog. A nontroduction? (Better suggestions will be cordially nonwelcomed if sent in.)

Approaching the subject of seating-in-motion from any starting point, we soon find ourselves in a world where many of the rules, traditions, preconceptions associated with seating-as-furniture, i.e., anchored more or less permanently in a room, are largely invalidated. The main reason for this lies in a variety of constraints so powerful that the designer has no choice but to put aside much of his painfully accumulated knowledge and start from scratch.

To get the picture, let us consider the elegant little plaything known as the "Windbuggy." Designed to cruise across level surfaces, such as hard-packed beaches, its seat looks like a folded oversized diaper with a pouch at the foot. There is little here to remind us of a "seat" in the familiar sense.

A normally padded human posterior can be set down without undue discomfort on practically anything—a rock, log, step, or the ground itself—or nothing at all. Squatting on one's heels passes for proper sitting in more than one society: all it takes is a skill that has to be learned in early childhood. In some highly developed societies, with Japan the prime example, a tatami-covered floor has been accepted for centuries as a perfectly good place to sit, even for the Son of Heaven himself.

However, once invented (and reinvented in a myriad of times and places), the chair was promptly subjected to all the social pressures brought to bear on artifacts used indiscriminately by different social classes. What I am referring to is the conversion of a simple, functional object into a symbol of status and power. A South Pacific islander might have a chair made out of a shaped log, but only the chief would be allowed to decorate his with inlaid shells. It doesn't matter in the least what the status-giving device is, so long as it is rare, expensive, and excluded from common use.

I am reminded of an incident, many years ago, at the American Academy in Rome. The Academy, which enjoyed a quasi-official status in the diplomatic community, had seen fit to invite Mussolini for a visit, and the invitation was accepted. As the Great Day approached the building was ransacked in a search for a suitably imposing chair—a throne, in effect. Several massive chairs were located, most of them enriched with carved Renaissance decoration, and after several heated discussions, one was finally chosen and put in place. Eventually Italy's well-protected Leader arrived and was ushered to his seat of honor. Photo lights went on, and the newsreel cameras, tucked away in an improvised jungle of potted palms, started turning as Il Duce sat down. Then there was a moment of shocked silence: the chair was too high. There sat Europe's shortest dictator—gleaming military boots dangling helplessly 6 inches off the floor—glowering like an angry baby with a heavy five-o'clock shadow. An interesting example of a symbol backfiring, so to speak.

Seating-as-furniture is subject to other conditions which differentiate it from the mobile variety. Since all a chair has to do (putting aside considerations of status and fashion for the moment) is hold up a body, there is an unlimited range of possible solutions. The designer has too much freedom. Freedom is something students are always demanding, but the professional knows that without rather stringent limitations, designs have a way of not working out very well. Nature abounds in splendid designs, all developed under conditions of no freedom at all.

The difference between static and mobile seating lies right here: mobile seating is so limited by its constraints that the viewer accepts the results without questions of style or good taste ever arising. It looks the way it does because it has to be the way it is, and we tend to see such objects as beautiful because of the impression of rightness they convey. The seat of a racing bicycle has to provide support and at the same time give total freedom to the rider's thighs. Whether or not we find it "beautiful," we know it is right.

Another object which has been given the place of honor in more than one exhibition of industrial design is the tractor seat, which has adorned farm machines for at least a century. The tractor seat is a minimal design, a contoured tray of cast or formed metal. It is perforated for lightness and is bolted or welded to an upright support. It is in every sense a classic: nothing can be added to improve it and nothing can be taken away. A tractor seat *can* be changed, but only by changing the constraints which brought it into being. A machine with a cab for the driver, for example, no longer requires a seat fully resistant to weather and under these circumstances an ordinary automobile seat can be substituted. Curiously enough, when this does happen, the elegance associated with the original product disappears.

This kind of observation applies in a great many situations. Why does a wood house of the early 18th century look so much better than a developer's house today? In all sorts of ways the new model is better: it has insulation, automatic heat, air conditioning, a dishwasher. Yet there is a general consensus that the earlier house is more beautiful, and there is more to the judgment than nostalgia.

Elegance in artifacts has to do with our almost in-

Windbuggy. Courtesy Windbuggy Mfg. Co., Newport Beach, Calif.

Tractor seat, 1974, John Deere. Designers: Henry Dreyfuss Associates.

stinctive responses to the expression of "fitness," and also dignity. Most people find the lion a nobler beast than the hyena, and a better-looking one. Each animal is perfectly fitted to its way of life, but we admire predators more than scavengers. We think highly of houses because they shelter families, and we consider farm machinery important because we have to eat. The elegance of the colonial house stems from the strong, intelligent, and economical response to a situation characterized by a limited materials supply, a small inventory of tools, an inherited tradition, and a new lifestyle.

John Dewey, if I recall correctly, observed that in admiring an ancient artwork or artifact we are not responding so much to the literal message of the object, but to the skill of the maker and the emotional intensity he brought to the problem. Not even the Greeks believe in the Gods on Olympus anymore, but we all continue to admire the Parthenon sculptures. The same goes for classic cars, few of which are worth much on a freeway or in a downpour. It's as if ancient objects were a kind of time machine which instantly transports us back to the situation when they were created. It is most interesting that such responses are made quickly and unself-consciously by the most unsophisticated of lay people. The quality of sympathetic and admiring understanding appears to be universal.

Technological societies tend to become preoccupied and ultimately derailed by their accelerating desires for comfort. It all starts harmlessly enough: a metal hoe is better than a stick and riding on wheels is faster than walking. Ultimately, however, when we find that we cannot live without an electric carving knife and demand air conditioning in climates where there may be four uncomfortably hot nights in a year, we not only begin to exhaust material and energy resources at a dismaying rate, but we lose the basis on which great design has always rested.

One of the most interesting aspects of mobile seating is that, as we move up the technical scale, comfort loses its high priority and survival needs take over. When this happens, when freedom truly becomes a recognition of necessity, elegance emerges once again as the minimal, inevitable, beautiful response to a vital need. Thus it is the form of the jet plane, rather than the seating inside, which really excites us. The form of the plane has to do with survival, the seating, admirable and ingenious though it may be, has to do with the comfort of the customers. The astronaut's couch is subject to many more limitations, not the least of which is survival under acceleration pressures for which the body is poorly equipped. Here we have a

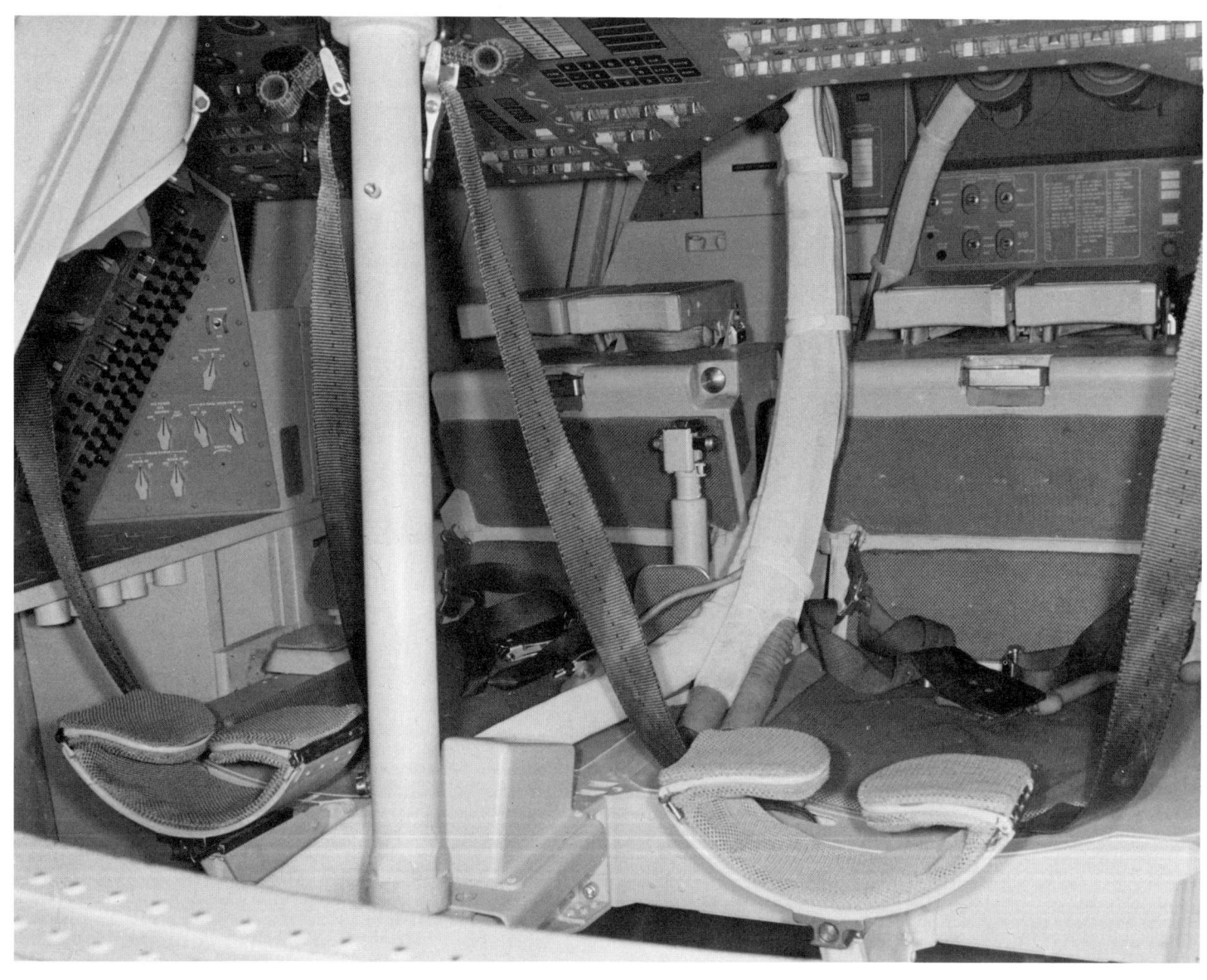

Couch for Apollo. Courtesy NASA.

kind of cocoon, a form-fitting cradle which has to support body and spacesuit at hundreds of carefully calculated points. Getting the human organism safely out of Earth's gravity is a very serious business.

A few years back the idea of connecting seating with survival would have seemed fantastic, but the future has caught up with us. At the leading edge of technology there are always survival problems.

The point about relating design excellence and survival needs is made simply because this is the area in which we can see most clearly what design is all about. It is one of the factors too, which is changing our views of Nature. The Victorians, we may be sure, never saw a green landscape as a complex of oxygen-manufacturing devices, but we are beginning to, thanks to massive air pollution. A flower garden may be a thing of beauty and a satisfaction to the gardener, but all those colors and delicate shapes are also the flowers' weapons in an implacable struggle for survival.

Are we perhaps making too much of survival imperatives as the basis for elegant design? What about the Parthenon and the Taj Mahal and Versailles and the Bugatti Royale and the Le Corbusier chair? Obviously, any statement can be turned into a dogma and thus drained of its truth. It is equally clear, or should be, that there is no such thing as automatic great design, created simply because one situation is tighter than another. Where artifacts rather than natural organisms are involved, there is always the matter of human intervention, and some designers have more talent than others. The powerful effect of necessities, such as survival, merely strips the irrelevancies away from a problem, forcing the designer to put all his energies, psychic as well as intellectual, into a concentrated effort.

Freedom and constraints can be arranged on a scale with survival needs at one extreme and the vagaries of consumer product design at the other. The novelty ball point pen stuck into a facsimile of a golf ball is a silly idea, but it does not endanger life or limb; it is not important anyway. Massive products, like Bugatti's classic Royale, are more important because they consume energy and money, and are conspicuous because of cost and rarity. The real importance of such a car comes from the immense significance of the automobile itself, plus its expression by a great designer. Versailles was important because it was part of a big European power play. The "freedom" of its architect involved accepting Louis XIV's need to be recognized as the greatest power in Europe, and his job was to design a palace that would

Bucket seat. Courtesy Recaro USA Inc., Carson, Calif.

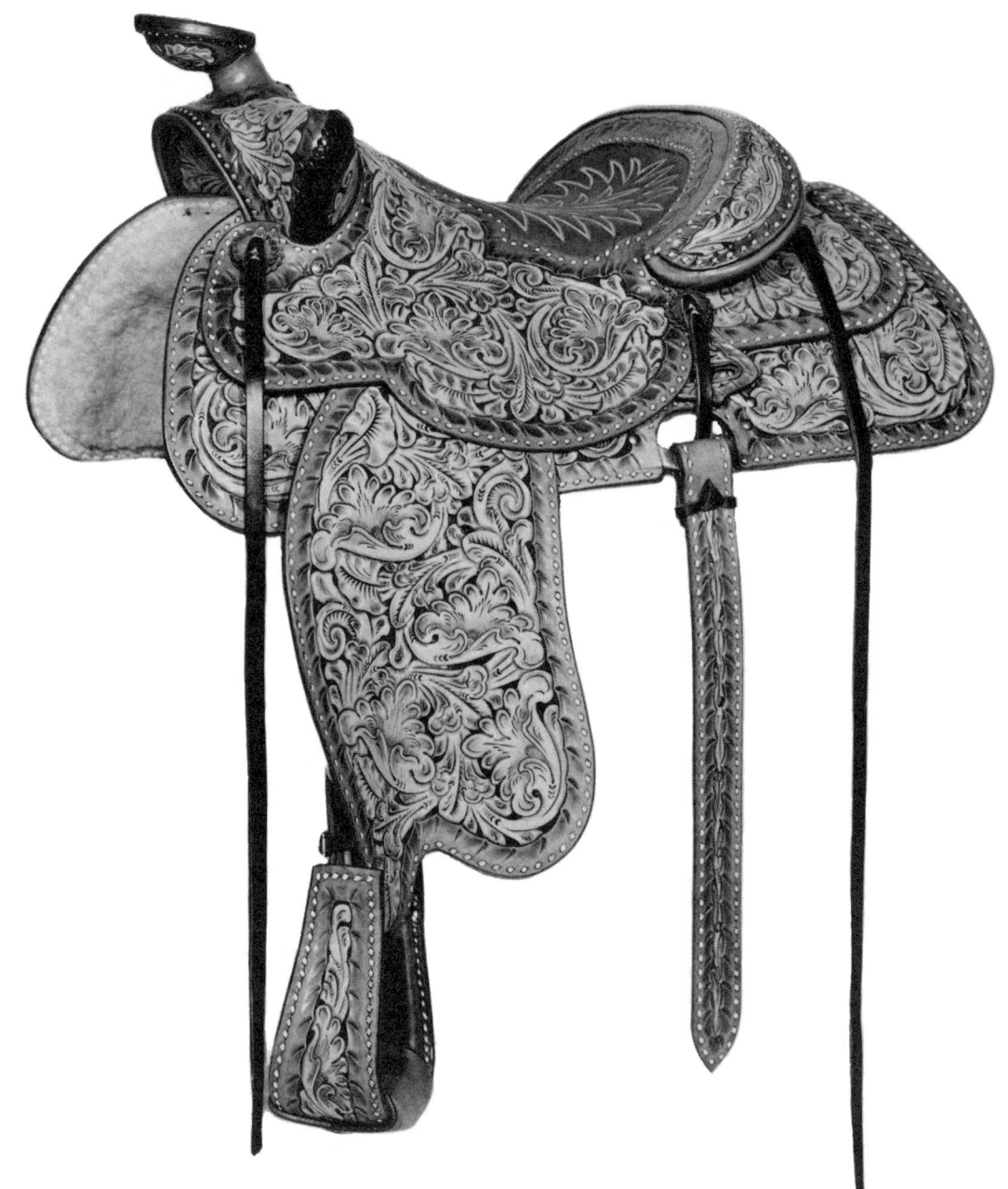

Western saddle. Courtesy H. Kauffman & Son, New York City.

make this clear to other monarchs. Generally the tighter the constraints the better the design. The extra interest we find in mobile seating, and the acceptance of designs often too radical or complex for sale in the home market, is again a reflection of our understanding that these objects are called upon, in their daily use, to meet situations that never arise in the case of household or office seating. In looking at them, we sense the critical importance of the performance specifications.

Conventional static seating takes a variety of forms which may be described as the lump (stool or hassock), the plank (any park bench), the sling (common in beach and patio furniture and hammocks), the catcher's mitt (beautifully expressed in some of the all-foam seating of the Italians). Mobile seating tends to fit some of these familiar categories simply because bodies in motion are still bodies, with limbs, spinal columns, and backsides to be taken care of. The early as well as modern automobiles found their seating solutions in the simple sofa. The bucket seat must have originated in connection with racing cars, for fast cornering called for something that would keep the occupant from being thrown out. Adoption of the bucket for family cars was part of a general trend to sporty-looking cars, but it is also snug, feels safer, is more comfortable for long trips, and makes the car interior seem somewhat more spacious.

In a sense, mobile seating is more difficult to design than static furniture, simply because of the demands made upon it, but it is also easier in that the designer knows what it is he has to achieve, and he does not have to worry about acceptable styling.

What comes out of all this, I think, is a general enrichment of the design vocabulary. The designs with the most potent influence are always those at the top of the scale of social importance. In the area of movement, we find that planes set the style. During the period of propeller planes, streamlining became fashionable in cars, home appliances, and even pencil sharpeners. With the advent of the jet, the profiles of the earlier planes looked suddenly fat and sluggish and sharp edges came in.

Still another factor in the case of so much new seating-in-motion is the simple fact that it *is* new. The saddle, which is where it all started, has had centuries in which to evolve.

"Mobile" seating is something of a misnomer, for in practice it is more rigidly located than household or office furniture. It is hard to imagine a saddle in any location other than the back of a horse.

The future of mobile seating, while it will continue to take many forms, includes the possibility that the evolutionary process will take seating and container and weld them into a single formal statement. This expression, even in its most modest form, makes the statement that the enclosure exists only to contain the seating and that the latter has meaning only in the sense that it makes the enclosure habitable. With this, it may be affirmed that mobile seating is beginning to show signs of maturing, for, to the extent that the statement is correct, the overall design becomes a single development of form rather than an assembly of piecemeal items.

From left to right: Ebony pencil, Rapidograph, Aurora, Parker "Big Red," Montblanc Diplomat, Lamy, Osmiroid, Pentel. Courtesy HARPER'S; photo by Terry Stevenson.

Great Writers

This one happened in 1973 because a beachside holiday deprived me of the services of my faithful electric portable and I had to backslide in time and technology to get some writing done. It was a welcome lesson, applicable to more than writing instruments, to be forced to remember that the *Iliad, War and Peace,* and *Hamlet,* among others, were somehow created without the aid of an IBM Selectric.

This piece produced a flood of mail from users, some of it reminders that I had left out the great Parker 21 or some other old-time favorite. It was reassuring to learn that lots of people everywhere really care about the quality of their tools.

I've been pushed by circumstance, of late, into thinking about writing. Not the deathless-prose variety but the business of putting words down on paper. At first blush it hardly seems possible that the modest implements involved would provide much in the way of evidence of good or bad design, but the subject is less barren than one might suspect. The stores have never been so full of new and different writing tools, each with its particular defects or virtues.

There are uncounted varieties of ball-points, now offered with a entire spectrum of points, from extra-fine (accountants, it says on the box) to bold (waitresses and credit-card holders). There are all the markers, also from fine to jumbo, with felt nibs or nylon; china markers; laundry markers (indelible); and kid markers (nontoxic). Plus mechanical pencils (one brand, Pentel, has leads so thin you need tweezers to pick them up), the good old plain pencils (mostly hexagonal so they won't roll off desk tops), carbon pencils, charcoal pencils, and fountain pens. There are also special types of pens, many of them superlative for writing, like the Rapidograph, which feeds its ink down through a fine tube with a wire inside that jiggles when you write, so the ink won't clog. The Osmiroid pen (made in England, $3) comes with interchangeable nibs that offer a variety of writing styles. I tried my illegible signature with one of their italic pens, and it came out with an unfamiliar kind of 18th century elegance.

When I was in high school, more than a few years back, one of the most gratifying graduation presents, if Father couldn't come through with the 1923 bright red Buick roadster, was the red-and-gold Parker, recently reissued for the nostalgia market as "Big Red." It isn't a fountain pen anymore, just a nylon-tip job with a replaceable cartridge. A comparison between the two models provides an interesting commentary on the value, then and now, of $5. The original was made, I would guess, out of a rod of some heavy plastic, drilled and tapped, and it had a lot of gold plating on the nib and clip. Big Red isn't in the same class at all, although it is a perfectly good fine-line marker. Automation and near-miracles in the plastics industry are not enough to match the quality a crew of conscientious mechanics could turn out back then.

Mostly when I write I use a typewriter. The typewriter in my office is an electric, the Olivetti Praxis, designed by an old friend, Ettore Sottsass, Jr., who lives and works in Milan. It is a very crisp little object, very Italian in its elegance and sophistication, and it works admirably. In the country I have a manual machine, the rugged old Olivetti Studio, which kept me contented for years, until I got used to the electric.

Anyone who does a fair amount of typing knows that switching back and forth from a manual to an electric machine creates problems that could easily lead to madness. Brush a key with your finger and the electric will give you an unwanted character on the paper. The manual, given fingers accustomed to the electric's no-pressure typing, becomes sheer labor, and the printing is all of different weights, depending on how hard each key is struck. The speed, of course, is like trying to run in childhood nightmares. John O'Hara, who used to be a neighbor, had a portable so old and beat-up that it must have gone back to his earliest newspaper days. Still, it banged out a fantastic dollar volume of best sellers that could have paid for IBM Selectrics by the gross, but he loved it and never switched, at least during the years I knew him.

The relationship between a craftsman and his tools is always a very personal thing. I remember a very good photographer who remarked that while he used a Leica, a mass-produced article identical with all other Leicas, his camera had a feel, through years of use, that made it different from all others. Use, in other words, creates an almost organic linkage between implement and user. There are many familiar images: Sherlock Holmes and his magnifying glass, Marshal Dillon with his infallible six-shooters, the Japanese carpenter with his plane. True, it is not that easy to visualize the writer with his typewriter, possibly because it doesn't fit the hand. A fountain pen would be a better symbol of the writer-tool relationship, but even this doesn't work. Nothing has ever really replaced the image of the quill pen. I suppose fountain pens are not sufficiently photogenic, and anyway, they are supposed to be obsolete.

Obsolescence is an odd process. In a disposable-consuming society one tends to assume that as soon as a better product comes out, the old one becomes obsolete. But in reality it is not quite that simple. Brooms were supposedly made obsolete by carpet sweepers and then vacuum cleaners; bicycles were "replaced" by motor vehicles. But these days the roads are full of cars with rack-mounted ten-speed bikes on their roofs, and it would be hard to find a household without at least one broom.

What often happens as new designs proliferate is not obsolescence but an increase in specialization. This fact is sometimes used as social criticism, the proposition being that Americans are gadget crazy, but in factories, which are not gadget happy at all, the same thing goes on. A plant fully equipped with power-driven screwdrivers will also have the older hand models around, and for good reason. When the original Reynolds ball-point was inaugurated with much fanfare at Gimbels in New York about twenty-five years ago, everybody rushed to buy (at an outrageous price), and predictions were rife that the fountain pen had had it. But things didn't work out that way. The fountain pen simply moved from the role of a near-universal writing tool to that of a more specialized device.

I discovered one of these roles on a trip when I had some writing to do, and the portable typewriter was just too heavy and too bulky. So I bought a large bottle of ink and stuck my pen, a Montblanc Diplomat model, in a pocket. The Montblanc is a giant among pens, with a barrel almost a half-inch thick, and my guess was that it held enough ink to write the first half of *War and Peace*. It wasn't quite that good, for it dispensed ink as generously as it took it in, but it was okay. Anyone with a writing chore and a deadline is always looking for some legitimate way to goof off from time to time, and refueling the pen, in this respect, was ideal. Not only did the reservoir and nib have to be washed out in water each time but when the pen was finally filled it had to be wiped carefully with tissue, or your fingers would be semipermanently stained. All this took at least five minutes, and with a little practice I was able to stretch it to ten.

The great thing about being stuck with a pen rather than a typewriter, however, was not the fussing around: it was the rediscovery of sensation, the feeling of a nib sliding across paper and the pleasant manipulation of the instrument so that all strokes were full of ink and not two thin parallel lines with a void between. Then there was the fascinating interaction of pen and paper, with one result on smooth paper and a different feel and look on paper with some tooth to it. What I am trying to say is that stepping down the technological scale, from modern typewriter to the relatively primitive pen, changed the act of writing from an "operation" to an experience.

One of the most subtle dehumanizing things technology does is to eliminate experience. When I was a student, I went on a bicycle trip through the hill towns of Italy, and most of what I remember of the man-tool relationship was that I walked up a lot of hills. Still, it was good for the appetite, sleeping was no problem, and trying to beat a thunderstorm down a 10-mile hill late one afternoon was something to remember. I don't think there would have been that much to remember with a car. As flying moved from open cockpits to the closed fuselage and pressurized cabins of high-altitude jets, experience

Praxis, Olivetti electric portable typewriter. Designed by Ettore Sottsass, Jr. Photo courtesy Olivetti.

diminished—which is why they can sell those inside seats in the 747s: there is nothing to see if you look out. Chevrolet has been suggesting that the best way to see America is in one of their cars, but on the big interstates you don't see America. I am sure that the revivals of camping, hiking, bicycling, home-baked bread, and the other do-it-yourself activities have come about because of a growing mass feeling of sensory deprivation, and the feeling reflects a very real and unpleasant reality, which is that technology, except in very carefully rationed doses, is not really good for people.

I can see some astute reader pointing out that the big Monblanc is a product of modern industry, and I would not argue, but, compared to a typewriter, it is not as impersonal, probably because the engineering is less sophisticated.

One also buys products because one cannot resist their looks, and as a designer I am especially vulnerable. The first really modern fountain pen I ran across was the Lamy, a West German pen introduced in the U.S. a few years back. One is always inclined to think, when dealing with shapes and functions as simple as those of a pen, that not many variations on the theme are possible, but the Lamy stands out as having a very different look. It is all black, not shiny but matte, and the only visible added element is an elegant clip of what appears to be brushed stainless steel. A very beautiful nothing, so to speak, and I bought one in tribute to its anonymous designer.

I used the pen and liked it, but eventually I found that the designer had succumbed to styling temptation instead of respecting a functional need: the finger grip tapers in such a sleek way from the barrel to the nib that I found my fingers were always sliding down the taper. I still use the Lamy from time to time just for the tactile pleasure it gives, but that flaw bothers me—so handsome a tool should have remembered that it is first, after all, a tool. Or perhaps I squeeze too hard; some good tools find one kind of hand better than another.

The next encounter I had with a pen came as a gift. The Italians have been proving, during the past decade, that if they are not the best industrial designers in the world, there are none who are better, and Marco Zanuso is one of the best of the Italians. The gift was his new Aurora pen, produced by a manufacturer in Italy, and it is at this writing one of the half-dozen most elegant small industrial objects in existence.

Externally, the pen is a slim (about pencil thickness) tube of stainless steel, plugged at both ends with black plastic. The cap, in some mysterious way, does not slip *over* the barrel—as is the case with the Lamy, the Montblanc, and all the other pens I have ever seen—but it ends up flush, so that the closed pen is a smooth tube with no visible taper. The clip has a perky little fillip on the end, and it slips into any pocket without fuss. A finger grip of black plastic is fluted, so there is no problem of a positive grip for fingers. The nib looks, in some odd way, like an old steel pen's, and the writing quality is superb.

After the gratifying trip with the Montblanc, there came another, also with some writing to do, when I decided to slide down the technological scale another few notches. This time it was a handful of Ebony pencils, Eberhard Faber's #6325, Jet Black, Extra Smooth, twenty cents at all good stores. I had accidentally discovered that the feel of the Ebony point on Goldenrod paper was comparable to sipping Dom Perignon for the first time, and I wanted to spend a week swimming in such inexpensive sensuous pleasure. It was great. And as a substitute for the ink-filling routine, if you take one of the tiny brass pencil sharpeners that art supply stores import from Germany, you can spend even more time putting a perfect point on that jet black extra smooth lead. The reason for insisting on the little brass pencil sharpener instead of the more common aluminum one is not quality: both use special razor-type blades and work equally well. It is the nice feel that comes with a bit of added weight. Since the price of either is under eighty-five cents, this is no place to cut corners. There is another thing to be said for writing with the Ebony: it is sheathed in an aromatic wood, cedar I imagine, and the fresh scent of the shavings adds still another thrill for the hungry senses.

I don't want to drop the Ebony pencil without noting that it is probably one of those real rarities, an absolutely perfect design. The shaft is without incident or decoration, aside from the necessary manufacturer's information printed in white. The grip is as good as a finger grip could be: it fits and nothing slips around. The fingers never touch the lead. The point is instantly put into perfect condition with a cheap and simple tool. It never leaks, not even in pressurized cabins, and I imagine it would write under water if it had to. It is close to weightless, for all practical purposes, and it functions during its entire life without need for supplies from the outside world. If you lose the little sharpener, any knife with an edge will do a perfectly good job. I am not suggesting that all these estimable qualities are the doing of Eberhard Faber, but merely that the pencil is, from the most critical point of view, a genuinely classic design.

The reason for my fix on Goldenrod paper (standard

product, any office supply store) is that it has exactly the right amount of tooth to make the physical act of writing sheer delight, and also because the deep yellow-orange color makes it easy on the eyes in bright sunlight.

The Montblanc is different from the other pens in that it is not a sophisticated modern design. In fact, I suspect that it is not a modern design at all. It has a funny kind of pudgy gold clip (which works just fine), it is decorated with three separate sets of gold bands set into the shiny black plastic cap and barrel, and it looks rather like a fat black cigar. The gold nib looks just like the nib people have been putting on fountain pens for more than a generation, and the finger grip has a rim on it so that fingers will not slide down to the nib and get stained. It is old-fashioned, for modern tastes, never a candidate for museum recognition. It is, in fact, nothing more than an absolutely marvelous design for writing, and I hope it goes on forever, like its guarantee. A couple of years back I damaged the point while in Vienna, found the company representative in an ancient loft, got a complete new nib installed in half an hour—and an indignant lecture on lifetime warranties when I attempted to pay.

A couple of days ago some young designer friends from Paris came by for a visit. I had discarded my jacket and had the Montblanc stuck in my shirt pocket.

"Aha!" said one of them. "So you own that fat old Montblanc too!"

There was nothing to do but admit the fact, since there it was.

"Funny," he said, "not a single designer we know would do a pen like that." I agreed. We talked for a bit about Zanuso's beautiful new Aurora. "But we all own the Montblanc," he went on. "All the designers I know own one. Funny, isn't it?"

It really wasn't funny at all. Why shouldn't designers recognize a great design when they see one? Even if none of us could bring ourselves to design anything quite so unstylish?

"How to Wrap Five Eggs"

This introduction to the book *How to Wrap Five Eggs* was, I think, the hardest writing assignment I was ever given. It seemed harmless enough: a beautifully illustrated book, first published in Japan, written by Hideyuki Oka, a man who had collected, for years and with great devotion, example of traditional Japanese packaging. Pages from the Japanese edition, still unbound, were flown in from Tokyo. I studied them as carefully as I could, made notes, and six months later the introduction was still unwritten.

The problem was that I was simply bowled over by the incredible "rightness" of these deceptively simple wrappings and couldn't find anything to say that was not being said by the photographs themselves. Then, in a spirit of some desperation, I began to wonder how a society with such a wealth of sensibility could devote so much time and skill to tasks with no apparent value. After a few more months of frustrated

The carrier was developed by farmers in northern Japan. The author remarks, "It is an example of packaging born of rural necessity. Interestingly enough, it seems to emphasize the freshness of the eggs." All photographs from How to Wrap 5 Eggs *by Hideyuki Oka originally published by Bijutsu Shuppan-sha in 1965; English publication by Harper & Row in 1967. Photos reproduced by permission of Bijutsu Shuppan-Sha and Harper & Row.*

looking, some unexpected answers presented themselves, and I wrote them down.

The less we prize delight as a reason for action, the greater the distance we put between the hand and the final product, the more we will chafe at the price to be paid for the blessings of technology.

We have brainwashed ourselves into equating the new with the good, and the newest with the best, and the only remaining holes in the synthetic padding wrapped around our uneasy convictions are those intermittent fits of modernistic anxiety, so often expressed in nostalgic fads which fill the stores with "provincial" furniture, early Aztec TV sets, Art Nouveau lampshades (made of paper and imported from Hong Kong), distempered dishwashers and refrigerators.

We have come a long, long way from the kind of thing so beautifully presented in this book. To suit the needs of super mass production, the traditional natural materials are too obstreperous—too uneven, too resistant to automation—and one by one we have replaced them with the docile, predictable synthetics, and these are now, for better or worse, the larger part of our environment.

What we have gained from these excellent materials and wonderfully complicated processes to make up for the general pollution, rush, crowding, noise, sickness, and slickness is a subject for other forums. But what we have lost for sure is what this book is all about: a once-common sense of fitness in the relationships between hand, material, use, and shape, and above all, a sense of delight in the look and feel of very ordinary, humble things.

This book is thus a reminder, a deceptively simple statement of the way things once were in a certain place, and a tantalizing hint of how things might be if life and the values which shape it were different. But they aren't different, and they will not be different in the foreseeable future; so what we see here does not have to be taken as a sermon on changing our ways, which we cannot do, nor as a guide to aspiring young package designers, since there is absolutely nothing here they can copy.

How to Wrap Five Eggs—what a modest and deceptive title for a book that is a totally unexpected monument to a culture, a way of life, a universal sensibility carried through all objects down to the smallest, most inconsequential, and ephemeral things.

For what is packaging? Nothing more than a way of containing merchandise that would otherwise break or spill. A way of explaining contents, use, and preparation to a user. A device for tempting a purchaser. A cheap—usually, though not always—wrapping to be mutilated or at least undone on opening, and to be thrown away when the contents are used up. We all know what packaging is. The department stores and supermarkets are our living museums. But none of us ever saw packaging like this in any of these places.

The exhibits in this book are all old—at least in the sense that they derive from an old tradition, even when made today. Both wrappings and contents are largely unfamiliar to us. We cannot read the labels. Thus, for us, they are not examples of merchandise, but artifacts. As the archaeologists know, every artifact—not just the 2,000-year-old shards found in diggings—is a silent transmitter, programmed with a considerable quantity of information. All one needs is a receiver with the right wave length.

The sender, in the case of the material here, is quite clearly not an individual, or even groups of individuals: it is an entire society, functioning on a time scale of centuries. Designs like these are not made overnight. The things packaged are mostly very common—bean curd, candies, *sushi*, eggs, fish. The society is obviously preindustrial: there are no aluminum cans, blister packs, or squeeze bottles. The materials are natural, and common: **straw, wood, hemp,** bark twine, bamboo leaves, vine ten-

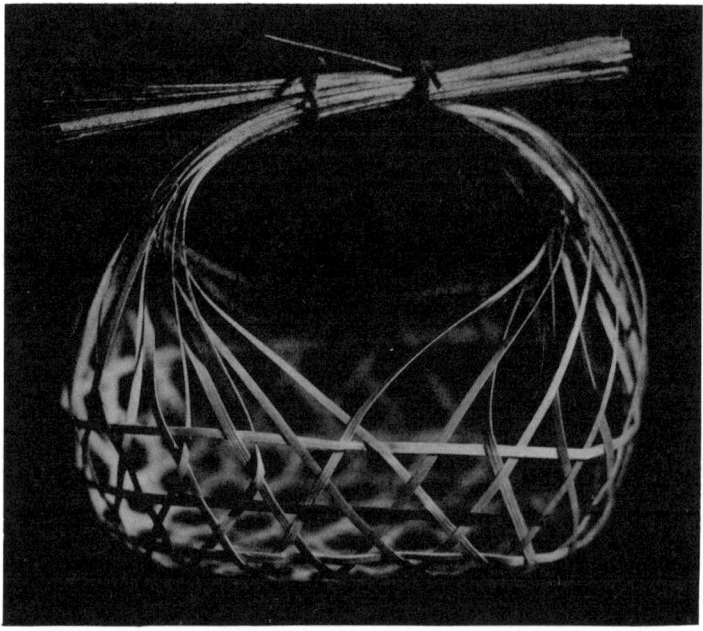

Baskets woven of split bamboo are used almost everywhere in Japan, in a rich variety of local styles.

drils, ceramics. There are edible containers, and containers which can be re-used as utensils. The latter is an approach we also use. The processes include woodworking, weaving, woodblock printing, rice-paper making, pottery—all of them normal for a society without production machinery. If some of the examples shown happen to be modern—respectful imitations of earlier designs—this does not change the nature of the message transmitted by the remarkable artifacts. The society, as already suggested, was one with a quite uncommon sensibility. Finally, it was rich enough to invest considerable time and energy in the embellishment of the simplest and most expendable of goods.

A curious fact about the collection displayed in this book is that, as far as I know, it is unique. The West has had its moments when the most highly prized social artifacts—cathedrals, for instance—also revealed wealth and sensibility. But where, in the history of our culture, do we find things like these? China or India, perhaps? Was there a place or a time when five eggs or ten dried shrimp would be so lovingly and deftly lashed together to make a beautiful, semi-edible chain? When papers and foils of unbelievable delicacy and richness would be used to enclose a few cents' worth of sweet paste? When marinated fish was sold in a container so elegantly made that it was not only airtight, but eligible for a place in a museum collection? If there was such a time in our part of the world, I have to confess ignorance.

What would have motivated this different society to treat generally cheap consumer items in this manner? On page after page we discover not only extraordinary variety of invention, but an almost obsessive concern with craftsmanship and a remarkable "rightness" of form and combinations of diverse materials. Why did they do it? One can understand this kind of lavish design concentration in a palace, a church, in the appointments of people of power—but why here?

I have been through these pages more times than I can count, not only savoring their riches, but pondering the question: Why—in packaging, of all places—did they do it? What made it worth the trouble? Who cared? My conclusion, after worrying these questions like a dog with a bone, is completely lacking in authority (I am not a Japanese scholar) but in any case it is my own and I pass it on for whatever it may be worth: I think they did it because they *had* to, because they were utterly unable to realize (as we do all the time) that there is a significant difference between an imperial villa and a jug of sake. Because the existence of a designed, man-made thing *demanded* that it be appropriate, a feast for all the senses, beautiful. Because the things men made were really like the things Nature made, and a complete man could no more tolerate

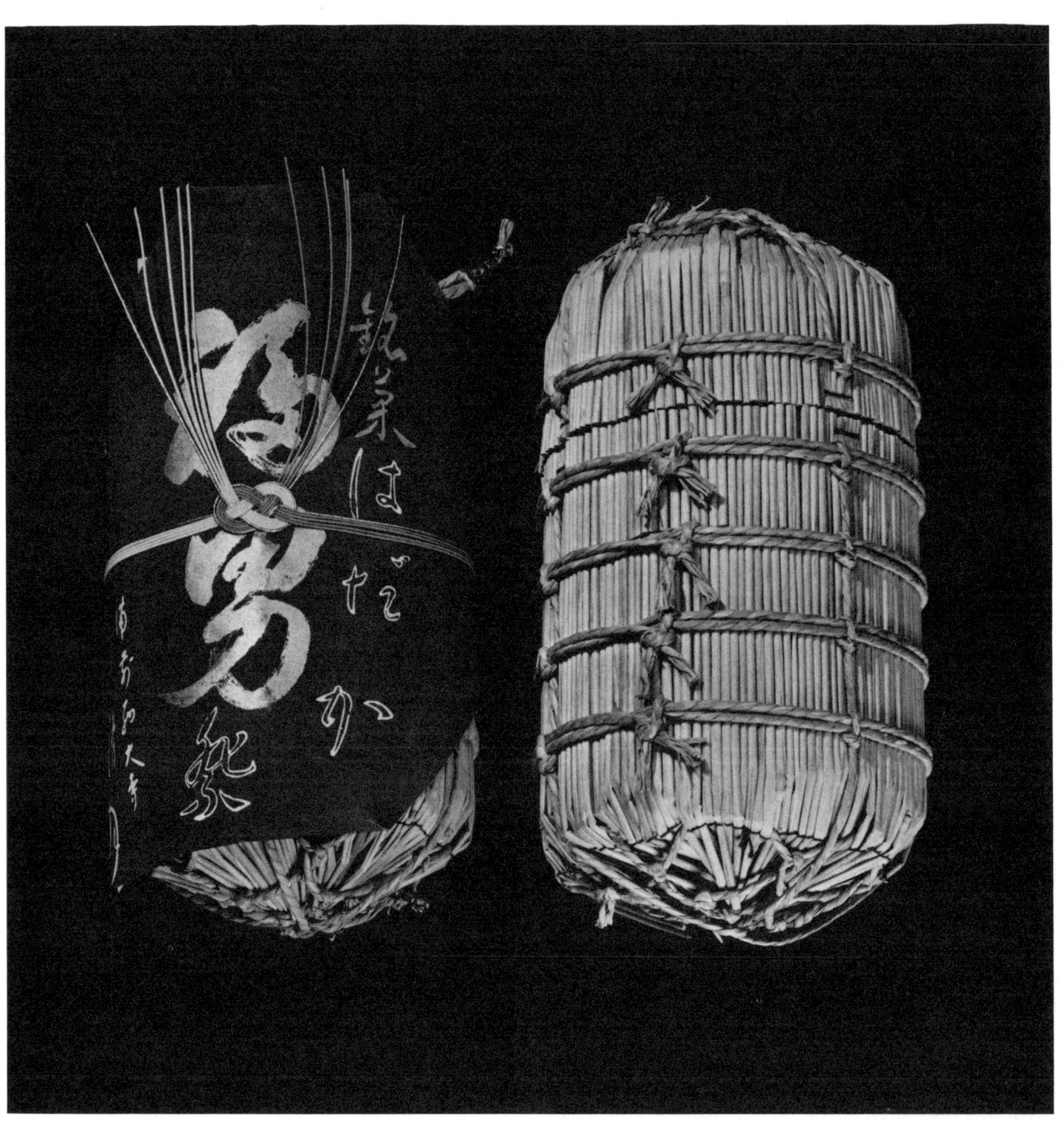

Sweets from Saidaiji are packed in miniature copies of old-style rice bales, made of the same reeds as tatami mats. The dyed paper label is fastened with the paper cords traditionally used for ceremonial gifts.

the sight or touch of a wrongly made thing than could Nature. In other words, their scale of values made it impossible for them to see that anything—a temple garden, hair ornament, a palace, or a package of dried fish—could be unimportant as an object. Wasn't it one of our Gods who felt the most acute distress when the humblest of his creatures—a sparrow, say—fell and perished? I think these people must have had things figured out in some way much as he did.

Imagine living in a world where all created things are of equal value, simply *because they exist!* I have seen many of the things made by these people, as we all have—the quiet temples, the roisterous baths, the ceramics and painted screens, the kimonos for little girls, and castles and great sculptures and tea ceremonies—and I sensed then in the vaguest kind of way that this might have been the way it was with them. But I never really *believed* it until I saw this book on packaging. For nobody treats packaging this way, nobody. Packaging is the bottom. Packaging is *never* where we expend high artistic skills and love on the thing itself. Packaging is slick propaganda, quick and cheap, offering something for nothing, full of surface seduction and "eye appeal," subject to jillion-dollar research projects, loaded with time-tested Madison Avenue goodies. That's the way we like it, because that's the way we are.

How nice of those uncounted generations of anonymous people to show us that this doesn't have to be the only way we are!

I salute you all, forgotten and invisible people, with gratitude and reverence. I should like to think that one day we might see the world with something like your humble vision and quite extraordinary sophistication. Now I can even hope that the time might again come when we, too, became unable to judge one created thing as more or less important than another, since *existence* is what makes anything and everything important.

And how clever of the author to have selected this particular subject out of the myriads offered by his admirable and beautiful country! For if the message is even roughly like the one I think I have decoded, this is really a thoroughly subversive document. To suggest, in no matter how discreet and tactful a manner, that the values of a society like our own are far from healthy, mature, or humane is less messy than sawing it off at the knees, but it comes to the same thing. Let us hope that thousands and thousands of copies are sold before the authorities get wind of it—it could do a first-rate job in our new Underground.

Above: A special Osaka confection has been packaged in a box with bold characters naming the contents. A sheet of dyed paper with family crests covers the top of the box.

Right: A container made of a section of bamboo, which was once used for preserved beans. The oilpaper cover is fastened with vine.

NET CONTENTS
IMPERIAL QUART - 0.946 LITER

The Future of Packaging

It was back in 1968 that a brief letter came from Walter Herdeg, publisher of *Graphis*, to say that another of his famous international annuals, this time on packaging, was in preparation and would I write an introduction to the American section. Herdeg, who lives and works in Zurich, Switzerland, has created one of the most prestigious publishing houses in the world, and a summons from him is not taken lightly. The question was what to write other than a preview of designs already accessible by turning a page. So the introduction dealing with packaging and litter was sent off and eventually it appeared when the book came out. There was no word from Herdeg other than a routine thank-you note from an assistant and I forgot the whole thing until I ran into him somewhere.

"Do you know," he said, "that introduction of yours scared me and I was sure it would offend our contributors. But eventually I decided to take a chance and I used it, as you know."

"I'm glad you did," I replied. "It got me a copy of that beautiful book."

"So am I," he said. "When you wrote it a year and a half ago it seemed radical indeed. But now it is timely. Things do change, don't they?"

I wondered. Do things change fast or is it just that we catch on so slowly?

As in so many fields of design where change is hopefully paraded as evidence of progress, packaging design reveals each year—each month—an impressive display of new forms, new materials used with extraordinary ingenuity, new techniques of shaping, folding, printing, embossing, and new ways of establishing style, attracting attention to the product, of creating for the customer the illusion that the contents will do something special and wonderful for him or her.

One wonders, as always, how anyone, no matter how ingenious, can think of still more unexpected and attractive ways of pleasing the buyer.

I find myself speaking as if "packaging" were a single type of activity, which of course is not the case at all. A beautifully engineered featherweight structure for holding six bottles or twelve eggs is by no means the same kind of thing as a subtly styled package-within-a-package containing a small bottle of scented alcohol which offers to change the male purchaser into a latter-day James Bond or one of the successfully lecherous monks of Balzac. Nor do these categories relate in any significant way to those packages designed to be kept as containers or travelling kits. And largest in bulk though smallest in "eye appeal" are those rugged cartons designed mainly to insure safe passage for the contents on their journey from factory to store and, sometimes, from store to consumer. These last are made to be opened—usually with certain difficulties—then thrown away as quickly as possible.

It is the last action—throwing away—going on daily all over the planet, entirely ignored by designers and manufacturers for good business reasons, that now provides food for speculation.

The global accumulation of waste, to which all packaging contributes its share, is becoming a matter of daily increasing concern. Some officials in large cities, when discussing this problem of waste disposal, begin to show traces of approaching panic. New York City, to cite one conspicuous example, has perhaps four or five years left before it literally runs out of disposal areas. In the meantime, while the hours slip by, 15,000 tons of waste are produced each day in the city and have to be gotten rid of somewhere. Population increases, naturally, exacerbate the problem, but *the amount of waste per inhabitant goes up faster than the population.*

Kaj Franck, the Finnish designer, eloquently describes the scene only a few years hence, when the entire globe will be covered with a layer of waste, a vast cocktail composed of everything megalopolis has to get rid of, for which he has coined the name "Urbanit." "Of what use for man to stand on Earth and reach for the stars," lamented this distinguished and perceptive designer, "if he is standing up to his navel in garbage?" Of what use indeed?

The direction packaging has been taking, with the full assistance of rapidly developing technologies, is, up to the present moment, one which makes disposal of the containers increasingly difficult. Paper can be burned, and even if dropped on a road or washed up on a beach, it presently disintegrates and returns to the soil. But the plastics, as we all know, do not behave in this way at all. No matter how violent the surf or how abrasive the sand and the stones, a plastic bottle or box remains indestructible. The aluminum beer can, so successful because it is light in weight and cheap enough so that it does not have to be returned to the store, tells the same story. The roadsides in the U.S. probably have more aluminum cans than wild flowers. The non-returnable glass bottles, produced by a beleaguered glass industry in response to the competition of the cans, are equally difficult to get rid of.

It seems unlikely that this new problem, an unexpected by-product of affluence and technical ingenuity, will be solved by the designers and industries responsible for it. This makes it the most modern of all problems, of course, for it is the same type of problem as created by the makers of cars, by industry and its poisonous effluents, and by nuclear fallout, probably the most sophisticated of all our wastes.

A recent published estimate suggests that it will cost roughly $60 billion to bring the problems just enumerated under control in the U.S. alone. The problems were created by the ingenuity of engineers, and now that the planet itself is in danger, it will be the same engineers who will be called on to rectify the situation. It is a most marvellous way to maintain a high level of employment in the technical professions and industries.

It should be an entertaining development to watch, for an entirely new series of design criteria will be established. The minimum package will become fashionable.

These containers which bulk three or four times as large as their contents will take on a suggestion of brassy vulgarity, and their makers will hasten to shrink them to meet the new tastes and thus maintain their sales. A new industry for dissolving plastics, glass, and aluminum will presently make its appearance, and achieve huge sales in the home market. Vast laboratories will spring up for the development of containers which disappear into thin air once emptied. Who knows? Maybe the antique beer can, once the symbol of working-class pleasure, may reappear, and long lines of trudging children will make their way between home and saloon. Anything is possible in this fast-changing world of ours.

All this is speculation. But one thing I am sure of: the greatest of ancient solutions to this problem will not be matched by technology. This too was described to me by Kaj Franck. It is the traditional lunch of the Finnish peasant. He goes to his work carrying a hard-crusted, round loaf of black bread. His wife has already cut a wedge from the top, inserted a large dollop of butter, and replaced the wedge. Once at his work the peasant puts it under a hedge, where its thick, shiny crust is immune to the attacks of the hungriest insects. When the lunch time comes, he takes it, breaks it open, spreads the butter and eats it. Nothing is left, for the package is the meal. If he drops a few crumbs, the birds dispose of them. The ideal, I suspect, is unattainable. But I cannot imagine a better symbol for the goals of the new generation of package designers, once the rising mountains of waste begin to blot out the familiar landscapes.

The Future of the Object

After the Gods have silently departed, and the acid rain starts falling on the ruined shrines and the defoliated woodlands, and the people are out of touch with the universe, then the world of things takes over, and the object, as hard and empty and fragile as a Russian Easter egg, moves to the center of everything.

The object, once shaped slowly by careful hands—the symbol and repository of mystery—now crowds the shelves of the supermarkets and the shiny pages of mail-order catalogs, coveted, bought, and discarded. It fills every view in all shapes and sizes, like fevered visions of UFOs. This is a good time to look at the object and think about it, for the winds of change are rising and it is time, once again, for it to shed its skin.

A good part of the power of Surrealist art stems from the unexpected and sometimes shocking manipulation of objects. Here, in Rene Magritte's Voice of the Wind, *three bells, blown up to monstrous proportions, turn familiar objects and a placid landscape into a haunting mystery.* La Voce del Vento, *Rene Magritte. Courtesy the Peggy Guggenheim Foundation, Venice.*

> "... And if it's you who gets the pneumonia I'll do a memorial to you to be set up in the yard of Scotland Yard—if Scotland Yard has a yard. It will be called Object."
>
> "Object?"
>
> "All my carvings are called Object now. It seems to be the thing...."
>
> *Judith Raven, sculptress,
> in Michael Inness's* Appleby's End.*

Our private and public landscapes are stuffed with objects; museums crawl with them; everything guides show surfeited tourists is an object. It is not news that humanity has been producing artifacts for a long time, but it may be news that the object, after 10 or 100,000 silent years in our midst, is no longer quite what it used to be.

Objects, silent or animated, have been used for a long time as a kind of code or cipher. The process begins early in school. The American Indian is identified by his association with a teepee, bow, or tomahawk. "Eskimo" equals igloo, sled, or harpoon. Classical Greek carries labels like temples, vases, and marble statues of gods and naked athletes. We identify modern technological humanity as the live kernel within a whole series of synthetic nuts called cars, office buildings, space capsules, submarines, planes, and elevators. Sometimes objects project so powerful a blast that onlookers are carried out of themselves: President Lyndon B. Johnson was reported to have reacted to his first view of the Taj Mahal with a series of piercing cowboy howls.

Two aspects of the contemporary object are entirely new under the sun: the first is the unbelievable quantity being produced and now in existence. "Before the Industrial Revolution," observed Richard Latham, "the only objects large and solid enough to persist and dominate the environment were architectural." Buildings, like everything else, continue to proliferate, but the synthetic landscape is now made up of much more, from litter and billboards to the monstrous gantries of Cape Kennedy.

The second aspect of the object we may consider new is that it is viewed today as something interesting and meaningful in itself. This was not true in the past, when the main justification for an object, aside from usefulness, was its existence as an embodiment or representation of a person or an idea. The object in itself was merely a material thing, to use the dictionary definition. Now the word itself has acquired a mysterious importance, as if objects, all by themselves, had taken over the organic world. Psychological jargon reflects this in such words as "love object," which refers to a person, not a thing.

It is typical of our time that people are not always sure whether they are individuals or things. A man makes a living, not as a man, but as an animate skill with a name or number. Warhol's soup cans attracted extraordinary attention because his choice of a tin container instead of a person was so unexpectedly perceptive and right a choice for a corporate portrait. In the life of a corporation, presidents and board chairmen come and go, but without the *can*, so to speak, the company is as nothing, meaningless and useless. Year by year the significance of people in these enterprises fades.... Who knows the name of the president of General Motors? Everybody knew Henry Ford. We move towards computerized, automated production in empty factories to provide merchandise for faceless hordes of consumers. It is no wonder that the object dominates.

It is no wonder, either, that artists have been turning, for more than a generation, away from people and towards objects. Artists have a very keen nose for what is real. It is more than a generation since André Breton coined the phrase "found object," one of those flashes of insight which is no less remarkable because it is (after the fact) so obvious. People have been picking up shells and driftwood on beaches for millenia and enjoying them. It was part of Breton's awareness of the realities of his time that he isolated the modern essence of the object, which is that it had begun to take on a life of its own, that it *existed* as an entity. Years before I had heard of Breton or the Surrealists, I came across a tin can lying on a road; it had been run over countless times by cars and trucks and it had been there long enough for rust spots to appear. The result was something unfamiliar and visually exciting. For a time I collected these objects and was pleasantly surprised to find that others had similar amusements. This was different from collecting sea shells, for these new types of objects were the result of violent, but appropriately modern transformations.

There was a time, not too long ago, when artists began rummaging through junk yards, instead of going to art supply stores for material. They had exhibits in respectable galleries and museums. Some artists even became known for their preferences and methods: Chamberlain, for instance, was admired for the things he could do with twisted bumpers and other automotive parts. César exhibited compressed junk, such as a Buick body

---

*New York: Dodd Mead and Company, Inc., 1945.

reduced to a cube by hydraulic presses. Lawrence Alloway, formerly of the Guggenheim Museum in New York, wrote critical analyses of junk sculpture: it was, he felt, a logical and appropriate expression of a materialistic culture. Indeed it is, but so is Rockefeller Center. The significant element in this development was not the use of junk, but the apotheosis of the object. It didn't matter in the least what the material was, and it is no surprise that the passion for junk as a sculptural component burned itself out in a hurry. One of the manifestations which supplanted it was Pop Art.

Pop Art replaces derelict artifacts with new ones. Jasper Johns' flags, beer cans, and targets, Claes Oldenburg's monster light bulbs and 20-story bananas are all fresh merchandise, just off the shelves. And since people, in the contemporary value scale, are more interesting as objects than as human individuals, they too appear in Pop Art as lifelike effigies in plaster and do not appear to be dead: it is more as if they had never been alive to start with. Pop Art, because it pretends to reproduce the familiar objects of popular culture with naive realism, has terrific shock value. It becomes the mirror in which we recognize ourselves with no pleasure whatever. It is like waking up to the horror of incarceration in a madhouse, only to realize that we have been living there for years.

The artists' preoccupation with the object has been carried recently to an extreme called "Minimal Art." In this expression very large objects are constructed, much as buildings are built. The artist makes a dimensioned sketch or model which is turned over to a fabricating shop. Tony Smith is said to have achieved some of his best pieces by phoning in dimensions and specifications. There is a kind of factory in New Haven where large objects by a number of artists are manufactured and sold via catalog. In this phase of development, it is no longer considered necessary to reproduce a familiar item: anything, provided that it is large enough, becomes an object suitable for sculptural purposes. Noguchi's huge cube, installed in front of the Marine Midland Bank building in Lower Manhattan, is one of a rapidly growing number of such installations.

It is easy enough to deplore or ridicule such manifestations, although both critics and public are becoming increasingly fearful of sticking their necks out and thus getting out of step, but the fact is that artists are less crazy than the rest of us, and infinitely more perceptive. It is also a fact that there is nobody left but the artist to give us a hint of the shape of the new, post-modern world now in formation. The engineers never look up from their slide

Cesar's cube, a compressed car body from a wrecking yard, was a sensation in its day. The Yellow Buick, *by Cesar Baldaccini, 1961. Compressed automobile, 59½ × 30¾ × 24 7/8. Collection of The Museum of Modern Art, New York; a gift of Mr. & Mrs. John Rewald.*

rules, business executives are too involved in the big rat race, and it seems most unlikely that the pious, idiot-child babble which emerges from the televised mouths of the mighty are going to cast much light on the confusing scene around us.

At any rate, the latest word from the artist types on our far-flung newsfronts is that the object is "in" and people are "out." But while the artists are celebrating, for the moment, the triumph of the inanimate object, every part of the planet is sprouting discotheques, which are artistic manifestations with a totally different message. Discotheques blend electronic and optical techniques with primitive tribal dancing to arrive at a seemingly unstructured event. Here again, we have an art form with global reach and a message diametrically opposed to the first one. Both reports, incidentally, are correct. We are watching a confrontation between the antihuman forces generated by technology and the prohuman forces made up of young people who do not like what their elders have in store for them.

The importance of the object stems from the fact that it is the most pervasive force in the modern world. Technology, for the time being, is largely devoted to the outpouring of objects. It is this immense agglomerate of "things" of all kinds and sizes which is the symbol, not any particular object. This is why artists can home in on any object at all, and still make their point. It doesn't matter whether it is a can, a plaster hot dog, a plastic girl, or an aluminum shape five stories high. One works just about as well as another. The situation has nothing in common with, say, the medieval framework, a common language with a vocabulary of accepted symbols.

Transformation

A peculiar quality of the contemporary object, in addition to its heightened psychic voltage, is the extent to which it represents a transformation of some kind. My little collection of flattened cans was a simple example of an unstructured transformation: a shiny tin cylinder, emptied of its contents, becomes an entirely different kind of object under the wheels of passing trucks. We respond to such expressions with varying degrees of intensity to the extent that we sense the entire epoch as an expression of transformation. The most dramatic example is not an art work, but a formula. Einstein's $E = Mc^2$ is pure transformation. Matter becomes energy on an undreamed-of scale; a busy city can be changed into rubble in milliseconds. We can no longer think of resisting change, as did our more deeply rooted parents. We have no roots—only wheels. Cities, we say, will all have to be rebuilt within the next generation. The only question is how? Frozen foods have transformed marketing, refrigerators, shopping habits, meal planning. Having been earthbound for a million years, we send out young men with Hasselblads to take snapshots of the Moon's surface.

Transformation is our daily fare, and it should not be unexpected to find that artists are having their say about this, too. Their statements, as usual, are made in symbolic form, since this is what artists do, but they are not too hard to decode.

At the Museum of Modern Art a few years back, a show entitled "The Object Transformed" presented examples. One item, produced by Man Ray back in the 20s, consisted of a simple old-type flatiron, the kind women used to heat on top of a coal stove. The object was normal in every way except one: the artist had soldered a row of carpet tacks down the center line of its smooth bottom. The effect on the beholder was like that of scratching one's fingernail on a blackboard. Another exhibit showed a cluster of glass milk bottles "transformed" by a welding torch. The bottles, naturally, had been deformed and partially fused together under this treatment. A third example consisted of open books of various shapes and sizes which had been sprayed with heavy automotive paint in vivid colors.

The theme of the show is made clear in these examples. In every instance a very familiar, ordinary object was treated in some unexpected and inappropriate way, deprived of its original functional attributes, and transformed into something mutilated and monstrous. The fact that the effect of the exhibition was exceedingly unpleasant did not keep it from being exciting at the same time. Since I keep insisting that art is one of our few valid information inputs in a period of great change and that artists are not on the fringes of life but working at the center of it, I will try for another illustration which may help clarify the "Object Transformed" show. I am thinking of Darwin, Marx, and Freud.

In the case of these three 19th-century men we find that each triggered social transformations of very large dimensions and that the work of each was, in his time and even now, regarded by many as something indescribably monstrous and evil. Darwin, if one takes only his proposition that humanity had not been "created" but had evolved like other life forms, dealt established religion a blow from which it has not yet recovered. Marx—to vastly oversimplify matters—postulated a noncapitalist society which could function and compete with the older systems. It happened. Freud isolated the unconscious as a source of our deepest motivations, thus opening a can of worms with which we are still trying to cope. A common element in the work of all three was the destructive—perhaps fatal—impact on established beliefs. Marx saw religion as an instrument of deception, subjection, and oppression, and the socialist countries which emerged under the Marxist banner are conspicuously uninterested in fostering religion, regardless of the degree of religious freedom they permit. Freud was perhaps the worst of all three, for he deprived religion of the Devil. A Christianity without a believable Satan is like a Western or a TV spy thriller without Bad Guys.

The artists in the "Object Transformed" show shattered a familiar world of irons, bottles, and books. Our three worthies of the 19th century did exactly the same thing. The fact that shattering is a common aspect of transformation, just as eggs are broken when transformed into omelettes, doesn't make the people like the transformation any better. However, the extent to which one familiarizes himself with the codes used by artists and designers can help cushion the shock when it comes.

Objects are the fingerprints left by a culture on the walls of its particular cell in space and time. Anyone can learn how to read fingerprints. Part of the meaning of any object is exactly what the sponsoring culture says it is. That ornate gold cup over there may look to you or me like the Hepzibah M. Perkins Trophy, awarded last year to the Curling Club of Upper Hydrangea. But if the society which created it says that it is the Holy Grail, then that's what it is.

Another part of the meaning of any object is what the culture *really is, and not what it says it is*. Take, for instance, one of those 1969 deluxe station wagons, spattered with vinyl, chrome, and fake wood. Read the advertisements and you see words like "luxurious," "tasteful," "elegant," "pride of ownership," and similar rubbish. Read the *object* and different words come to mind like "vulgarity," "fakery," "pretentiousness," and others less printable. The information provided by the object is invariably more reliable than the advertising copy.

Magic

Magic is a very special quality possessed by some objects which allows the lucky holder to do extraordinary things. One of the difficulties it presents today is that its miraculous properties do not show up in testing laboratories, and it only works if there is unquestioning faith. In the fairy tales of earlier cultures this was never a problem and they are consequently full of cloaks of invisibility, rings which make the wearer invulnerable, potions which cure anything. The wand owned by Cinderella's fairy godmother is an excellent example: it turned a ragamuffin into a princess, a pumpkin into a gilded coach. Imagining for a moment that Karajan's baton were an exact replica of the fairy godmother's wand, there is no way he could manage the pumpkin-coach transformation. Nobody believes that it will work, so it doesn't.

Another example is the pointed bone favored by the Australian bushman: after it has been anointed with the proper incantations and aimed at the hapless victim, he promptly goes off in the bush and presently dies. He dies because he understands the lethal qualities of the bone. If we shared his convictions we could save some of the immense expenditures we make on fusion bombs, and reduce atmospheric pollution as well.

But it is a great mistake to assume, from these cultural changes, that objects no longer have magical properties. Think of mink coats, for instance, and the extraordinary transformations they can produce in a perfectly ordinary girl. The Ford Motor Company, after the initial success of the Mustang, accumulated a large file of letters from happy owners who, in many cases had Cinderella-type stories of an overnight metamorphosis from a social drab to a dashing fellow with more dates than he could handle. This, unless I am way off the beam, is still magic and it is still working because of the simple faith of girls that if picked up by a character in a red Mustang, they will be transmogrified, and the equally complete belief on the part of the owner that with this magic vehicle he is now irresistible.

A royal crown which, in a few remaining places, still retains its ability to turn a perfectly normal human being into someone very special is another sample of that old magic still at work, and on a surprisingly large scale. Modern man and woman can exorcize all sorts of devils by buying a new dress or set of golf clubs. Huge investments of energy are made by all sorts of industries to keep turning out a vast and ever-changing assortment of placebos. In fact, this is one of the reasons why the countries of the West have become so rich. The placebo industries, which are legion, do not have to worry about customers. They are supplying addicts.

Objects with magical properties depend to a large extent on exclusivity for their effectiveness, but a given individual's perception of exclusivity varies greatly within social groups. What a mink coat does for one can be matched by dyed rabbit in another. But a million crowns put on sale at Woolworth's would be ineffectual, unless reserved for small chidren, who know exactly how to transform 69 cents worth of plastic into something truly glorious.

Proliferation

Proliferation is not only a million crowns, but tens and hundreds of millions of everything else. We, the spoiled children of a rampant technology, suffocate in a welter of materialistic excess. A common reaction of some of the more thoughtful rebels among the young is to strip themselves of all possessions, much like the medieval orders sworn to poverty. Yet, accepting the mystics with their voluntary poverty as interesting, honest, and valuable, I do not quite believe that one can dismiss proliferation as materialistic excess or gluttony. There are times when it seems more like an imitation of Nature, which can be very prodigal in its output.

In the earliest factories a single motor drove all the machines. Water power and later steam provided the power to drive shafts to which all machines were connected by leather belts. With the advent of electricity all machines were quickly equipped with their own motors. Now this is indeed proliferation, but hardly neurotic greed. Factories so equipped are more flexible.

The same goes for a surprising number of things in the dwelling. We have a dishwasher. I have special affection for this machine for it relieves the family of at least three hours at the sink daily, work we all consider unrewarding. It is hard to find uplift in the washing and drying of the same dishes over and over again. Now if a dishwasher will do this for us, it should presumably do the same for 40 million other households within our boundaries. Proliferation? Of course. We can continue the search for something really wicked, really destructive of the national moral fiber, but I doubt if we will find it in the proliferation of such objects.

The proliferation of household goods also reflects the increased pressures on family time, especially for women. Much is invested in these tools because of the value put on time and energy saved. Toys are proliferating madly, partly because industries can turn them out in huge quantities, because city children are boxed in, because parents feel guilty about neglecting their children, and because grandmothers have money to throw around. Sporting goods are proliferating in large part because a man made to feel like a nothing in his job can recover some of his self-confidence on a golf course or by a trout stream. Amateur photographers, as they develop skill, begin to emulate professional photographers, who always have lots of cameras.

Then there is the proliferation of slums, another area in which the U.S. bids fair to lead the world.

Social

Let us consider the slums for an instant, for they fit into our theme. The U.S. is the richest country anywhere. It is riddled with slums it seems powerless to eradicate. Switzerland and Denmark, to pick two smaller but also prosperous countries, do not have slums. To answer the questions suggested by these statements could occupy the energies of an army of researchers, but I suspect that the real reason the small countries have no slums is that *they refuse to have them*. The U.S. doesn't really care whether it has slums or not, so long as the inhabitants of the ghettos stay out of sight.

There are amusing examples of the interactions of social convictions and social action. Puerto Rico has been a hideously poor country until very recently, but in the early 1900s its water and sanitation installations proliferated until they reached a level of excellence completely out of character with the country as a whole. This happened after our army of "liberation" moved in, in 1898, with officers and families who refused to expose themselves to the diseases associated with improper sanitation. Slums, however, presented no such threats and hence they continued to proliferate, so that even today our "showcase of democracy" in the Caribbean has some exceptional displays of hillside and waterside slums, all very picturesque.

We are only now getting to the point where we, as a society, can begin to sense that proliferation is not an inevitable, automatic process, but one that can be controlled. The slum example is a perfectly good one. If one industrial society has slums and another does not, then it follows that *any* industrial society *may or may not have slums*, as it chooses. That the three countries cited have different histories, political attitudes, and so on does not really alter the possibilities, since the means for slum eradication exist.

Competition is another factor in the proliferation process, and a curious one. As a people we are emotionally tied to such concepts as individual enterprise and free competition, although it is pretty evident that less and less enterprise is individual and that more and more competition is not free. Even so, the concepts are a very important part of our image of ourselves. One of the things which makes it even possible for us to conceive of a noncompetitive society is the existence of such systems in places like Russia, China, Cuba, Yugoslavia, and the Soviet satellites.

I encountered one of the leaders of the Russian

design profession at a UNESCO conference in Soviet Georgia in the spring of 1968, and he told me with great satisfaction that the USSR was going to surpass the U.S. in the production of high-quality refrigerators (more proliferation) in the near future. Having seen the few pathetic examples available to the Soviet public, I felt that what he was describing was not likely to occur for quite a while. Nevertheless, I asked him how this new triumph of socialist technology was going to be achieved.

"Do you know how many models of refrigerators are being produced today in the U.S.?," he demanded. By some oversight I had neglected to arm myself with the necessary data before leaving home.

"It doesn't matter," he said impatiently. "The number is 156!"

It did seem like a lot of models.

"Consider the waste!" he cried. "Consider the tremendous cost of all that unnecessary tooling! We have analyzed the needs of households and we know that fewer than a dozen models will take care of everyone. We are going to study these models in great depth, arriving at a degree of perfection you have never reached, we will put them on automated production lines, and then you will see what happens to sales on world markets!"

It was marvelous. He was talking just like an American of forty years ago. All the assumptions of Henry Ford, all the oversimplified theories of a now-obsolete industry, all the brash presentations of warmed-over ideas as something new were there. Nevertheless, there was also a kernel of truth. We could unquestionably make all the refrigerators we need in fewer plants and with substantial reduction in the costs of tooling. Part of the price of doing this would be an accompanying reduction of "individual initiative." There is indeed social waste in uncontrolled competition, but our experience also suggests that the payoff is not so bad either. Socialism theoretically discourages waste, but observers back from Russia find the country riddled with it.

Ownership

As the outpouring of goods continues, spreading from one continent to another, other problems begin to emerge which alter, in profound ways, traditional attitudes towards the object. I have an example right behind me. It is a new high-fidelity set which keeps blowing its fuses. There is no way I can repair it, for its insides are a mass of printed circuits. To get it fixed will take a round trip of 130 miles, for the set and I are in the country. In the city, the trip would be shorter but the inconvenience would be about the same. This morning there was a little trip, only 18 miles, to pick up a replacement for a broken tail light. The garage had forgotten to order it. A broken electric shaver head, taken into New York for replacement, is regarded with amazement by the clerk. It is an antique (over eighteen months old) and he acts as if I had come in with the Dead Sea Scrolls.

Such tales, in an infinity of variations, represent the weekly experience of millions of families. Fewer and fewer products are made which can be repaired by the ordinary householder, because manufacturing is moving in the direction of complex components which are pulled out and replaced if anything goes wrong. Can anyone imagine trying to repair a transistor? They need microscopes to make them. When one adds the shortage of competent repairmen, the frustration involved in getting one consumer product after another back into working order is taking a good bit of the glamour out of the ownership of objects.

Now there is one completely common product which presents few if any of these problems: this is the telephone. No user has to *own* this attractive and indispensable device. Anyone for a telephone? it's simple: get a dime and call the phone company. A man shows up. *With* his tools. He brings his tools because he knows he can't stick you for that extra trip to the shop and because his boss is a hardbitten pro who knows all the tricks. So there he is. Where do you want the phone? He puts it there. What model, what color? You get them. An hour or two later you can start building up the phone bill. You can call Rochester or Rio, Karachi or maybe Kamchatka. It works. When it stops working, another dime brings the man. No bill. There is nothing like the $10.00 paid to a self-styled TV expert for passing his hands over an ailing set, plus $49.76 for the replacement of perfectly good parts. One thin dime, and the man comes and takes care of everything.

It is absolutely inevitable that a generation of telephone subscribers should finally begin to wonder about the so-called joys of ownership. Let another generation pass, and certain keen minds begin to separate the concept of ownership from the concept of service. Then entire categories of objects begin to lose their old values. It happens to all of us. My office had need, a while back, for some new dictating machines. The salesman came and we got ready to buy. Then our business manager looked thoughtfully at the phone and said, "Why don't we

rent?" A week later one of the machines went completely haywire, with the playback sounding like all four Marx Brothers talking at once. The man came. "It's a factory job," he said solemnly. "I can get it back to you in about five or six days." Our business manager smiled sweetly at him. "You don't expect us to pay rent on a machine we can't use, do you?" "Well," said the man hastily, "it just so happens that I have a brand new machine in my bag. Now if you would care to have me exchange them. . . ."

A great change in the status of the object, unpredictable in its ultimate consequences, takes place when modern man, burdened like an old-time scissors grinder with all his hard-won possessions, begins to get it through his head that *the service is all he needs*. Messrs. Hertz and Avis got the idea long before he did and they are doing very nicely. One can open a business office with everything rented down to carpeting and desk calendars. The yellow pages are full of rental offers of all kinds.

One might assume that a possessions implosion is well under way, but there are few trends these days which go in only one direction. People's behavior is too contradictory, for one thing. Having just cited the telephone as the ideal example of a rented service, it is necessary to acknowledge that people are now *buying* phones too. These are mostly refitted antiques and copies of antiques. Why? Probably because they get bored by the good-looking sameness of the standard phones and want something different. On a larger scale, companies can buy entire systems for their offices which compete with the AT&T products on the basis of features, price, or both.

Another factor in the growing disenchantment with ownership is the mobility of U.S. households, a sizable percentage of which is always going somewhere else. Here too with freight costs being what they are, plus the nuisance of packing and unpacking, there tends to be a revival of nomadic attitudes, which includes a healthy skepticism about the value of bulky furniture.

In an odd way, the entire tendency to reject ownership of objects in favor of the rental of services becomes a kind of invisible bridge over the generation gap. Large numbers of the young are turning away from the piling up of possessions because they disapprove of indiscriminate accumulation as a way of life. Their elders are doing a similar thing for quite different reasons.

Anonymity

The Industrial Revolution sealed the fate of handicraft production, bringing factories and mass manufacture instead. Not only people, but objects themselves were affected in the process. Objects which had formerly been "personal," showing distinct traces of the maker's involvement, now became impersonal. Objects which had an individual identity (handmade things are never exactly alike) now became anonymous, unidentifiable. We have all come to appreciate these attributes of impersonality and anonymity, for they mean uniform quality and precision. Another unforeseen result, however, was that the bonds which link people to things were weakened.

It is hard to become attached to an object which shows no evidence that the maker cared what he was making. It is normal for a person who has and uses good things, well-conceived and carefully executed products, to become attached to them, to keep them in good condition, and to take pleasure out of the way they work, look, and feel. Deprived of this association with inanimate objects, he becomes more vulnerable to the alienation which has become so conspicuous and worrisome a characteristic of the modern individual. It is far from the most significant element in the sickness, but it exists.

I sometimes wonder if the passion for male gadgetry, like guns, fishing equipment, cameras, and tape recorders, so clearly expressed in constantly climbing sales figures, does not reflect a desire to renew some of the old attachments to objects. The items enumerated are all tools of one kind or another, and it is hard for a tool to remain impersonal and anonymous no matter how it is made. The professional photographer buys the same Leica or Nikon as you and I, but constant use in his hands produces imperceptible modifications, so that the mass-produced object finally becomes *his* in a completely real sense, and he would be quite right if he refused to lend it to his best friend. I remember a carpenter who worked on a house we had designed; someone had stolen his set of wood drills and he was inconsolable. He could have bought an identical set, but as a good workman he knew that they would not be the same. The microscopic changes in an object which are brought about through use are quite apparent to its owner, and the effect of the coordination of man and tool helps give him a sense of solid identity which is all too often lacking elsewhere in his existence.

Isamu Noguchi's red cube is one of the most successful of the geometric and abstract objects that adorn the new commercial plazas. Red Rhombohedron, Isamu Noguchi, Marine Midland Building, New York. Photo by Ezra Stoller; courtesy Skidmore, Owings & Merrill, Architects.

It is impressive to observe how far the move towards anonymity has gone on an international scale. What purchaser thinks when he buys a Sony or Panasonic TV set, a Teac tape recorder, or a Nikon camera that all these objects are *Japanese*? Substitute a kimono, a woodcut, a *kokeshi* doll, or a Noh theater and there is instant recognition of a special place and culture. Not so for those admirable industrial artifacts which freely circulate throughout the world, giving no hint whatever of country of origin. My office once designed a traveling exhibit on industrial design and deliberately inserted into one section of it a collection of unidentified products from a dozen countries, challenging the viewer to sort them out. It was practically impossible to pick the place of origin unless one happened to know the item.

The reason for this situation, which is quite new even in the modern industrial world, is that *technology recognizes no country or culture*. Under its domination there is no meaning to national identity, only a best way of designing and making things at a given moment. The fast spread of communications systems, also a facet of technology, makes it possible for anyone anywhere to know what is happening elsewhere. Obviously, if I am working in Rhodesia on a highway interchange, and I see yours in a magazine and realize that it is better, I am going to follow your lead. It would be stupid not to. So highway interchanges everywhere begin to take on the same look. Politics and nationalistic sentiment are thus at odds with technology at the present time, and the only thing one can be sure of is that this aspect of technology is going to win.

Even cities behind the Iron Curtain are beginning to sprout examples of the international look, in buildings, vehicles, and smaller objects. The attempts to jam the radio, censor mail and publications, and all the other efforts to build a wall around the population simply come to nothing. The supposedly powerful Marxist ideology has no effect whatever on the forms of objects. Technology overrides everything that can be subjected to it. Soviet cities are different from those in the West only because urban planning is not an area in which technology can play a decisive role.

It is both easy and fashionable to deplore sameness, anonymity, and impersonality, but we must do our deploring judiciously, for these qualities are not always negative. Who would want to supplant an international code of highway signs and symbols by new, individually designed information systems at every frontier and state line? Drivers would go out of their minds and the accident rate would climb even higher. When the airplane stewardess, in telling you to fasten your seat belt, extinguish cigarettes, and put your seat upright, says the words used by all stewardesses in all languages, it is a comfort for the traveler, for the ritual phases remind him of what to do and he doesn't have to listen. Would those insanely "individualistic" neon jungles called Main Street, U.S.A., be even uglier and more depressing if a similar bit of order were introduced? New York's Park Avenue is worse, not better, for having small differences in the design of the fifty-story buildings which now flank it. These office structures are all there for one reason, which is to permit their investors to mortgage out after a few years of occupancy. The so-called corporate identities established by minute exterior styling differences accomplish virtually nothing beyond massaging professional and corporate egos.

What makes Park Avenue better than the typical Main Street is that the differences between buildings *are* so small, and it thus achieves a certain discipline and monumentality. But after the first awed glance at all that glass, there is very little to look at. These places are very, very dead. At street level one only sees banks and an occasional industrial exhibit. Main Street, bad as it is, has at least shop windows and other incidents along the way. The architects of the New Sterility, who are merely doing what their clients tell them to do, have not solved this elementary problem of human interest, and it is quite possible that they do not know that it exists.

Behind the glittering, empty facades of new highrise buildings there is an entire story of swift technical evolution. The same holds true for smaller objects. Any industrial or architectural object of 1900 has more interesting details, a more direct revelation of working parts, than artifacts currently in production. This shift from articulated to closed form has been dealt with elsewhere, and the reasons for it are logical enough. Beyond the logic there is the immense prestige of technology's major achievements. The rockets and supersonic planes, for example, the Diors and Cardins of the industrial design world, show an elegance dependent on simple but powerful forms and the visual suppression of all working parts. The automotive world bends its knee to these dictators of design fashion by introducing disappearing headlights and windshield wipers. But these eliminations are only the latest in a long series. The same look filters down to radios, refrigerators, and lawn mowers. In all periods a certain common look is to be found; it is established by the most significant objects and then diffuses itself through all production.

Instant Obsolescence

The main line of technical development takes us through a series of objects, each one of which does more with less than the preceding generation of designs. These objects, however, are conceived as reasonably permanent, using whatever time scale is considered appropriate for that object. Then, as design and manufacturing become more sophisticated, the old nuts and bolts type of fastening, for example, is replaced by glued or welded joints. These are replaced by complex castings or molded plastic. Replaceable vacuum tubes go to transistors which are then swallowed up into integrated circuits. As we have already noted, this process leads to replacement of elements rather than repair, and the throwaway component comes into existence. From the component it is logical to move to the complete object, at which stage it is ready for the consumer. Kleenex is the great symbol, of course, but the family of expendables or disposables has now become very large.

One of Finland's outstanding designers, Kaj Franck, spoke his mind on this subject recently. Man, said Franck, has always been an "uninhibited producer of waste and there is now an accelerating series of events which break down natural landscapes, changing them into a new material, a conglomerate cultural waste.... Man has always tried to change nature, but now, the former slow shaping of daily life has switched to a merciless system of extracting, producing, distributing and consuming which cannot be stopped without serious change in the mechanism of society.... The entire process lacks that quality of *renewal* which characterizes biological systems." Franck even coined a name for his conglomerate cultural waste, "Urbanit." The word is a play on the many names for building products, like "Eternit," which are current in Europe. He foresees a thick layer of this Urbanit eventually covering the entire planet. Even if one assumes deliberate exaggeration to make a point, the picture, as we all know from experience, is not fantasy.

To cope with the new mountain ranges of junk and garbage, we use rather primitive methods. The stuff is hauled to dumps, burned, and bulldozed into the ground. Desperation sometimes generates ideas described as ingenious, but which are merely desperate. One, which got a fair amount of publicity, was the dumping of wrecked car bodies into the water, where they form artificial reefs. It is claimed that the fish love them. There are different kinds of waste disposal problems, of course. Paper products will burn. Organic wastes can be processed. Plastics are much more difficult to get rid of. Public agencies are traditionally expected to repair the damage done to the environment by private industry, but this is due for drastic change.

As if throwaway components and products did not present enough of a problem, we complicate it enormously by packaging which, in the case of some items, bulks larger than the object contained. Since people almost invariably get rid of packaging as soon as they get home and since more and more of the containers are made of plastic, the entire problem is raised to another level, and the mountains of junk begin to take on Himalayan proportions.

The process by which packaging eventually takes on such proportions begins innocently enough. Crackers used to be sold out of barrels. The shop proprietor took them out with his hands or with a scoop and put them on a scales. Then they went into a paper bag. All sorts of foods were sold in this way. The next step was to put them into boxes, which were less unsanitary, reduced spoilage, and—this was the revolutionary advantage from a business point of view—had six surfaces which could now be used for advertising. As the package rather than the product became the focal point of competition, increasing amounts of highly paid talent were pumped in, to the point where the package has become, in many cases, *the* object on which marketing depends. Around 1966 there was a news item which suggested how far the proliferation of throwaway containers can go. It was reported in *The Wall Street Journal* as "The Can Opener Craze" and described the sudden enthusiasm for cans to package all sorts of nonperishables such as candles, toys, puzzles, pajamas, belts, dresses, hats, and other items. One can carried greetings printed on the label and had nothing inside but air, an impressive example of a "product" which was practically nothing but waste and a kind of waste it is not easy to dispose of.

There is a great deal to be said for the attractive packaging of objects. It protects them, gives pleasure to the buyer or recipient, and adds color to a life which, for most of us, could use more of it. The problem arises with the side effects, at which point it is inevitable that one begins to wonder if the package is worth the candle, so to speak. Somewhere in the near future it is inevitable that people will begin to decide that legislation is necessary to control waste. A tiresome prospect, for most of us feel that there is probably too much legislation, but given a private industry which has an almost unbroken record of ignoring the social consequences of its activities, it is hard to think of other action. One also begins to wonder if the demand for superconvenience may not be carried to the point where it becomes silly, and a menace to boot. During World War II very few cans found their way to the dumps because people flattened used cans and saved them for the metal scrap drive. In this case, the waste problem was eliminated by recycling it through industry. There have been moments in history when drinking beer in very large quantities produced no waste because it went from keg to glass to gullet, or from keg to beer pail to home to consumers. All the containers in the cycle were washed and used again. If, for reasons beyond our control, it became necessary to return to this inconvenient old way of doing things, one doubts if the beer drinkers would suffer greatly. The beer pail could be replaced by a thermos without damaging our space programs or defense efforts.

Systems

It seems apparent, as we pursue our investigation of the object, that almost everything that affects it these days tends to downgrade it. Proliferation takes a lot of the fun out of owning special things; automated production removes the human element from making, which lessens the old attachment to man-made things; expendability eliminates it, for people are simply not going to put old pieces of Kleenex away in lavender-scented drawers; and the problems of owning things which cannot be kept in shape through normal maintenance and repair lead people to prefer renting them. The trends thus appear once again to be contradictory: on the one hand, the object has become the prime symbol of an entire culture and on the other, people seem to be getting fed up with it.

It is more precise to view what is going on as a process of transformation, with both positive and negative elements, rather than downgrading. Nothing illustrates this more clearly than the tendency of the object to lose its identity, its separateness, and to become swallowed up in a system of one kind or another.

"System" is one of those words which have been gaining currency at a very rapid rate of speed. Systems design is now recognized as a new kind of design. To identify something as a "system" rather than as a mere object gives it new authority and glamor.

Nature is a series of self-renewing systems, and the investigation of how these systems really work has kept many able people working for lifetimes during the past century. All systems, by their every essence, tend to be more complex than isolated things, which is probably why the proliferation of computers has led to the proliferation of systems (and vice versa).

For our purposes we can take an example which has the virtue of familiarity, although it too represents problems of considerable complexity. I am thinking of the kitchen. Anybody's kitchen. A kitchen is a space where food preparation and the cleaning of utensils go on. Whether we eat there or not is irrelevant. It is a work center equipped with tools.

Originally the kitchen was a place where a pump, a basin, and a fireplace were located. When plumbing came into general use, the basin became a sink, with built-in elements which let the water in and drained the liquid waste out. It was "designed" as a piece of primitive industrial sculpture, free-standing and fitted with its own legs. At the same time the stove emerged as an object, sometimes decorated with cast iron ornaments. The icebox, a third major object in the kitchen, gradually transformed itself from a wooden container into the electric refrigerator, but it retained its identity as an autonomous object until the late 50s. A kitchen of thirty years ago looks, to our systems-conditioned eyes, more like a museum of domestic appliances than a workplace. When I began to work with the General Electric Company as a consultant in 1950s, it was still necessary to argue the proposition that the *kitchen* should be treated as the basic product, not the different appliances. The appliances, I insisted, were not true objects anymore, but really components, since they functioned together as part of a housewife-directed process. It was hard going. It was not easy to persuade the high-ranking manager of a department—say, refrigeration—which did a business of several hundred millions of dollars a year that his beloved product was nothing more than a mere component. He viewed this as another subversive downgrading of the object. I lost the battle, after eight or nine years of interesting work and lively controversy, but won the war. Any appliance store will show what has happened.

Today's kitchen is styled as a system. That is, the separate appliances are no longer isolated sculptural objects, but matching modular boxes which fit together in a

Man Ray's iron does not lose its power to disturb the viewer simply because the nightmarish contrast between the smooth iron surface and the tacks transforms a simple tool into an impossible contradiction. Gift, Man Ray, 1958. Replica of 1921 original, 6 1/8 × 3 5/8 × 4½. Collection of The Museum of Modern Art, New York; James Thrall Soby Fund.

variety of ways. Furthermore, many of them are designed to be built in (oven, cooktop, sink, dishwasher, garbage disposal unit, laundry machines, refrigerator) or to *look* as if they were built in. This look is the "in" look in kitchens today, just as the systems look is "in" practically anywhere in industry.

Cars, unlike kitchens, are still styled to look like freestanding objects and are sold as such (General Motors alone sold 20,000 a day during October 1968) but when one sees these objects strung out along a highway, or massed in a parking lot, they are as alike as peas. It is this essential "look-alike" quality which reveals that the car is in reality a systems component. The system does not function well as a system, for it breaks down when the car gets within the city, and even the new highways, frequently overloaded as soon as they go into service, are more like linear parking lots at rush hour than high-speed roads. In-city parking, service, and even fueling present more and more problems as the pressure increases. Large numbers of vehicles have motors with 250 and 350 horsepower, but on parts of the system a driver is lucky to average 5 miles per hour, a speed the feeblest of compacts or any fifteen-year-old jalopy can achieve with no trouble at all. Given the prices of suburban lots, he pays through the teeth for the privilege of letting the car sleep on the premises, and if he drives to work he has to get another car for his wife, who cannot shop or get the children to school without it.

Some systems work better than others, naturally, but as one compares them it is quite clear that what was said about the object tends to apply to the system. We noted earlier that objects made for the direct use of people were generally inferior designs and that those with a non- or antihuman purpose were almost invariably better. The same holds for systems: private automotive transportation works poorly, Apollo 8 performed superbly. All the clues from both systems and objects suggest very strongly that Americans and others subject to the full blast of technological influence feel very much at home with *things*, but are completely thrown when confronted with problems involving people.

It is likely that the problems raised by the automobile and such system components as roads and service facilities may never be adequately solved without a decision to redesign the totality of transportation networks so that they function in a mutually supporting way. In other words, not even a trillion dollar automotive system is big enough to cope any more. If this is true, then the dimensions of the systems problems directly ahead are staggering, and somewhere along the line the designers (planners, politicians, business leaders, architects, engineers, industrial designers, and others) will have to learn that no action can be undertaken without an assessment of possible side effects and also that hardware alone will not solve these problems. Our blithe but battered assumption that technique solves everything will have to be qualified. Technique solves technical problems. It can not solve human problems unless deliberately and intelligently directed to human ends.

Nowhere does this show up more sharply than in the cities, where an accumulation of problems ignored for several generations is suddenly reaching critical mass, and behind the pious platitudes issued by political leaders there is already more than a touch of panic. Cities, as they have evolved in the U.S., are a complex of interlocking (and now malfunctioning) systems, created for purposes that have changed. The problems of an orderly transition to an environment in which the human qualities in people would be enhanced rather than brutalized will not be solved by 19th-century minds or fragmented interests, and there is no assurance that the results will be more than new patchwork. We have too long and too often demonstrated our incapacity for dealing with large problems involving people.

Dr. Glenn T. Seaborg, head of the Atomic Energy Commission, assuming the role of the clear-eyed optimist, says that we are getting past this stage. "In spite of the many foolish things we still do today, I think we are now much more analytical, farsighted and wiser than we have been, particularly concerning our own survival." One can only hope that he is right, for it would be just fine for everyone if we were wiser about our own survival. Humanity could probably "survive" on a planet covered with 6 feet of "Urbanit," or "survive" in the rotted hulks of cities spotted through a landscape ruined by housing tracts and other junk yards, but as what? Dr. Seaborg is probably right in suggesting that we are more "analytical and farsighted" than formerly, simply because we are beginning to be able to see what might be described as the "ravages of peace." This is the first moment in history, as far as I know, when war and peace have presented roughly similar problems of survival.

This survey of the object takes us far afield. It is typical of the situation in which we find ourselves that a survey of almost anything takes us far afield. "No man is an island" has taken on meanings John Donne never dreamt of. Everything is connected.

The future of the object, it should be clear by now, is to be seen in the present of the object. No matter what happens, the object in its transformations, disappearances, shrinkages, and proliferations will continue to reveal through its design the real concerns, priorities, values of the society which permits it to come into being.

We can see now, by examining the objects we do produce, what many of our culture's real values are. Man's ancient preoccupation with killing is still very much with us, and in this respect, so-called educational advances do not seem to have accomplished anything at all. This is probably because education is designed, like the object, to fit the society's real purposes. In the case of "defense" one has only to scan the astronomical budgets to see what the society's purposes are. These purposes are identical for the U.S. and the USSR and presently, no doubt, China. If one of the new nations should show signs of a peaceable disposition, there are master salesmen from both the West and East to parade tempting samples of military equipment for sale on very reasonable terms. These weapons are among the most sophisticated designs we produce, the most disciplined, the most elegant, the most beautiful, and they clearly reveal the very high priorities assigned for their design and manufacture.

The other truly great objects to which we can point are those made for scientific exploration and for the increase of our physical power over Nature. Since both of these are connected with war-making potential, we are really looking at one large category, the contents of which are either antipeople or nonpeople. In some ways the immense collection of objects in these related categories is uncomfortably reminiscent of the Egypt of the Pharaohs: huge projects totally unrelated to the needs or aspirations of the population, an obsession with death (it's on television, right now), wars, of course, and a rigid control over the population.

Below the dizzying heights of design excellence expressed in spacecraft, ballistic missiles, and particle accelerators, we find ourselves in the world of objects made for hundreds of millions of consuming individuals. Here, if we look hard enough, there are some admirable things to be found, but taking all the objects generally available, the landscape they form is mediocre, with extremes on the low end (mass housing, for instance) worse than anything ever perpetrated by earlier cultures. Boris Pushkarev, chief planner for the New York Regional Plan Association, puts it this way ". . . we find that the beautiful objects of our contemporary man-made environment tend to be grouped at the extreme ends of the scale, the micro and the macro, while the intermediate range, the so-called human scale, contains most of the ugliness."

Objects are always precise reflections of value systems, not because they are new versions of the old crystal ball, but because their forms reveal the degree of concern with which the design problem was tackled. Top priority objects are developed under extreme pressure, nourished by unlimited funds, and designed by the most brilliant problem-solvers. Such objects always impress us as beautiful for reasons discussed earlier.

Low-priority items do not attract the best talents since the problems are not that challenging. The pressures are not so great and the funds are anything but unlimited. The technology used in such devices rarely represent breakthroughs, but rather adaptions of discoveries made at the high-priority levels. Furthermore, the ultimate test is not life or death, which tends to sharpen wits to their finest point, nor is the judge of excellence the enemy's Chiefs of Staff. The judge, for such objects, is the consumer.

The modern consumer, poor little alienated bastard, is the most upward-mobile character who ever lived, but his problem is that he isn't quite sure where "up" is. His new affluence, a heady brew compounded of some cash in the bank and a large amount of installment credit, teaches him that the basis of status is dollars and there is precious little in his environment to suggest anything else. The central philosophy of a technocentric culture is based on a faith in "efficiency," in its most narrow and localized sense, and in quantity. The effects of this philosophy are to make people feel helpless and insignificant, to encourage conformity, to cripple the faculties needed for living a full life, and to discourage both thinking and feeling. People, in this context, tend to become objects themselves—things—and hence their judgment in such matters as design is not reliable.

If further transformations of the object are to take place—changes caused by a new concern for human needs and qualities—it is obvious that this can happen only if people and their values change. People never change simply because they would like to change, but because new situations present new promises and threats to which they react. We are thus confronted by the old circle, vicious or beneficial, in which situations and people are modified through interaction until something new emerges on the scene. Such transformations are now going on at a constantly accelerating rate, and viewing with alarm, deploring and exhorting, contrasted with this massive process, are nothing more than parlor games for the faint of heart and pseudo-intellectuals. The only constructive behavior possible within the modern maelstrom is based on obser-

Few artworks on the modern scene have made as great an impact as Warhol's soup can. Part of its appeal is shared by the whole Pop Art movement: making the familiar and unnoticed become strange and highly visible. It also functions as a subversive symbol, hinting that the item sold is more significant than the people who make it. Campbell's Soup, Andy Warhol, 1965. Oil silkscreen on canvas, 36 1/8 × 24 1/8. Collection of The Museum of Modern Art, New York; Elizabeth Bliss Parkinson Fund.

vation, reaction, change of attitudes, action.

Even the mass so bitingly described by Tom Wolfe as the *lumpen bourgeoisie* is in ferment. Everyone, during this extraordinary period, is developing new awarenesses and insights through experiencing the shake-ups produced by fast change. As one crisis after another comes up to confront us, the need to think is intensified.

The role of the designers—the millions who play a significant part in giving form to objects—can be played with intelligence and sensitivity or with heavy-handed stupidity. As the creators of the synthetic environment they are responsible for everything around us, which is no small responsibility. However, one can only speak of the designers' responsibilities with precision if it is understood that the role is also played by the client, public, and the professionals who execute the designs. Designers taken by themselves—architects, engineers, planners, industrial designers, and all the rest—are not a power center and hence cannot make the decisions—except through persuasion—which control their activity. In the period just passing, a dominant designer group has been the engineers, a breed not noted for its esthetic sophistication or its awareness of the consequences of its activity. Here too, the winds of change are blowing. An editorial in *Science and Technology* tells its readers that now that the engineers have pretty much fouled up the landscape they had better take another look and start repairing the damage. A pretty sentiment indeed, but it is going to take more than engineers to do it.

As the object continues to show occasional signs of disappearing, either into larger systems or growing heaps of "Urbanit," the possibility of future surprises for future objects is always there. One eminent sociologist, Dr. Nelson Foote, when queried by one of the industrial giants regarding possible consumer wants in the year 2000, studied the available data with his customary scholarly thoroughness and came back with the answer that the most desired commodity at that no-so-distant time might conceivably be . . . conversation.

STATEMENTS

The Office Revolution

In June of 1977 an office furniture system of our design, manufactured in Canada, was shown at Neocon, the annual show of contract furniture in Chicago. Some months later, probably because of the Canadian connection, I was asked to talk at a similar event in Toronto.

Futurology is in, these days, no matter what the area of activity, and the "office of the future" is as popular a theme in business circles as the growth of regulation. The trouble with almost all our predictions is the assumption that any possible future contains an even greater overload of technology than we are carrying now.

The question of present trends and possible futures is an important one because it looks as if the year 2000 is going to see practically everyone working in one kind of office or another. It is not the most attractive future I can imagine, for it would simply be another sample of a world closing in on itself. My feeling is that the core of the

Crowded open work areas, with private offices at the edges, were characteristic of the early 1900s; the pattern persisted into the 1940s. Typical office, c. 1910–1940. Collection of the Library of Congress.

problem is to rediscover productive inefficiency again, a notion which so far has not turned up many takers.

The contemporary office is about to undergo a series of transformations which might well continue into the middle of the 1980s, changes so massive and far-reaching that they can only be compared with the mechanization of agriculture. Not only the physical facility itself will be affected, but the effects will be felt throughout the society.

These changes are being brought about by a series of astonishing breakthroughs in electronics, a process of consolidation within the furniture industry, big alterations in the nature of office work and social attitudes as they impinge upon the behavior of business.

While we are accustomed to thinking of ourselves living in a period of constant change, the shifts in the way we live and work are not overnight affairs; some sections of the society move more rapidly than others. Also, the process of change is not mysterious: there are always forces working to bring it about, there are always reasons for what is happening, although it may take time to figure them out.

In an effort to fill out these statements and make them more intelligible, I am going to present you with a grossly oversimplified capsule history of the modern office. My main purpose in doing this is to make the point that this process of change is not moving at a constant speed, but is steadily accelerating. This is very important when one is dealing with an industry which is more attached to traditional procedures than many and which is not geared to high-speed responses to new situations.

Starting with the traditional office, inherited from the late 1800s, we can describe it as a place where the working equipment consisted of wood two-pedestal desks, some rolltop desks for the management, and an assortment of chairs and tables, also in wood.

In 1947 my firm designed a series of pieces for the office, also largely in wood, the most notable feature of which was the L-shaped desk. This format has been standard for quite a few years, and it takes a mental effort to remember that thirty years ago it was viewed by the industry as a radical departure. It took several years for the manufacturers to realize that the new Herman Miller product was acceptable to many architects and designers, but in the early 50s copies began to appear. I did not realize it at the time, but this product was the first step in the breakup of the old kneehole desk toward the format we now call the "workstation."

This happened in 1947. In the mid-1950s something

The first step in breaking up the old two-pedestal desk configuration, this group offered modular storage and an L at typing height. EOG marked the beginning of the evolution from desk to workstation. Executive Office Group, 1947, designed by George Nelson for Herman Miller, Inc.

else happened: a management consulting firm in Germany, the Quickborner Team, invented the open office landscape. The basis for this idea was not interior design or decoration, but *process*. The German group had studied the movement of paper—projects or jobs—through the office and then began to make layouts which reflected the flow of such material through the office. The results were strange looking, with curved lines of flow rather than straight lines and right-angle corners.

The effect of this radical planning concept on furniture was not visible for a long time, and when groups of enthusiasts began to lay out such offices, they were restricted to furniture designed to fit into smallish offices with square corners. Even with such handicaps, the new trend gained ground.

Once again, what had happened was not immediately apparent. The elimination of solid partitions looked like a way to save money, but it also raised problems like noise transmission, status, and so on, and these details obscured the revolutionary nature of what was going on.

The concept was revolutionary, not because it suggested laying out furniture in curved lines, but *because it suddenly connected paperwork and factory production*. In factories, planning based on the flow of materials and components had been accepted for years. Now for the first time, a hint was given that the evolution of the office was taking it in the direction of the factory. Nobody took the hint.

Nobody, that is, except Bob Propst of Herman Miller, and in 1967 the upheaval initiated by the Quickborner group was matched by a full-scale response, Action Office, a *system* rather than office furniture.

The industry looked at Miller's collection of screen partitions and wall-hung components and then went back to sleep for a while. Today, however, to buy an office furniture system that is not a Chinese copy of Propst's Action Office takes a bit of doing.

Around 1973 my firm found itself with a planning problem of unusual dimensions, a new headquarters building for the Aid Association for Lutherans, a fraternal life insurance company in Appleton, Wisconsin. The building was to have 500,000 square feet on two floors and the number of workstations required was close to 1,000. A survey of available systems was made, and I found myself dissatisfied with the labyrinths created by the panels and also with the claustrophobic effects that accompanied the proliferation of head-height partitions. The client shared these reservations and urged us to try for a more open, and presumably more humane, solution. This was done, and on approval of the designs we began work with Steel Equipment, a company primarily engaged in the manufacture of high-quality file cabinets. The office Workspaces system was finally presented at Neocon in Chicago during the summer of 1977. It was the first time in ten years, to the best of our knowledge, that a genuine alternative to the now-dominant panel systems was available.

Now let us look at the time scale. First, a period close to a century, during which the traditional wood desk underwent few significant modifications.

Then, in 1947, the L-shaped desk appeared, with the first hints of systems to come. In the mid-50s the open office concept appeared, but the furniture suitable for it had to wait until 1967. Then, ten years later, the Workspaces system was presented. You must note the shrinking times involved: first, about 100 years, then, from 1947 to 1967, we have twenty years. Then, from Action Office to Workspaces, ten years. Now what?

Now we are in the midst of a series of extraordinary breakthroughs in electronics, based initially on chip technology, which promise machines of fantastic capability in ultracompact forms and at affordable prices. These include electronic telephones with memories, word processing equipment, electronic editing devices, optical scanners, terminals where computers can be programmed in ordinary English—a host of devices now on the boards or already on sale.

These are going to be throwing people out of work,

Propst's radical office design for Herman Miller permitted, for the first time, the use of open planning in large spaces with screen partitions of various heights for privacy, sound absorption, and some storage. Note that everything, including desk surfaces, is supported by the structural screens. Action Office; courtesy Herman Miller, Inc.

just like earlier tools. Already, one can see the reduction of clerical staffs where the equipment is being installed. They are also going to be creating jobs, primarily for people with a different kind of training.

Beyond such happenings, which always take place when a major technical advance is made, we have to consider the effects on the physical structure of the office itself. These developments are raising a host of new questions: Will the "paperless office" really become a reality? What will this do to the manufacture of filing equipment? Will these events have a major effect on the open office concept? What will electronic mail do to office routines?

We have been thinking about these matters, naturally, since two of our major areas of activity, furniture design and space planning, are affected by all these new developments. Only recently we completed a study of probable trends in the design of offices. While the telephone company has no interest in furniture production, to the best of my knowledge, the systems it does make and now has in development do relate to the physical form of the office.

Still more recently we have begun more specific and detailed studies which could lead to experimental prototypes. These studies are being conducted with particular attention to the impact of electronics and to the growing demand for more humane working environments. "More humane" means, among other things, "less monotonous."

I would be very surprised if we were alone in these activities, and our own work strongly indicates that a workable model of the electronic office could go on stream in the early 80s.

Now we have to take a last look at the curve I have been building: it goes from 100 years to 20, then to 10, and now to about 5. I don't think there can be much argument about the fact of constant acceleration, for we are looking at an exponential curve which is about to run off the top of the chart. It is almost vertical and still rising. Eventually, the wave of breakthroughs in electronics will subside, but that time is still out in the future.

Earlier I used the phrase "electronic office." It is a convenient shorthand for what we are discussing, but it is also an oversimplification of what is really going on.

Technology is not the only force acting to transform working spaces. There is now enough time between us and the Quickborner office landscape concept of the 50s to see that this was not a dream of a new Garden of Eden or any other kind of garden. The "landscape," so-called, was in reality a speed-up of the transformation of the office from a kind of modified domestic interior to something that now appears to be no different in essence from a factory.

This means, among other things, that the distinctions between blue- and white-collar workers are beginning to break down, not only because salaries are no longer that different, but also because the size of office staffs in factories, relative to the size of production staffs, is growing. In both areas the bottom groups are being weeded out by technical innovation (automated quality control devices in factories is one example) while better trained people are moving in to take care of the jobs that are left.

If offices are becoming more like factories, the reverse is also happening. One may ask why such an evolution has to occur; why can't offices remain nice, cozy places full of fake Georgian woodwork and coffee-breaks? Some of the answers lie in the numbers. It is predicted that despite the electronic assists, office staffs will have doubled by 1985. This revolution seems to be going on because our communication needs have no visible limit.

A plausible picture of modern society in another generation might show 5 percent employed in agriculture, 5 to 10 percent in industrial production, and a very large number in the tertiary industries, all of which carry on their activities in offices. The volume of information flow would then be very large indeed, and factories are the only places we know which process large quantities effectively. Right now there are very large offices which fit all the descriptions of a factory except for their interior styling.

It is also a fairly safe guess that the styling is going to change, moving away from the furniture look toward something more industrial in character.

We get a clue to this when we look at electronic products in offices today. Mostly they are put on desks, because these provide the needed horizontal surfaces. Putting a terminal on a desk—both expensive items—seems rather silly when one thinks about it, for the terminal immobilizes the furniture and merely creates the need for another surface. The sensible way to deal with this problem is to provide stands of suitable dimensions, much as is done for light machine tools. As a matter of fact, this is what many electronic equipment producers are doing already.

As this solution begins to become visible in offices, some interesting questions come up: Are these equipment stands furniture or something else? Are they sold with the electronics or are they part of the furniture system? Who makes them? Are the stands and the furniture visually compatible? If not, which will be the preferred look?

To put it differently, if the equipment and its supporting stands have an industrial look and if the furniture has a different look, which is going to dominate? The answer is the look that has greater money value.

Another way to put the matter is to ask who has more status and power, the electronics industry giants or the furniture makers? There is no point in even asking these questions, for the answers are out there for all to see.

As the office moves in the direction of the factory, the furniture, for entirely different reasons, will begin to take on a look which would be at home in an industrial environment. Another aspect of this development is that the big manufacturers will get bigger, and the smaller ones will either get swallowed up or fall by the wayside. The primary advantage of bigness is not only, as we might imagine, the economies inherent in large-scale operations, but vastly superior management and marketing skills.

The largest North American producer in the field has sales of roughly $300 million. There are about a half-dozen with sales over $100 million. These are businesses which can afford to bring customers to their factories in private jets, exploit computerization in the factory and office, and which have been reaching out to foreign markets. They can also afford research, consultants in a variety of areas, and the marketing programs necessary today. Many of the small producers have yet to learn what marketing is. As in other industries, the gap between small and threatened and large and successful becomes wider. In the U.S. there are currently several large companies in difficulty, for even size is no protection when competitive tools include management skills, design, marketing in all its aspects, and access to money.

As the crunch develops, the competition will become keener, not more relaxed, and credit will become tighter for the weak enterprises. It takes no foresight to predict a North American office furniture business with consolidated factory sales of $2 to $3 billion and with 75–85 percent of the business done by a handful of large manufacturers. It is the same old pattern and it is emerging here for the same old reasons.

In this deadly serious battle for survival and domination, a few small companies may manage to stay in business, but they will have to meet at least one of two requirements: they will either produce merchandise in quantities that do not interest the big manufacturers, or they will make products at a quality level beyond the reach of the mass market. Such products will have to represent something very special in design and quality of performance. In the latter case, such companies may become tempting acquisitions, for reasons of prestige, diversification, or profit, but it is hard to imagine many small producers qualifying since the great majority relies almost exclusively on copying. The consolidation of furniture manufacturing will also push product design in directions which enable it to take maximum advantage of tooling and automation.

We now have two major trends: one, a move toward saturation with electronic equipment, and another, a growing pressure to reduce the number of manufacturers. From a styling point of view, both will lead us even further away from the fake Georgian paneling, so to speak, but what they do lead us to may be even worse in some respects, for the dominant trend in industry is a nonhuman or antihuman direction.

This takes us to a third factor, which is the response of people to developments they perceive as desirable or undesirable. The question we have to ask here, of course, is what kinds of people are going to respond or fail to respond. The tendency within industry, shown in an extreme form on the high-speed production lines, is to favor people who are docile, lacking in temperament or imagination, whose behavior is uniform and predictable. But people are not inanimate objects (Chaplin's "Modern Times" made this point many years ago), and there is a limit to their ability to tolerate such pressures.

A part of the Nelson Workspaces system, this movable conference unit is surrounded by acoustical panels and topped with a nylon umbrella as a ceiling. A curious spinoff is the conviction of many users that the space is "totally soundproof," although, as the photograph shows, this is obviously impossible. Courtesy Storwal International.

The increasing use of electronic equipment has created a growing demand for flexible access to power and communication lines. The Sunar system makes the solution for these requirements a central feature of its design. Plug-in frames above the raceway can carry lightweight sound-absorbing elements and ambient lighting units. Designer: Douglas Ball; photo courtesy Sunar Limited.

The tendency in the society in general, which became visible with the counterculture explosions of the 60s, is in direct opposition to the traditional attitudes of industry. The growing interest in sensory experience, which covers an enormous range from the drug culture to things like transcendental meditation, yoga, jogging, bicycling, and cooking, is leading more and more people into a search for a better quality of life. They are a minority, but a very articulate one, and their numbers are going to increase.

The confrontation of two distinct ways of being is a contemporary reality and it isn't going to go away. Furthermore, managements are also being affected, with more and more companies accepting the view that humane working conditions are desirable and that they have community and environmental responsibilities.

Societies today have people problems to a degree that earlier societies did not. For one thing, people know more. Modern people have inherited a number of ideas which took hold in the 18th century, having to do with equalities of certain kinds, rights to life and liberty, a license to pursue happiness, and so on. They know about poor boys who became rich, and it matters less to them today how they became rich than in the days of Horatio Alger and the pure Protestant work ethic. As affluence has spread in the industrial and mineral-rich countries, so have experiences. People by the millions visit foreign places, read paperbacks, listen to LP records, sign up for adult education, watch public and commercial television. They can still be manipulated on a huge scale, to be sure, but the thrust generally is in the direction of greater freedom in every sense. The gradually emerging awareness that freedom demands responsibility will become a strong force in taking populations to a level of greater maturity.

At this point we are looking at three ingredients in what may appropriately be described as a revolution in the office: we have the electronic developments; the tendency for furniture and equipment to evolve rapidly as sophisticated industrial systems and products; and the growing interest in what we may call "humane working environments."

Under the influence of the last, we are beginning to ask questions, many of which are new to us: What is a humane office? What is the connection, if any, with efficiency? What are the real, desired values in work? What are the roots of high morale? What is the role of status symbols? How do we learn more about predicting people's responses to environments?

My own guess, in looking at the three main influences on the further development of the office, is that what we discover in the people area is the most likely to take us to breakthroughs. Innovation in electronics is beyond the capability of anyone outside the field itself, and using the products as they come out is going to be a relatively simple matter of finding appropriate ways to install them. With human motivation and behavior still a dark and mysterious area, anything we discover here is bound to have an effect on both furniture and interior architecture, not to mention planning patterns. It looks as if a new breed of psychologist may presently be in demand.

The reason for all the current interest in the office today does not lie in the natural interest of designers in new problems, although this is a significant element, but in the immense and growing visibility of the office as a *primary place of employment*. It was Peter Drucker, I believe, who predicted that the current ratios of production and office workers in industry may well be reversed by the mid-1980s. In any industrial society this represents a social upheaval of truly enormous dimensions, and the side effects will be felt in every section of society.

For the professionals in the field—manufacturers, marketing people, production engineers, designers, and others—these sketch images of what may be right ahead of us suggest that there are some uncommonly interesting opportunities, although there are manufacturers with whom I would not care to change places.

When talking about possibilities for the office of the day after tomorrow, it is almost impossible to avoid referring to trends, tendencies, evolutionary patterns. The danger in this kind of talk is that we come to view change as the outcome of large, impersonal forces and to conclude that there is nothing we can do about them. There is some truth in this feeling, of course, because the forces *are* large and impersonal. But at the root of all change you find people, who function as large groups—entire populations—and as individuals.

The movements we see as trends are created by people; they do not just happen, and the role of Herman Miller is particularly instructive in this respect: the office built of screen partitions with attached components might have just happened, but it didn't. A designer with vision and a manufacturer with uncommon nerve *made* it happen. The same holds for everything we are going to see in the very exciting period of rapid change which is now upon us.

The freedom to make important changes is the mirror image of the responsibility to humanize our technology.

The Universal Necessity

For several years the Canadian Government's Office of Design has jointly sponsored a series of lectures and seminars for manufacturers, with Electrohome Ltd. Speakers are always invited from abroad and in 1974 I was tapped for the job. This essay is a modification of several talks, and it is in effect a kind of primer, an elementary statement of thoughts about designers, particularly in their relations with manufacturers.

I lectured in several cities and the whole thing was very pleasant. The experience left me with the feeling, however, that whatever it is manufacturers need, it is not lecturers and seminars in their present form.

The real problem is how to build bridges of communication and understanding between groups—designers and manufacturers—whose mentalities and skills are different. The problem is not Canadian, or even North American; and it is not even restricted to the private industry of the

West, for I have heard an influential Russian describe the situation in identical terms. I see here a splendid opportunity for some idealistic and perceptive young people in design and business. The problem, regardless of who tackles it, is well worth the trouble.

Design has become a matter of interest for business and industry. The big surprise in this growing interest is not that it exists today, but that it took so long to appear. Design, after all, is a very basic activity, as old as mankind. You cannot build or make anything without a design of some sort, even if it is nothing more than some scratches in beach sand, or a glint in someone's eye. Every piece of the entire man-made environment had to be designed before it could be made.

It is not without profit to concern ourselves briefly with some speculations on the reasons for the disappearance of an ancient, universal activity as a recognized necessity. We should also consider what put new life into it, so that today design is seen as a legitimate and effective tool for business and industry.

I can give you my own picture of what happened: through thousands of years men made the things they needed, doing the best they could with available materials and traditional techniques. Since *making* was the visible act, design was taken for granted. Furthermore, because changes came very slowly during the thousands of years of handicraft activity, designing was largely copying and modifying. Things got made on the basis of familiar, traditional models. Innovation was not popular, or even very respectable. If you were a farmer who was going to build some furniture during the long winter months, you did not *design* it: you looked for a pattern or model to follow. Houses were built from books prepared for carpenters and cabinet makers.

Since the attitudes of modern industry—the attitudes, that is, not always the standard practice—frown on copying (which we often call design piracy or plagiarism) we may wonder why copying was once so respectable and what happened to produce its fall from grace.

A reasonable explanation is that for the overwhelming majority of its time on earth mankind lived in very close proximity to Nature. In Nature, all designs of all organisms are based on *reproductions* of types or species. Mutations, which are Nature's equivalent of innovations, have an overwhelming history of failure. It is true that evolution proceeds on the basis of successful mutations, but statistically, successful innovations are extremely rare. Nature is very conservative.

Handicraft societies are very conservative too. It takes years of painful work to acquire the skills needed to make a chair, or the blades with which one cuts moldings in wood. The only practical way to learn is to work as an apprentice for someone who has those skills. The pupil tries to copy the master: it is the best way to learn. Changes do occur, but, as in Nature, these changes are small, and it takes decades or even centuries for a significant change to become visible.

Consider the bow and arrow as an example. What wood for the bow? How is it shaped? What makes a good bowstring? How long did it take for someone to think of putting feathers on an arrow? How many years to go from the primitive bow to the laminated bow of the Parthians, or to the crossbow of the Middle Ages? Take any such familiar object, make a time-lapse film of its evolution and, in many cases, a ten-minute film will show millennia of copying, small improvements, and the ultimate development of a highly perfected design.

We, of course, do not work on such time scales. In less than a century we went from the first flight to supersonic planes and rockets; from gunpowder to fusion bombs; from unlimited natural riches to the spectre of planetary depletion and the exhaustion of natural resources.

In a handicraft society, everyone knows how things are made and designed, because they see it happen. The shoemaker (who actually *made* shoes), the silversmith, the cabinet maker, the blacksmith, and the baker were all right there in town or village. Kids grew up watching these people work. They also appreciated the difference between a good design and a bad one, because the common criterion was performance rather than taste or esthetics, and the designs they saw taking shape had been selected out over centuries. Designs had to be good: there was neither the wealth nor the energy to indulge in expensive fantasies. Things had to be done economically, with few tools and with few hands.

When the Industrial Revolution exploded in the middle of the 18th century, suddenly a way of doing things that had been valid for centuries came under attack. Machines took over work that had always been done by hand. The role of the craftsman, who was traditionally maker *and* designer, was split. He became a worker, making what others had designed.

Since people had no place to turn for their models except to the existing inventory of handicraft designs, the first products of the machine tended to copy the earlier designs. But soon it became evident that machine production was different from hand production and that machines tended to produce shapes that had no counterpart in the world of hand production. In the middle of the 19th century, for example, England produced great greenhouses of prefabricated metal and factory-made glass. The crowning achievement in this area was the Crystal Palace of 1851. Others included bridges, railroad stations, and exhibition structures such as the Eiffel Tower.

As we trace these revolutionary developments, it should be remembered that the first evidence of a new machine esthetic appeared where there was no precedent. The ancients had not built metal bridges, or 1000-foot towers, or huge glass buildings, or grain silos, or huge factories, or railroad terminals. So, for the design of such new objects, there was nothing to copy, except details. Thus, we discover an enormous railroad terminal shed of metal with Gothic or Roman details in cast iron. But the shed itself was something truly new under the sun.

This was not the case with small objects. A cast-iron stove, for instance, still got feet that looked like the paws of lions or the claws of eagles.

Where the object had something familiar about it, the handicraft look prevailed. Our world of antiques is full of Victorian relics that demonstrate this.

Along with this kind of inappropriate copying, the idea grew up that household objects made in factories were cheap and shoddy. The expression "Grand Rapids furniture" was an expression of disapproval. Socially acceptable things were made by hand, which, of course, limited their use to the rich. So the way to show that you were rich was to have things crafted by hand. For the not-so-rich, who have always worked very hard to emulate their betters, the machine-made fakes which pretended to be handmade became the favorite means of showing one's social status. This is still with us, although it has become rather negligible in its applications. People still buy grandfather clocks with electric motors and useless pendulums, period furniture of all types; and there is a market for television sets housed in cabinets which claim some ancestry such as Italian Renaissance, American Colonial, or French Provincial.

By the early years of the 20th century there were people stirring, most conspicuously in England and Germany, who pointed out that machine forms were just as valid and hence just as respectable as the old ones. By the early 20s there was the Bauhaus school in Germany, which produced all sorts of common objects, such as chairs, made of modern materials like steel tubing with a look which clearly stated that these were machine-made products.

In other words, it took from around 1750 to about 1950 before great masses of ordinary people found the new forms produced by machines to be familiar, even beautiful.

Obviously, during these two centuries of confusion about how an object should be put together and what it should look like, the traditional designer had little to contribute. Architects continued to pour old wine into new bottles. Canada, the United States, and Europe are full of buildings which pretend to be Greek or Roman or Gothic, although these styles were no longer meaningful in their new applications. Real changes in architecture came from the engineers who didn't see themselves as designers spearheading an esthetic revolution, but simply as men engaged in solving problems in a realistic and economical manner. This practical, nuts-and-bolts attitude was closer to that of traditional design than the gentlemanly fantasies of the architects, designers, and decorators.

The designer came back into the picture—now as a consultant to business and industry—only when the machine esthetic, the acceptance of new forms that originated in factory production, became familiar and acceptable to large numbers of customers. We can put the date of the resurrection of the designer at about 1930.

Today, almost half a century later, thousands of producers are still trying to get used to the idea that the designer, still regarded by many as an esthetically oriented type who puts consumer frostings on industrial cakes, belongs with management and production.

While the industrial designer works in a manner which is basically traditional, his environment is vastly different. New elements include the existence of immense anonymous publics, of advertising and marketing. The old designer-craftsman worked for people he knew, and he created his artifacts to meet their specific needs. The designer today is working in an atmosphere which is characterized by the drive to create markets through arousing consumer wants.

Societies produce designs for a variety of reasons. They design to survive, to express their deepest beliefs, and to embellish existence. Survival designs include weapons for attack and as means of defense. The medieval castle and fortified town were survival designs. A house, at least in cold climates, is a survival design. Designs which express a faith include churches and temples. Designs produced to embellish existence cover a vast spectrum, and each of us could list dozens of examples.

Of these three major categories, designs for survival are always the best and the most powerful, for the simple reason that one tends to turn out a better job if one's life hangs on the results. This, I imagine, is why God was not only the first designer, but is still the best. Everything in Nature, certainly every living organism, is a survival design.

Any inspection of natural organisms, whether large or microscopic, can produce some truly astonishing insights for anyone interested in a better comprehension of the design process.

The most dramatic aspect of design in Nature is that each organism has virtually *no freedom in determining its form*. Our idea of "creative freedom" seems to have no counterpart in Nature, where all designs emerge as responses to environmentally determined necessities. We also learn that, regardless of our habit of considering many organisms as "beautiful," Nature seems to have no interest whatever in good taste or beauty. An organism either survives or fails, and that is that. Furthermore, the outstanding characteristic of natural forms is economy. There is no example, to my knowledge, of superfluous decoration in Nature. The most is always done with the least, and the least, in the organic world, still goes way beyond anything we have been able to produce. There is no man-made product comparable to, say, a dandelion stalk, which holds up a flower, transmits fluids as needed, can bend without breaking, and weighs almost nothing. We come closest to these fantastic performances in the IC chips, but generally, we have a long way to go.

Survival design has produced some spectacular results in the case of insects which can camouflage themselves. The Sumatran leaf moth, to pick one out of thousands of examples, has wings which duplicate exactly the veining of the leaves on which it rests. The veins have "painted" highlights and shadows to create the illusion of three dimensions. It has a set of tiny muscles whose sole function is to make the wings flutter exactly like leaves in a breeze. And all this is done by a self-duplicating organism which weighs a fraction of an ounce.

It is a matter of common observation that predatory animals have eyes set in front so they can see their prey, that grazing animals have eyes set at the sides of the head so that their fisheye view of the world will give advance notice of danger.

Over and over again, as we speculate on design in Nature, we are led to the conclusion that organisms and their environments form an unbreakable unity. Orchids grow in jungles, but Alpine meadows abound in plants like the edelweiss. Polar bears and penguins are not encountered in Amazon rain forests, nor are alligators and anacondas discovered in the Arctic. Furthermore, these relationships are more complex than simple cause-and-effect mechanisms: they are two-way or, perhaps, twenty-way-streets, systems of great delicacy which are always adjusting themselves to stay in balance.

Because design in Nature is always trimmed to a limit of economy, the lines between survival and extinction are thin. A study of migratory birds showed that those which made the trip across intervening bodies of water invariably had bone structures weighing only a few grams less than the skeletons of the birds which failed. Good design, in the case of these birds, equals survival.

No animal has the freedom to design itself. A hyena cannot decide to become a lion. So our little foray into the natural world brings up an interesting question: who does design these animals? If a creature cannot design itself, someone or something must do it. The protective camouflage of a leaf moth or a stick insect cannot possibly be coincidence. How does it happen?

Forced to abandon the theory that God figured it out and did it all in six days of work, we are driven to a very strange notion: this is that *the prey is designed by the predator*. The mechanism for this is not simple, we can be sure, but we can describe it simply. If a given bird feeds on certain kinds of insects, it is only going to eat those insects it can see. Hence, those creatures which have some resemblance to their backgrounds are less likely to be eaten than those which can easily be found. The survivors pass on their traits to their offspring. And, as mutations occur from time to time, some will inevitably make the insects even harder to find. These survivors pass on their traits, and so on and on. Give this process a million years, and you end up with insects which are extraordinarily hard to find.

It is possible that the predator is also designed by its prey. Given a group of leopards living in an area where there are gazelles, we may assume that those leopards best equipped to catch gazelles are most likely to have a chance to pass on their characteristics to their descendants.

Now how does all this apply to designs made by people? In the military area, something similar appears to go on. If you have groups of fighter-bombers in the same area as groups of ground-to-air missiles, it seems safe to assume that if too many planes are hit by the missiles, they will have to be sent back for design modifications. On the other hand, if too many launching sites are knocked out by the planes, someone will have to do something about the missiles. Since weaponry falls into the survival area, the efforts to maintain a balance will go on regardless of cost.

The message we get from all examples of survival design is that the "creative freedom" we sometimes talk about is as nothing compared with *an effective response to the pressures of necessity*. There is also a hint that wars may be won or lost as often by designers as by generals.

The notion that the prey is designed by the predator seems to hold very often in Nature and in the sphere of military action. What about less critical situations?

We might do worse than speculate briefly about a building. Most buildings are not primarily survival designs, although in these latitudes we can hardly dispense with them. But the example I am thinking of has no trace of survival needs in its program: this is a Greek temple of the 5th or 6th century B.C., say, the Parthenon, since we have all heard of it.

The Greek climate is relatively mild, and nobody lived in the Parthenon anyway. We might place it in the category of "acts of faith." Athena, the goddess of the temple, was a member of the Olympian elite. Nobody in Athens at the time would have seen anything odd or wasteful in putting up an expensive temple on the Acropolis in her honor. But what of the design? Can we say, in such an instance, that the prey is designed by the predator? It doesn't fit: there is no prey. What we can say is that the object (in this case the temple) and its environment form a unity.

The architect for the Parthenon was Iktinos. He had been given the job in recognition of his talents and, presumably, he was "free" to design the temple as he saw fit. But here again, with even a superficial probe of the situation, we find that his freedom was very limited. Everyone in Greece knew what a proper temple was: it was a structure with a gable roof, covered with tiles; it had columns on all four sides, and all it needed inside was room for a larger-than-life statue of the deity. There was no assembly of a congregation indoors. The citizens of Athens also knew that a temple should have sculptured friezes and pediments illustrating stories related to the god or goddess. Effectively, the architect had two choices of material: wood and marble. He also had very good stonecutters available; the temple was probably considered too important for wood.

In very much the same way, an architect today, entrusted with a highrise office tower, finds that his choices are limited to materials and techniques available at reasonable prices and to forms generally accepted as proper for the purpose. City ordinances impose all sorts of limitations. We take it for granted that such a building today has windows that do not open, that its walls are curtain enclosures of lightweight insulating panels, or perhaps precast concrete frames, and that when the structure gets to the top floor, it stops.

In both of these examples we find that object and environment, which includes not only landscape, climate, and available materials, *but also technologies and ideologies*, tend to become mirror images of each other.

In neither case is it likely that the architects are particularly frustrated by their lack of freedom. One doubts if Iktinos could have even conceived of a nonstandard temple, and the architect today accepts the limitations surrounding his work.

Another point on the subject of freedoms and limitations: it is more than likely that the *limitations* are a major reason for the high degree of perfection reached by the Parthenon and for the sophistication shown in recent skyscrapers. It is only when the same problem is solved over and over again that the object finally reaches its most elegant form. The same goes on today for aircraft and superhighways: each successful change becomes the springboard for the next development.

When changes take place in the design of man-made objects or of natural organisms, it is usually because something has happened to the environment. The air-conditioned highrise building is now under attack because it is wasteful of energy. A study of the World Trade Center in New York revealed that these twin 100-story towers consume as much energy as the entire city of Schenectady, N.Y., which has a population of 80,000 people. Given the energy crisis, we can be sure that this new factor will have a visible effect on the design of future office structures.

A shift in social values can have the same effect. There are critics who will claim that, while the design process employed in the Parthenon and highrise buildings is roughly the same, the resemblances stop right there. The towers, they say, are perfect expressions of the Age of the Body Count, ideal housings for bureaucracies and alienated individuals, while the Parthenon was a conspicuous celebration of all that the Greeks found divine in man.

When we slide down the scale of objects until we come to consumer products, there are also questions of the predator designing the prey. The motorcar manufacturers tell us that their big, flashy cars are accurate responses to consumer demands. Critics like Ralph Nader tell us that this is not really so, that the consumer has been so victimized by the manufacturers, and given so few real choices, that he has to buy something he might not really need or want.

We could go on indefinitely, multiplying examples of the interactions between artifacts and their environments. The moral of all this is that *design for industry is more than styling for mass taste*. To whatever degree the manufacturer can relate what he is doing to processes and principles that cover long periods of time, the more he expands his vision of what is really going on in the world, the better are his chances of establishing programs which lead to successful design solutions.

I have been referring to design and designers as if there were a kind of automatic challenge and response, and that individual insights and talents were inoperative, or at least inconsequential. I must correct this impression if it does exist. An illustration is the case of the commercial plane. The world's major airlines fly North American or European planes. Nobody buys Russian commercial planes except the Russians and countries within the sphere of Soviet influence. The reasons are that the Russian planes are not as well designed, not as economical to fly, as the others. Whether this reflects Russian incompetence or indifference I cannot say, but clearly, while all planes are equal in that they are able to fly, transposing George Orwell's famous phrase, some are more equal than others. Responses to surrounding conditions are necessary, but by no means automatic. The intelligence and sensitivity of the response and the motivations of institutions make a big difference.

In case the thought has not occurred to you, let me stress the point that institutions such as corporations do indeed shift their motivations with the passage of time. It was high corporate taxes, plus scientific curiosity, plus defense and space projects that led to America's massive expenditures on research. Current corporate concerns with the quality of the environment are relatively new, but they are becoming very real.

I have another example for you: ten or fifteen years ago, it was standard procedure for our clients, when confronted with an innovative design proposal, to become alarmed by the risk and to remind us that "after all, we are in business to make a profit." Nobody tells us this anymore. The new message is that business must indeed make a profit, but there are other reasons for being in business. This represents an extraordinary shift in attitudes. What has happened?

There are no answers I could swear to in a courtroom, but some theories seem valid. The counterculture, created through the post-war decades by millions of angry and rebellious young people, was based on values which were essentially nonmaterialistic. Many of these people are now grown up, and hold positions of power and responsibility. The values of their youth persist.

Another element is the new and powerful pressure to correct environmental damage, an awareness that the industrial world cannot go on indefinitely squandering irreplaceable resources. So there is an uneasy feeling that our earlier visions of unlimited growth cannot be maintained indefinitely. And it is in the nature of the human animal that if you take one goal away, he will presently find another.

Finally, I believe that in an advanced industrial society, business becomes the best game in town, so to speak. Our upper-class young do not aspire to Church or Army as respectable careers. And if business is really the liveliest and most challenging game around, its basic appeal is the fact that, aside from the much advertised attraction of endlessly growing profits, it is exciting and rewarding *as a game*. Also, as many have found, the satisfactions of doing something regarded as socially useful and rewarding can be substantial. I cannot vouch for the accuracy of these guesses, although they must hold some truth; in any case, they suggest that in a period of eroded profits and other problems, and even if our values are shifting from materialistic to nonmaterialistic, business remains an exciting and rewarding activity.

One value of the designer who is worth his salt lies in the simple fact that *he sees problems differently from management*. I spent many years as a consultant to one of the divisions of General Electric and was interested to note that when GE management talked about the "customer" it meant the retailer. For the designer, the customer is always the end user. The difference is that the retailer's image of the perfect product is something that keeps moving off his shelves, while the user's concern has to do with direct value and performance. Working for the retailer will rarely lead to innovation, whereas thinking about the needs of the user almost always opens up the possibility of improvement. Manufacturers spend a lot of energy keeping their dealers happy. What the designer does is bring in a comparable concern for the buyer.

In making this distinction, I am not suggesting that the designer is stuffed with virtue and that his client is a callous, greedy fellow, but simply that the manufacturer never meets the end user, for all practical purposes. Distributors tell him how the public responds to his efforts. Similarly, the designer's concern for the ultimate customer is a reflection of his situation: he has to design or redesign a product, and about the only way he can get a grip on the problem is to imagine himself as the user.

This concern with the user and his needs is not an unalloyed blessing so far as the manufacturer is concerned. It can lead to radical proposals for change. Yet without this occasionally disturbing element, business growth may be stifled.

It requires cool judgment to determine the value of a proposed innovation. There is always the possibility that the designer's estimate may be incorrect. Detroit still talks about the spectacular failures of the old Chrysler Airflow and the Ford Edsel. And yet it is tempting to try something new, for this is an element in business competition. To deal with this complex of risks and temptations, the team approach offers safeguards.

The designer, whether team or individual, is the latest of the human resources available to business in its eternal struggle to remain successfully competitive.

Eames lounge chair and ottoman. Courtesy Herman Miller, Inc.

Plagiarism, or How to Be Creative When No One Is Looking

The Business and Institutional Furniture Manufacturers' Association (BIFMA) is a trade group whose members manufacture furniture and equipment for offices. It is impressive because its members have the most advanced production methods and the best design, by and large, in the furniture industry. The problem was how to respond to an invitation to speak at its annual meeting in 1976.

For whatever reason, it struck me that plagiarism would be a lively subject, since the practice is widespread throughout industry, and the differences between lip service and behavior are conspicuous. Of all the subjects one might pick, this was easily the most touchy and yet I felt it to be important for the vitality of the industry. The problem of how to deal with the subject matter was resolved by directing the discussion to the question of how plagiarism affects the plagiarist, and this saved me from a possible polite lynching.

Actually, having to write it all down was very instructive, for what I had always seen as a black and white case turned out to be very complex, and richer in its ramifications than I had imagined.

The activity is so old, so totally diffused, that entire vocabularies have grown up to describe it. Plagiarism, which has the special meaning of theft of another's work and taking credit for it, was familiar to the Romans. *Plagiarius* is Latin for a kidnapper. Current U.S. words are "ripoff" and "knockoff." "Design piracy" recalls those unreconstructed characters who roamed the seas under the *Jolly Roger*; their land-based descendants are beyond counting. Then there is the umbrella word "copying" which covers an entire spectrum of moralities and legalities. The student painter who goes to a museum and makes a copy is considered a serious artist dedicated to the improvement of his skills. The man who makes copies of a Vermeer and sells them as originals is a rascal. Forgery is a specialized skill of a high order but is considered reprehensible when applied to the production of currency. In Japan, as *The New York Times* has reported, where small appliances are concerned, "competitors are quick to copy any hot-selling item. . . . Product cycles are much shorter in Japan because copies—good copies—proliferate. . . faster than anywhere else in the world."

It is hard to know what position to take on this last item, for it suggests that product evolution goes faster in Japan than elsewhere *because* of the intensity of the knocking-off process. It thus appears to be one of the explanations of Japan's success in world markets. Copying in Japan also has its own special traditional flavor; I was once shown a magnificent piece of porcelain in Tokyo, with an astronomical price, which was proudly described as a 17th-century Japanese copy of a Chinese original. It was an expression of reverence for a masterpiece.

There is another word in the vocabulary of copying: "infringement," and with this a new set of conditions comes into view. One can only infringe a design, or any other intellectual property, which already has some degree of legal protection, such as a patent or copyright. Sometimes the protection, while legal enough, is illusory because the cost of protecting the property may be prohibitive.

The nature of patents can be illuminating, because the distinctions between what is patentable and what is not show up the real values of the society in which patents are applied for. Our belief that everything of significance can be weighed and measured shows up in the priority given mechanical patents. Things are far more difficult for an "intellectual property" which does not lend itself to some form of mechanical exclusivity. Another kind of protective system which covers the work of composers and playwrights is ASCAP, a policing organization set up to keep an eye on the uses of the work of its members.

It is when we come to design that protection gets exceedingly difficult, in part because few products display mechanical uniqueness or, as in the case of furniture, are created at a very modest technical level and rely on their comfort, or utility, or esthetic appeal in dealing with their markets. A case in point is the 1967 Action Office system developed by Herman Miller from designs by Robert Propst. If a visitor to the Chicago Merchandise Mart goes to the ninth floor, which is devoted to the display of contract furniture, he can see the original Action Office in Herman Miller's showroom and about two dozen systems in other manufacturers' showrooms that in some instances are so close to the original that only a professional could tell them apart. Design piracy would be a correct description for what has happened here, although some of the manufacturers have introduced elements of their own devising.

Detroit's cars fall into a roughly similar category as far as styling goes, and the public has become accustomed to the slavish way in which the leaders are followed. When tail fins were the thing, all cars had them; opera windows, vinyl roofs, and other features have enjoyed equally wide emulation. In the automobile industry it is taken for granted that every manufacturer has spies in the others' design departments.

Most TV commercials, whether for soft drinks, foods, toothpaste, detergents, or deodorants are copies of successful ones. Networks copy networks. Best-selling books trigger imitations.

One area in which every trick imaginable is used to steal technical information is, of course, the military, and Heaven only knows how many international spy thrillers would have perished unborn if this were not the case. Here copying has the immunity from criticism that goes with activity at the highest levels of power: the U.S. government offers money to Soviet pilots who defect, if they bring their MiGs with them. The Soviets bribe government employees in other countries. All this is seen as a complex and dangerous game demanding personal courage and a high degree of professional skill. The justification, presumably, is that national survival is involved.

The loudest outcries about the unethical nature of design piracy come, as one would expect, from those least able to protect their creations. Small items, including furniture and any number of household accessories, fall into this category. Part of the noise made by the victims is due to frustration, for so far there are few defenses. Some years ago I sat as an expert witness on a case in which an ingenious and economical molded plastic coat hanger had been copied by a competitor. What I remember mainly about the case was the utter indifference of the judge to the obvious similarities. Like most educated people he was a visual illiterate, and he was genuinely puzzled, or so it seemed, by all the fuss about something as inconsequential as a design. For such individuals, who lack the remotest notion of what the design process is about, a design is something that just happens to be there. Such people are truly the new barbarians and the seats of the mighty are filled with them.

The reason plagiarism so frequently comes up as a subject for discussion is that it hurts the originator financially, and the damage is sometimes great enough to wreck or seriously damage the business involved.

Developing a new product is a genuinely risky affair and most manufacturers avoid the process if they possibly can. One of the best ways to avoid the risk and the costs is, of course, to steal the design of an item that is already a market success.

Crime may not pay, but the savings made by piracy can be very substantial. The innovator starts with an idea of something new, and he must go through a series of stages before he can tell whether the idea will work or not. Sketches, models, engineering calculations, estimates of market, and all the rest are part of the preliminary work. Eventually there are appearance models and working prototypes, then pilot runs, the whole debugging process, revisions to reduce cost, and, finally, a first production run.

Then the expenses start up again: the product has to be packaged, taken to market, demonstrated to salespeople and dealers, introduced to the press. All these costs go into the sales price of the product and they can be very high. The ripoff operator starts at the end of the process, with the production sample. This can be reengineered and subtly downgraded, reduced in price, and introduced to susceptible retailers as "just the same" for less money.

If the originator tries to protect his creation by heavy advertising and promotion, he may get away with it if he is big enough, but more often than not, the copy gets a free ride on the advertising too. The path of righteousness has never been smooth, and for the innovative manufacturer it can have more potholes than a New York street.

My own most vivid memory of this kind of thing came many years ago when we designed a line of hybrid office furniture, built of both wood and metal. The design apparently caught on, for within months there were some twenty-six copies on the market, some of them better made and all of them cheaper. The original manufacturer was forced to drop the line before the year was out. Total sales of the imitations were in the millions.

Another case involved a product we called the "Bubble Lamp," a hanging fixture made by spraying a self-webbing plastic on a wire frame. We were not able to patent the design. Again, there were about two dozen copies on the market within a few months. This time, however, we were less naive and persuaded the manufacturer to put an initial price of $50 on an item he could sell for $30. The product did very well from the start, and with the extra profit all development costs were amortized with great rapidity, which meant that when the copies began to appear, the manufacturer was able to compete easily by cutting his price. The lamps, as a result of this action, were able to stay on the market for over twenty-five years and are selling today better than ever.

These stories do not always have so happy an ending, and they vary all over the lot depending on the nature of the product and the size of the industry. The automotive producers, for instance, do not seem to have much concern about the design piracy in which they all indulge, since marketing is such a big factor in sales, and items like mass-produced cars rarely show spectacular innovations. Oddly enough, radical change is frowned upon by the car makers because one of their main objectives is to hold their customers. Since people keep cars for an average of about three years, drastic change in that period would lower the trade-in value of the old car. Thus it has become standard practice to make a big thing out of inconsequential styling changes. Automobile advertising is full of examples.

Plagiarism, whatever one's view of the ethics, seems to come down to someone getting hurt financially. In the case of the Ming porcelain copied by a Japanese craftsman, there was no commercial element: the original artist might well have been dead when the copy was made, and in any event, there was no "market" in the contemporary sense.

The difficulties in dealing decisively with matters like plagiarism lie in the fact that no matter how deplorable the practice, the lines defining it are anything but sharp.

Civilizations advance because, as someone once put it, "we stand on the shoulders of giants." The most normal and healthy way to learn is to copy: a child could never learn to talk if it did not copy the sounds it heard. The history of science is a story of concepts developed by individuals specially gifted in generalizing from scattered data. When made public, such insights become the property of the entire scientific community, which then tests the proposals, modifies, enlarges, and thus moves on to new discoveries. The protection of the originator lies in the attribution of the discovery and the literature is full of names like Boyle, Galileo, Newton, Einstein, Planck, Heisenberg, all of whom are credited with the laws or theories linked with their names.

The scientist, like the artist, is in essence an explorer. Explorers do not invent, they *find*. Technicians invent. Sometimes the roles are blended, as in the case of Louis Pasteur, whose discoveries led to techniques such as pasteurization.

The difference in this regard between scientists and designers is instructive: no scientist can present a paper, apparently, without referring back to the work of his predecessors, for he has to use their discoveries to give credibility to his own proposals. I have never yet run across a designer who did this, although we are all powerfully affected by the ideas and accomplishments of others.

It seems clear that there are at least two ways of looking at copying: from one viewpoint it is an absolutely essential part of an evolutionary process; from another it is barefaced theft. Theft is only possible where there is something of value to be stolen, and in our kind of world value is generally defined in terms of money. Shakespeare's "who steals my purse steals trash" sounds almost naive these days, for that aristocracy of the spirit which prizes a good name over money, and has existed since the beginnings of civilization, is not much in evidence at the moment.

In our crowded time, when so many voices clamor for attention, a good name is more likely to be manufactured to order by a publicity agent. Marshall McLuhan, almost a household word a few years back, was "manufactured" by a fan of his in the public relations business, Raymond Gossage. The fact that McLuhan had some extremely interesting things to say has nothing to do with the process: the quality of his ideas was a bonus. Ivy Lee, a generation earlier, had turned in an even more spectacular job on the Rockefellers, whose public image in his hands was transformed from utterly ruthless greed to a gentle philanthropic concern for the well-being of humanity.

I seem to have drifted a bit, and it is time to leave our initial concern with plagiarism and its victims and consider the process itself, which is by no means as simple as one would wish. One example which meets our needs is the story of the 35mm camera.

The first such camera was the Leica, invented by Oscar Barnack around 1913, and manufactured in Wetzlar, Germany. It was a startling departure from the cumbersome boxes then in general use, employing standard movie film, rangefinder, and fast lenses. It was tiny, by current standards, pocketable, and it opened an entire new field: candid photography. Its popularity made imitation inevitable, and it was followed by many, the best of which was the Zeiss Contax. It is hard to pin the label of plagiarism on the Contax, for it had a number of significant improvements and the concept of miniature photography was too basic to be restricted to one product. When our troops moved into Japan after World War II, the press photographers were surprised to find the Contax there too, under the name of Nikon. It was a cold copy, sure enough, but the lenses were of impressive quality and presently the cameras began to drift into the States.

One of the significant developments in the design of these small cameras was the emergence of the single lens reflex, and the camera I recall was the Exakta, made in Dresden, Germany, by Ihagee. A reflex camera is one which allows the user to look directly through the lens with the aid of a mirror or a prism. Its introduction in the small camera field quickly made interchangeable lenses a practical reality. Today such cameras are standard, and even Leitz, which started the whole thing off with its first rangefinder model, had to bow to the inevitable and follow the trend. But the story doesn't end here.

Small cameras are mechanical devices which depend on very precise manufacturing for quality and durability (the analogy to the traditional Swiss watch is obvious), but the electronics revolution has been again changing the designs, replacing mechanical linkages with electronic components. A new generation of equipment is now coming on the market, with miniaturization and automation the qualities most sought after.

It would be hard to find a better example of the complex interactions between copying and technical progress. Others that come to mind include digital watches, pocket calculators, typewriters, and computers. Unfortunately, if we are looking for a villain, they do not help us much, for imitation and innovation are so tightly interwoven that it is virtually impossible to disentangle them. Also, if copying is part of the way children grow up and how the race evolves socially and technically, then it can hardly be "bad" in itself. To stop copying would be to stop education, or at least to slow it down to a crawl.

If the real evil in plagiarism is the financial damage done to innovative designers and manufacturers, then the root of the problem has to lie in the social values themselves. The patent laws show clearly that mechanical inventions are viewed as more worthy of protection and reward than concepts which cannot be weighed with a scale. What all this leaves us with is the plagiarist himself.

There seem to be two different breeds of copyists: those who start with what is there and by adding something, move it up to another level, and the parasites. The former, of course, are far more interesting, but the latter are in the great majority. Why is this? Since there is infinitely more stimulation, pleasure, and satisfaction in creation, why isn't this the norm?

Questions like this are unanswerable; the problems they raise are central in psychology, philosophy, art, and education. If one starts with the assumption that all children have creative potential and a depressingly large number of them grow up to exhibit none of it, it is reasonable to guess that something was done to them while they were growing up. This takes us right back to social values again and their expressions in the schools and in the home. The society apparently, despite its vast assortment of technical breakthroughs, must still be functioning on a rather primitive level, not unlike the Roman model, with great dedication to the tranquilizing of unruly populations, to the elimination of curiosity in both schools and places of work, to the glorification of material values, and to the 19th century distortions of the survival-of-the-fittest doctrines so useful to the Victorian establishments. The inevitable result of all this is to take the miraculous potential of children and squeeze it, like Wonder Bread, into the uniform shape of mediocrity. Mediocre people do mediocre things like plagiarizing and they are taught how to do this in mediocre societies.

None of this really answers the original questions: it merely describes a prevailing state of affairs. Design piracy is not only a way of life for business people who indulge in it, but also an expression of a personal philosophy. We have to keep in mind, moreover, that it is very, very old and it has been practiced wherever people lived.

It is evident that the material rewards for the theft of designs can be very gratifying and they include a large assortment of corporate fringe benefits. It is also a fact, although less in evidence, that the price for such activity is not negligible.

The plagiarist is, by any reasonable definition, a parasite and his host is the creative, innovative individual or company. A parasite (the root word is Greek and means "one who feeds at the table of another") survives by feeding off another organism. The result is that the parasite never develops muscles of its own. The race has survived so far because living in jeopardy, which is its normal situation, provides all kinds of stimulation and incentives to solve problems. A company can be entirely parasitic in its behavior, which may seem to work out just fine as long as the host remains in good health, but a built-in weakness of parasites is lack of mobility. If something happens to the host, the source of ideas, say, the parasite is in trouble. If change comes too fast for imitation to catch up, the parasite is also in trouble. And if its spiritual and mental flabbiness is suddenly challenged by the need for innovative behavior, the parasite is in even more trouble.

In most businesses problems are getting tougher, not easier. The accelerating rates of change, if nothing else, create survival problems, and the difficulties in which Canadian industry finds itself today provide a large-scale example right next door. This is not to say that Canada is more addicted to plagiarism than any other place, but rather that the current requirements for independent constructive action are simply not being met at acceptable levels of performance.

The parasites, going back to companies which live by theft, are poorly equipped to stay in the kind of game now going on with rising intensity the world over. A reliance on imitation tends to play an antisurvival role when the going gets rough simply because it undermines the vitality and resourcefulness of the player, and as competition is stepped up, the player needs everything he has.

All this comes close to meeting the imperatives of corporate attitudes and behavior (plagiarism is bad for you or the company because it flabs all those conceptual muscles; time to start a bit of creative jogging). It is compatible with TV-sponsored samples of poetic justice (sure, he goes to Acapulco every weekend in the company jet, but look at the spiritual price he has to pay).

But this isn't quite what it is all about. There are the various meanings of work as they relate to the enrichment or impoverishment of existence which are rarely discussed since they cannot be measured and hence may not even officially exist. There is the possibility that sometime, sooner or later, the rats will get tired of racing. Maybe the dogs are not really that crazy about eating other dogs. Maybe things change in depth as well as in the headlines.

In a reasonably civilized society the parasitism of the plagiarist would fare much worse than it does now. The Mickey Mouse mentality, so comforting to the modern masses, would vanish, and the practice could be seen much more clearly for what it is: behavior eminently suitable for a timid, helpless, sly, not very bright, and rather lazy little rodent, but quite another matter when viewed at humanity's proper scale.

Miniaturization, Ephemeralization, Dematerialization

Writing, over and over again, reveals itself as a way to expose and correct one's sloppy thinking. Here, for example, the overly simple notion that a main drive of technology is to make things smaller and lighter turns out to be much more involved on close examination. Hence the mouth-filling title.

This very short essay was written for the British magazine *Design* in 1978; since the space allotted was less than 1,000 words, it became an exercise in miniaturization itself.

Trying to say a lot with a little is a very old discipline: the sonnet form which allowed fourteen lines, no more no less, within a framework of rigid rules, has challenged generations of poets. Even more demanding is the Japanese *haiku*, where large thoughts have to be compressed to as few as two lines; the sparse elegance of these mini-poems is easier to admire than to emulate.

For the designer who also writes, the dif-

With a storage capacity of 64,000 bits of information, roughly equivalent to 1,000 eight-letter words, this chip is the most densely packed ever produced by IBM. Courtesy IBM Corporation.

ferences between selecting and organizing words with a minimum of overkill, and the kind of things he does in his daily work are, as it turns out, very small.

As a title, it would be hard to imagine one more pedantic or polysyllabic, but I can't think of a more compact summary of what seems to be going on.

We use the first of the words all the time in reference to the widely publicized shrinkage going on in a variety of products, notably electronic. Ten thousand transistors can now be made to fit on the head of a match, far more than the number of angels theologians used to think might stand on the head of a pin. A fairly adequate little radio slips into a shirt pocket, assuming that one of the new microcassette recorders isn't already there. Two years ago General Motors "downsized" its cars, amid loud huzzahs from the buying public. Bulky office files can be squeezed onto microfilm or computer tape. The KGB and CIA probably have high-fidelity microphones which can be comfortably inserted into sewing needles, and if they don't now, we are unanimous in our belief that they presently will. Miniaturization. The No. 1 miracle of modern technology.

Ephemeralization means Kleenex and beer cans and felt markers and U.S. cars, items in the vast modern family of products used once, or briefly, or until the ashtrays are full, and then disposed of.

Mobility in all its forms encourages both downsizing and the creation of throwaways. Since mobility is the one commodity we have plenty of, its spinoffs are to be seen everywhere, including roadsides and public beaches.

Dematerialization occurs when performance that once required a "something" can now be achieved with a "nothing." Buckminster Fuller's great sphere at the Montreal Expo came very close: never before had so much space been enclosed with so little weight. The air-supported domes probably do even better, since there is nothing but a skin, sometimes restrained by a network of cables.

The materials handling industry now offers "rails" for automatic electric vehicles in factories and offices which are invisible control strips, sprayed on floors. Magnetically supported trains will presently follow, racing across virgin meadows where copper coils lie buried beneath the daisies. Domed cities for places like the Arctic would eliminate millions of tons of conventional building materials.

All this, and much, much more, the almost total

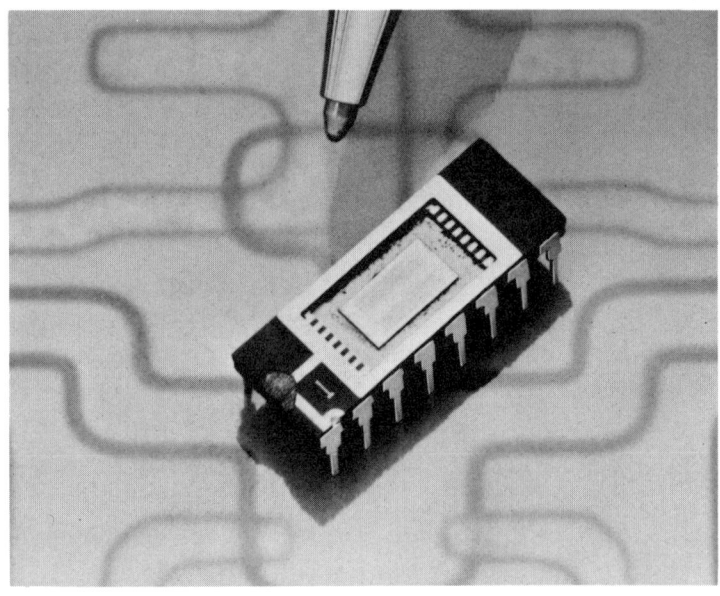

This tiny computer component contains 65,536 microscopic data storage cells. In the background, what appears as abstract drawing is a chip section photographically enlarged 1,000 times to show minute electronic components; the width of each is 1/30th the diameter of a human hair. Courtesy Texas Instruments.

Close-up of enlargement: areas between the lines are actually microtransistors. Courtesy Texas Instruments.

transformation of deeply rooted values in a few decades, is a truly astonishing thing, particularly since it happened without any fanfare at all. Nobody had to persuade anyone to go along with the idea. Furthermore, the *spread* of the attitude is extraordinary: anyone can understand that objects designed to be airborne must be pared down to minimums, but this is only where it begins. How many places are left in the world where conspicuously overweight women are sought after? Or men, for that matter? Entire populations seem to be on diets of one kind or another, and they all carry subminiature cameras and featherweight luggage.

No one disputes the absolute rightness of all this. Our faith is as unquestioning as that of a peasant before a reliquary holding a nail from the True Cross. Less is More. All that is needed is a translation into Latin set to music with a Gregorian flavor. The one truly funny thing in an otherwise dismal century is the spectacle of a generation of skeptics busily installing a new Age of Faith.

Actually, it is not an unpleasant change, for a change.

When we ask how it all happened a curious thing becomes apparent: there is no identifiable starting point, no unique prime mover. It is nothing less than a global change of sensibility which converts every possible circumstance into one more reason for miniaturizing, ephemeralizing, or dematerializing. One might call it a paradox filled with laughing gas, or the good old Marxist contradiction of a contradiction. In this new game everything turns out to be true.

It was the thrust of an infant science and technology that helped give the *coup de gráce* to the Middle Ages, rubbing out all traces of mysticism with an aggressive, abrasive materialism. Materialism is a belief in the reality of things you can feel, weigh, and count, and its base lies in the fact that a properly set up experiment always comes up with the same answer no matter how many times it is performed.

Believing in the reliability of material things leads to a growing understanding of physical phenomena and presently tremendous sophistication in manipulating matter. Finally some people get so good at these tricks that they rub out a couple of very tangible cities with a pitifully small amount of fissionable stuff.

If we superimpose $E = mC^2$ on a new awareness of Nature, seeing it as the unbeatable model of elegant and economical design, we begin to believe that less can indeed be more, and an unconscious slippage back in the direction of mysticism gets under way.

One of the lightest structures ever built, this transparent sphere made an extraordinarily successful exhibit space. It was subsequently destroyed by fire. Geodesic sphere by R. Buckminster Fuller, U.S. Pavilion at the Montreal Expo '67; photo by Jacqueline Nelson.

Accepting the hypothesis that the brighter we get, the more we can do with less, it presently follows that if this is a good thing, then doing *much* more with *much* less must be an even better thing. Then, if we cautiously extend the evolutionary line in the direction of infinity we come to the interesting realization that the ultimate goal of technology has to be *doing everything with nothing*.

This, of course, is precisely what God did, as reported in the admirably concise account in the Book of Genesis. One wonders if the conjunction of mineral reserves being depleted to an eventual vanishing point, and the real goal of technology doing everything with nothing, is serendipity or something more.

The more immediate problem, I suppose, is how do we determine when to start closing down the design schools?

Design and Technologies

Political events are something we read about in the papers and it always comes as a surprise when they reach out and touch us personally. This is the way it was for me as I read about the explosion of nationalist sentiments in Quebec. It was interesting to observe and probably a good thing in providing Canada with some political excitement, but my imagination did not reach far enough to anticipate a phone invitation in 1976 to give a lecture in Montreal.

"They want it in French," said the man at the other end. "Do you speak French?"

"My English is better," I confessed.

"They want it in French," he replied. "Will you or won't you?"

Everyone in the audience, as far as I could make out, was perfectly bilingual and there would have been no problem of comprehension had the talk been given in English. But the people in Quebec are feeling strongly about language

A 210-foot diameter antenna at Goldstone, California, used in space flight programs. Photo by Dennis Stock, MAGNUM.

these days, and the one they wanted to hear was their own. They were gently amused by the foreigner's struggle to do justice to their elegant mother tongue and were as pleased by the effort, I think, as by anything that was said.

On the way to the plane to Montreal, my taxi was stopped by traffic and I found myself fascinated by a message attached to the bumper of the car directly ahead. It read: "Keep America Beautiful."

I do not know how these matters are handled in Canada, but in the U.S. the traditional kiosk and the empty wall no longer serve as the primary gathering place for public messages. Since we spend less and less time looking at walls, and more and more time gazing at the rear ends of automobiles, the bumper sticker has come into wide use.

The message was "Keep America Beautiful," and as I looked out the window for the beauty we are being exhorted to maintain and failed to find any, I found myself with several reactions.

For one, where is this beautiful America? Certainly not in the cities, not in most rural areas, not along the seacoast. Whoever uses these messages, therefore, appears to me to be a combination of visual illiterate and idiot. America the Beautiful is what we found 200 years ago, not what we have today.

A second reaction to the message might be another question: How did we turn America the Beautiful into America the Ugly? The answer, these days, is to blame everything on the technological society which has created our man-made environment, along with ugliness, pollution of air and water, too much noise, and so on.

A widely held view of technology today, in other words, is to consider it a source of ugliness, as a danger to health, even life. This is not universal, to be sure, but it is rapidly spreading through many sectors of public opinion.

Just before coming to Montreal, I visited a client who had just returned from a two-day seminar on "Anti-Business." Many magazines are carrying articles dealing with the social responsibilities of corporations. The common theme in all these stories is that the technological society is under attack and also that it is transforming itself in ways which, only ten years ago, would have seemed visionary and impossibly radical.

Thus, when we attempt to talk about technology, we have to seek some degree of precision in our definitions. Preindustrial technology, which still exists for billions of people, is in the hands of artisans who, over generations or even centuries, have become specialists of one kind or another: they weave baskets or cloth, they make swords or ceramic bowls, they build houses of stone, furniture of wood. These days we look to them with a certain envy, for their work is more interesting than the production line and they do not pollute the atmosphere. Still, we do not know how to go back to these idyllic practices.

Technology today is in the hands of technicians, who possess much more knowledge than the old craftsmen, but also a more specialized kind of knowledge. An engineer in the aircraft industry, if put out of work, has difficulty in finding other work *as an engineer*. The technician also differs from the artisan in that he can invent on order: in other words, he can use a known process for making inventions that fall within the limits of his specialty.

The industrial designer is a relatively new member of the technological society, and manufacturers have a certain difficulty in understanding his role, mainly because he is not a pure technician, but a kind of hybrid with connections to both technology and the arts. He calculates, but he also works intuitively. He is not really an artist, but neither is he an engineer.

The industries making up modern society are dynamic, compared with their counterparts of the 18th and 19th centuries. Another word for "dynamic" is "unstable."

Business people and politicians are very fond of the word "progress," although more and more people are beginning to wonder whether the benefits of progress are equal to the damage done, but whatever the color of opinion, "progress" is another word for "change." Change creates instability.

At this point we encounter contradictions. Modern business and industry are dynamic, subject to change, but in some instances the rate of change is more than the enterprises affected can cope with.

There are many examples. Foam rubber emerges from the laboratory as a material suitable for production. The market appears to be very large. Expensive factories are built. Just as the foam rubber is ready for the market, foam plastic appears, and it shows a certain superiority to the rubber. The new factories are now obsolete before they open. Someone loses a very large amount of money.

In the computer industry, new developments come even more rapidly. Some of the largest companies have had to withdraw from competition because they could not move fast enough, or because their research was inadequate, or because they could not raise the money needed to stay in the race.

I have heard a report that one difference between the U.S. producers of TV sets and the Japanese is that the latter, over the past eight or ten years, have installed about $80 million of automatic quality control equipment. Because of this, one or more big U.S. producers may be forced out of the business.

Whether we use the words "dynamic," "progressive," or "unstable" in relation to modern industry, it comes out to the same thing: accelerated change. The degree of change is not the same in all industries, of course. A mouthwash or soft drink may go on for fifty years.

Engineers, designers, and research technicians are agents of change. After all, this is what they are hired for. I have never met a designer who was retained to keep things the same as they were—something new is always wanted: a new package, a new trademark, a new product, a new set of executive offices, a new corporate image.

The contradiction is that corporate management does not necessarily want change of any kind; it is costly and, above all, risky. To say that a management is not automatically enthusiastic about change does not mean that it is backward or reactionary: it merely means that management has an awareness of possible disaster not always shared by specialists who may be carried away by fantasies of personal glory.

Because any change means risk, and is thus a potential source of instability, modern business has become very skillful in creating *the illusion of change*. One simple way to do this is to leave the product alone, but change the package. Another is to call something "new." The new soap, the new detergent, the new aspirin—these are all familiar.

There is enough wreckage along the road to corporate success to cause any observer to proceed with caution. Not only factories made obsolete before they opened, but the history of cars like the Chrysler Airflow and the Ford Edsel. Now we have the case of the Concorde, a beautiful airplane but also a risk involving billions of dollars for reasons that have never concerned industry until very recently: damage to people through excessive noise and damage to the atmosphere through discharge from the engines.

The problems of business are being complicated, almost beyond belief, by the new awareness of the interaction of industry and environment, but the problems of business risk go back thousands of years. Merchants in the Mediterranean, trading caravans across mountains and deserts, the clipper ships that sailed to China—all these and many others were gambling for high stakes and enough of them lost to create a steady demand for fortune-tellers. We are still looking for them. In the old days it was the stars, crystal balls, tea leaves, the entrails of birds. Perhaps the most consistently successful was the Oracle at Delphi, the inspired priestess who bent over a fissure in the earth and made prophecies. The reason for the success of the Oracle was that it was never wrong. Its secret was the ambiguous answer, developed to a high degree of refinement.

The lesson of Delphi has not been lost: today it is being used in marketing, which is a kind of modern fortune-telling with scientific pretensions. At its most mediocre it can be described as a social disease which has reached epidemic proportions. A basic weakness of marketing is that it attempts to quantify material which is not always quantifiable, but the instability which afflicts modern business drives management to seek answers wherever they can be found.

Innovation is another answer to the problem of instability, but it is risky. But since marketing research is not infallible, the most popular procedure, internationally and historically, is plagiarism—copying—design piracy.

Copying is marvelous in its simplicity. If Manufacturer A has a best-selling product, Manufacturer B knows, without a doubt, that if he brings out a copy, it will not be rejected. Nobody was foolish enough to attempt a copy of the Ford Edsel.

Copying starts with the biggest and richest industries and trickles down from there. The most entertaining recent example has to do with the naming of cars. One manufacturer brought out a 1975 model named after a Spanish town; almost immediately the second car manufacturer brought out its model named after a Spanish town; this was quickly followed by the third manufacturer with another Spanish town. Fortunately, there are a lot of cities in Spain. Then, all three managed to state or insinuate that their new models were each copies, in one way or another, of the Mercedes. Now the Mercedes is a German car, but the name is also Spanish. The puzzle is just how everything in 1975 happened to take on this Iberian coloration. One possible explanation is that the automobile manufacturers may spend more money on espionage than on design.

Smaller companies do the same thing, but more cheaply. A furniture manufacturer recently told me, with a great show of pride in his cleverness, that his successful new line of Early American furniture had been "created"

The ruins of the famous Oracle sit in the fantastic mountain landscape of Delphi. Rumor has it that gases from a fissure in the earth served to put the priestess in a trance, during which her predictions were made. Photo courtesy Greek National Tourist Office.

by the theft of a leg detail from one successful model, the wood finish from another, and hardware from a third. He clearly felt that what he had done was more effective than anything that could have been provided by a professional designer.

Copying is quick, cheap, and generally safe, especially when one deals with a large public that has long since lost the ability to recognize quality. However, there are some small problems. Industrial leadership is based, at least in part, on the ability to innovate. The whole idea of progress as held by the technical-business community means change, novelty, improvement. If everyone copies, who is left to innovate?

The reason I am putting emphasis on these matters is that we are at a point where the roles of business and industry are in a state of almost revolutionary transformation, and such a period is always one in which new opportunities for leadership present themselves. Copying and leadership, obviously, have nothing to do with each other.

Many new industries have reached a point where a vigorous, creative, innovative position can be taken and maintained. Older models, like some industries in the U.S., no longer have the power to inspire that they had twenty years ago. Leadership in many industries, as the Japanese demonstrated brilliantly, is up for grabs, so to speak.

If Canadian industry still suffers from the inferiority complex my friends here are constantly telling me about, this is a good time to put it aside, for it is unproductive and probably no longer based on reality.

This, however, does not mean that it is wise to ignore what is happening below the border. The U.S., long a leader in the technological race, has also been the first to learn from the backlash of environmental impacts, it was the first to be attacked on the basis of social values by the counterculture in the 1960s, and it is the first of the modern industrial giants to demonstrate the rapidity with which decay can take place if antiquated attitudes toward business are permitted to continue.

The most visible weakness of technological societies, aside from damage to the physical environment, comes from the effort to convert people from living organisms into things. It does this in two ways: by subjecting workers to dehumanizing tasks which are devoid of meaning and satisfaction, and by turning people into "consumers." A consumer is a cross between a living organism and an automatic response mechanism, programmed to buy on order through advertising and other brainwashing procedures. The end of this process is a perversion of the meaning of work, the real value of which is to help the individual mature, and the mass substitutions of private fantasies and cravings for instant gratification. On a national scale this leads to a loss of morale, a lack of vitality, and a declining ability to compete.

Business and industry are undergoing a metamorphosis which may be illustrated by the proposition that there is a change from 19th-century mechanical models to electronic models. Weight and size thus become less important, while flexibility and fast reaction times become more important. A basic instability, characteristic of all forms of life, becomes a permanent characteristic of industry. All organisms live in jeopardy, and this condition is not to be deplored, but should be viewed as an indispensable stimulant. With the advent of the computer and flexible automated tools, many old arguments about centralization versus decentralization become obsolete.

As the engineer shifts from a mechanical to a less rigid working environment he will transform himself into a professional as intimately concerned with relationships as with things. The designer, in a certain sense, is already there, for his work has conditioned his viewpoint so that he sees the connection between products and people, and he is prepared by training to understand the relationships between quality of life and the performance of products and systems.

I am not projecting a Utopia, for it is almost certain that the future holds more crises and dislocations than the present. The tasks of protecting the environment and humanizing work are not a matter of good intentions, but rather a necessary response to the changing conditions of contemporary life.

It was Arnold Toynbee, you will recall, who advanced the proposition that civilizations prospered or failed to the degree that they were able to respond to new challenges.

In theory, at least, the smaller industrial nations like Canada have a better chance to perceive the challenge and the opportunity than the superpowers, whose paranoia precludes an objective view of any situation. In the present-day context, backwardness, so-called small size, a lack of imperial aspirations, a concern for the proper use of natural and human resources can be assets greater than accumulated power, fear as a motivating force, and intellectual rigidity.

The technological societies have had impressive success in developing intelligent and well-educated people. The new and most urgent priority is the need for *civilized* men and women.

Design and Human Needs

The difficulty in dealing with human needs is that we have lost all awareness of such intangibles, and there is no way to catch up now without a lot of laborious homework.

I had lunch a few days ago with some insurance company executives, who were expressing their bafflement over what happens to their efforts to make their offices more pleasant for their staff: in more cases than not these efforts are not perceived as improvements, or even perceived at all.

Designers are prone to such errors of judgment: when we have a great idea and no one else sees it as such, it comes invariably as a blow. The real problem is to learn how to get inside someone else's skin. . . . Maybe it is time for the design schools to try a new curriculum: humility, psychology, and the habit of listening.

This tightly packed housing near San Francisco reveals one of the mysteries of the ticky-tackies: how the repetition of standard boxes can lead to such appalling ugliness, while the identical process, expressed on a Greek island or an Italian hill town, has produced villages of great beauty. It could be that the problem lies in the abysmal quality of the individual components.

In midtown Manhattan, between 6th and 7th Avenues, there is a kind of minipark that cuts through the block between 48th and 49th Streets. It contains benches, planting, and a tunnel of clear plastic that penetrates a waterfall. My 18-year-old son and I used it as a shortcut on a quick shopping excursion and he was impressed. "If all of New York were designed like this," he observed, "it would be a terrific place. Why aren't cities designed for people?" Why indeed?

One reason an intelligent teenager can ask questions like this today is that so many cities are clearly not designed for people at all, and it is beginning to show; another reason is that such questions concern the young more than they did a few years back, and they may be taken as a reaction to the general decline in the quality of life throughout the society.

The voices raised with such questions as my son's, the slowly increasing concern with values generally ignored, are part of a large and radical social transformation, and they eventually affect the work of the designer. According to these new attitudes, he must be dedicated to serving human needs.

It is a noble aim, this idea of a career dedicated to the service of others, and we could do worse than spend time examining it, for it turns out to be less easy than it sounds. It calls for greater sensitivity than we commonly display, and it requires a great deal more homework than we are accustomed to devote to such matters. Part of the problem lies in the brainwashing to which we have been subjected since babyhood: as a society we have little or no interest in human needs and in consequence we know almost nothing about them. What we believe in is the expert, specialist *control of situations*: "Give us the problem and we will hand you the solution."

Last week at the 1978 Design Conference in Aspen, some 1,400 of us listened to the ex-astronaut Gordon Cooper say just that in the course of an absolutely unbelievable Disney commercial that lasted almost an hour and drove close to half the audience out in disgust.

Human needs are not a problem, they are an integral part of our common existence, and not even Disney can solve that one. But because we are so dependent on experts, self-styled and otherwise, we have acquired a kind of mass docility which makes us easier to manipulate. The fact that more and more solutions to the problems they present have calamitous consequences does not make us less credulous the next time around, and one of the reasons for this is that environments are contexts in which we exist, but we rarely notice them. We do not marvel every time we draw breath that the air pressure on our bodies is 15 pounds per square inch, nor does the fish think how amazing it is to live under water. We were raised in a world of technical specialists and experts and we have been conditioned to take their wisdom for granted. Furthermore, since most human societies are elaborate mechanisms for discouraging independent thinking, by the time we are out of grade school we have pretty much lost the habit of asking questions.

Last week, on the way to Fort Wayne's airport, I passed a new housing tract. The land in the area is wooded and rolling, but the development had been bulldozed flat and all the trees, of course, were gone. At the entrance to this instant wasteland there was a sign: "Wildwood."

This game, the putting together of actions and labels which flatly contradict each other, has been played by politicians for centuries, but with us it seems to extend to everything. The bumper stickers urging us to "Keep America Beautiful," for instance. America was beautiful long before we got our hands on it and it has been going downhill steadily ever since. But we have been trained out of the habit of asking exactly what the stickers mean. We buy "wood" station wagons made of sheet metal and order "home cooking" in restaurants where the chef's main job is to warm up frozen food packages. Plastic flowers and plants have all but pushed out real ones from the florists' shops. It goes on and on. Wildwood is everywhere. When you get tired of it, come to Marlboro Country.

The name of this game is the mass evasion of reality or the confusion of fantasy and reality. The problems it creates when we try to design for human needs are obvious: there is no way to satisfy a need we cannot identify.

Many years ago I was invited for the weekend to a modern house just built outside Boston. I had never spent a night in a modern house. It was raining when we arrived and it never stopped all weekend. After a half-day indoors I got claustrophobia.

The following weekend, by coincidence, was spent with friends who have an 18th-century farmhouse in upper New York State. Originally a standard colonial box, it had been added onto by succeeding generations, and there were a lot of rooms, most of them quite small. It rained all that weekend too, and we had a lovely time.

Without going into detail, it is clear that in one case some human needs were being frustrated and in the other they were not. What made the difference between the houses had nothing to do with style, but with spaces. The

A mid-Manhattan park/tunnel/waterfall, part of the ground space around a highrise office building: modest urban amenities like these are appearing in city centers all over the country and represent a new set of social values in action. Harrison and Abramovitz, Architects.

modern house was a two-story box with a splitlevel arrangement at one end, with a dining space down a few steps and a bedroom on a balcony above. Everything, except a bathroom and kitchen, was exposed to view. The whole interior was there to be grasped in a glance. In the old house, while the rooms were tight, there was always a door leading into another. Its spaces unfolded, so to speak, in a series of leisurely experiences.

Claustrophobia is produced, not by the size of a space, but by the feeling that there is no exit. Even though the modern house did, of course, have doors to the outer world, one's sensory impression was that of a trap. It made no difference that this impression was not rational. We are programmed as organisms to associate traps with threats to our survival and we learn early in life to fear and avoid them. An animal caught in a trap will gnaw off its leg to escape.

Design for human needs has to deal with such psychological responses and these have to do with our senses rather than our minds. This is surprisingly difficult for members of a society conditioned to believe that the logic of science answers all questions and that the methods of technology can cope with anything. We are learning from the lumps on our heads that this simply is not so.

For designers of things and spaces in an advanced industrial society at this time it appears that what we call "human needs" are more likely to be met through an understanding of the sensory, nonrational elements than by more technology.

Anyone who has traveled abroad knows that the older cities, built with far more primitive tools, are more "humane" than modern ones, and if we analyze some of the differences we find, just as we did in the example of the two houses, that the old cities give more exercise, so to speak, to our senses and that the sequences of visual experience are richer than in modern cities.

The new open landscape offices have a label which does not correspond to their reality. Such spaces are rarely perceived as open by their occupants, but as labyrinths densely cluttered with screen partitions and workstations. And if we call the usual sprinkling of plants (real or plastic) a landscape, we are right back at Wildwood again.

As a society we have become remarkably indifferent to people generally. Ordinarily we do not notice the evidence, but it is everywhere. In any but a tiny sampling of airports we can note that luggage and supplies are handled with tender care while the passengers are left to drag themselves through mile-long corridors. Most housing for the poor is so badly conceived, so destructive of the occupants' dignity and vitality, that it creates more problems than it solves.

In the field of housing, the experts have produced some astonishing disasters. The widely publicized Pruitt-Igoe project in St. Louis is perhaps the most spectacular, but by no means atypical. Built in the mid-50s at a cost of $36 million, it replaced 57 acres of slums in a high-crime district and was presented as a model of decent and safe homes for some 10,000 people. The subsequent history is one of disorder, rape, and robbery, with many units abandoned as no longer livable because of vandalism, and the ultimate dynamiting of a number of structures. The costs, finally, mounted to $57 million, with a possible additional $42 million for retiring the bonds. So much for Pruitt-Igoe's "economies." The damage done to the occupants and the city cannot be calculated so neatly, but what shines through as brightly as a campaign speech is that the experts' ability to assess human needs and to design for them could not be found without the aid of an electron microscope.

The most stubborn obstacles to humane design are our dominant social values, which have conditioned us to believe in the essential worthlessness and expendability of people. One reason we believe this is that so much has been done to make people worthless and expendable. This comes through in all sorts of ways, small and large. The use of devices to confuse fantasy and reality is part of the process. Last night I noticed an advertising blurb on a paperback thriller, a book about the hair-raising adventures of a mining engineer in South Africa. The blurb goes like this: "And hanging in the balance, the fate of a vast, vicious struggle between a clandestine revolutionary organization and a diabolically efficient secret police amid the ugly slums and breathtaking wilderness of present-day Africa. *This is what great entertainment is all about!*"

We are all entitled to our escape literature and the vicarious thrills that go with it, but this is not what the advertising message is saying. Many of us have met emigrants from South Africa, most of them decent people who can no longer stand the mass brutalization of both blacks and whites in their tormented homeland, and for those who haven't, there are the newspapers. To translate this tragic situation into "great entertainment" is about as good a sample of the substitution of fantasy for reality as one could find in a month of research, and it could only exist if people were indeed perceived as expendable items of no consequence.

One might object that this is just an ad for a piece of fiction and thus irrelevant, but nothing is irrelevant. There is a series of whodunits from Sweden which might be used as required reading in a sociology course.

The values behind the downgrading of people and the destruction of their dignity are in essence technocratic values which tend to equate live people and inanimate machines. They were once powerful assists to industrial growth, but in their old age they have become a kind of social poison.

I suppose that the most massive and destructive example of these values in action is the story of what has happened to farming in North America. Agriculture is not my area of competence, but the capsule history of what has been going is not that difficult to comprehend. Between 1910 and 1969 the farm population of the U.S. dropped from 33 to about 5 percent. Going from the numbers to the living realities, which include the forced migration of millions of farmers into the cities, what we are confronted by is the loss of a cultural base.

It is hard to talk about an immensely complex transformation without oversimplifying, so I will do just that. A modern industrial society may be seen as a mix of two mentalities: the farmer and the miner. The latter takes minerals out of the earth. He exploits irreplaceable resources. Nature, for him, is something to be dominated, raped. The miner mentality predominates in all exploitative activity.

The farmer, however, is an entirely different cultural product: he maintains, nurtures, works with Nature. When his land is taken over by agribusiness, the produce shifts from diversified to specialized and the values of husbandry are replaced by those of technology and finance. The land, in other words, now becomes another kind of mine, and since monoculture leads to depletion, the input of chemical fertilizers must be constantly increased to maintain output.

Fertilizers are heavily dependent on petroleum and energy, as are the machines, and their excessive use eventually creates the risk of polluting the underground water. Ultimately the national inventory of productive land begins to resemble Pruitt-Igoe.

In this process the farmer and his family, and their shared values which are based on work and a close relationship to Nature and its cycles, are destroyed.

I do not mean to suggest that the farmer mentality is "good" and that of the miner is "bad." We need both the food and the minerals, and we are just beginning to

The dynamiting of Pruitt Igoe housing in St. Louis is a complete statement of what can happen when technocrats are allowed to meddle with human problems. Wide World Photos, Inc.

learn that the work of the miner can be extended to the restoration of organic environments. As far as our relationship to the planet is concerned, however, the farmer mentality is the only one that offers any possibility of keeping it habitable.

Now what do these digressions have to do with the designer and his presumed concern with human needs? In my view they have everything to do with it. The farmer deals with life; so does—or should—the designer. And what becomes apparent as we scan pieces of the larger scene is that a preoccupation with life must inevitably spread to include *all* life. Thus, if the designer is going to deal creatively with human needs, the first thing he has to do is divest himself of those beliefs which dominate our thinking and make a radical, conscious break with all values he identifies as antihuman.

This kind of change is an intensely personal matter and it cannot be achieved by joining one more organization. It is also frightening, if only because it is a change. But it is not as bad as it may seem, for once the individual makes this shift he finds that he has a lot of company.

What we have to get through our heads is that the technical-specialist approach, being based on the concept of one solution for a carefully isolated problem, does not work where life becomes part of the equation. Pruitt-Igoe as a collection of modern buildings was an admirable performance; the only thing wrong with it was that it didn't work when the people moved in.

We must also realize that the promises of the technocrats contain price tags no one tells us about. We were promised two chickens in every pot, two cars in every garage, affluence, leisure, entertainment—in other words, happiness. Nothing was said about the pollution created by the cars, the massive slums and streets riddled with potholes that seem to go with the promised affluence. It is not a good scene, and the increasing radicalization of traditionally conservative people is a virtual guarantee of big trouble up ahead. Instead of the Garden of Eden what we are getting is Wildwood. Another name for Wildwood is "spiritual impoverishment."

We must also become more critical of what we are told. When the establishment leaders, speaking through the Department of Agriculture, tell us that getting rid of supposedly inefficient small farmers is necessary and ultimately beneficial, we are entitled to skepticism. When we hear that land prices make 50-story towers essential, we might wonder how true the statement really is. When we are asked to design for the marketing department rather than the ultimate user, we must feel obliged to question the meaning of what we are told.

As one shifts lenses and turns from the wide-angle view to the small closeup—in other words, to one's own work—it gets very important to decide whether one is working for the enhancement of life or its degradation.

Taking the small view, I doubt very much whether the real solutions to the problems we are customarily asked to solve have significant technological answers. This is not to put down technology, but merely to assign limits to its appropriate activities.

The present concern with human needs is, like so many other manifestations of the present time, a grassroots movement. It is not organized. The ideas no longer come down from the top, but spring up in random fashion.

An advertising manager of an international corporation suddenly quits his job, winterizes his summer cottage in a small town, and becomes a house painter, a restaurant owner-chef, or a cabinetmaker. He trades income for clean air and freedom from traffic noises and competitive pressures. When these individual decisions mount up into the millions, there is a change in the texture and beliefs of the society. In actuality the multiplicity of individual, seemingly random decisions can be as potent in a political sense as the organized lobbying of a pressure group.

Political action does not necessarily involve adherence to one or another of the dominant ideologies, nor does it demand membership in a party. It is particularly true in this case, for the issues do not define themselves in terms of a struggle for power, but rather as a search for life.

This search is going on at many levels all over the world. It ranges from a simple desire to keep the bombs from leaving their silos to a struggle for more habitable environments. In the eyes of political prisoners or people without food this last might seem very far removed from the realities of their existence, but they are all part of the same thing. Since all political parties claim to be pro-people and none show the slightest interest in the quality of life, the people involved in such a search tend to be scattered individuals or small groups.

When we come down to the smallest units of personal concern, one can only talk in terms of one's own life and work. Since I have been in and out of space planning and office furniture design for many years, much of my interest is focused here. The questions that come up, once routine attitudes and stereotypes are discarded, are difficult and absorbing. How does one eliminate the feelings of claustrophobia that are all too common in the so-called open landscape offices? Are there ways of creating acoustical barriers psychologically rather than with brute force and overuse of materials? To what degree can one reduce the overkill common to all available systems? What kinds of working environments will foster concentrated work? How does one define concentrated work?

There are more questions than answers. Can one create private environments without building traps? How much variation is there from one individual to another? Human needs are variable and frequently unpredictable; they certainly are not quantifiable; they are complex, subtle, and mysterious.

Another problem: What is the most advanced office design one can conceive of? Is it a system or something else? To what extent do status concerns affect the design? We have a suspicion that the more boring and monotonous the work the greater the preoccupation with status, but we cannot prove it.

I learned years ago that most of my clients were visually handicapped. Nonetheless, they persist in believing that they are fully competent to judge design and other visual expressions, something they would never dream of if the problem were medical or technical. So I became aware of what we now call "visual illiteracy," wrote a book entitled *How to See*, and am now working on a series of seminars to help people read nonverbal messages.

Do these private concerns play a significant part in bringing about a new and better society? Does the question really matter? One does what one can and leaves it at that. People who claimed they could redesign the world (names like Hitler, Stalin, and Mussolini come to mind) did not manage very well, and a more modest approach might have a better chance.

It is our fate, recalling the ancient Chinese curse, to live in interesting times. The heads of every one of us are full of lumps from these interesting times, and anyone may be forgiven for finding himself in a state of confusion. Still, there is one way to simplify an impossibly complicated situation which I find both practical and comforting. It is to look at whatever one is doing and to decide whether it is an act that will enhance life, even to the most minute degree, or something that will work against life.

What makes this kind of work worth doing? What is the payoff for the effort demanded? In my view the answer is simple: it is the only way to get an exit visa from Wildwood.

Edited by Sarah Bodine and Susan Davis
Designed by Pentagram, James Craig, and Jay Anning
Set in 10 point Times Roman